BODY COI

The War on Terror and (
in Iraq

Lily Hamourtziadou

BRISTOL
UNIVERSITY
PRESS

First published in Great Britain in 2021 by

Bristol University Press
University of Bristol
1-9 Old Park Hill
Bristol
BS2 8BB
UK
t: +44 (0)117 954 5940
e: bup-info@bristol.ac.uk

Details of international sales and distribution partners are available at bristoluniversitypress.co.uk

British Library Cataloguing in Publication Data
A catalogue record for this book is available from the British Library

ISBN 978-1-5292-0672-2 hardcover
ISBN 978-1-5292-0673-9 paperback
ISBN 978-1-5292-0676-0 ePub
ISBN 978-1-5292-0675-3 ePdf

Cover design: blu inc, Bristol
Front cover image: John Spragens Jr./ScienceSource

To the people of Iraq

Contents

List of Tables

Acknowledgements

To Hamit Dardagan, John Sloboda, Josh Dougherty and Kay Williams, I want to say a big thank you for your dedication to this project and for your commitment to documenting this human suffering. Bulent Gokay, I am grateful for your friendship and guidance. Diego, without your patience and calming presence, I don't know if I would have been able to carry out this research through the worst years, 2006–2008.

Finally, to Peter and Valentina: thank you for your love. It is through those we love that we understand what true loss is.

Foreword

How many Iraqis have been killed as a result of the country's 2003 invasion and its long-drawn-out and bloody aftermath? The truth is, no one knows: what we do know is that Iraq Body Count's huge public database of civilian deaths and the incidents in which they occurred (as of mid-2019, numbering over 200,000 killed and more than 50,000 incidents) is sufficiently well documented to be essentially undeniable. This is no 'estimated' number, but quite literally a painstaking and transparent count, with each database entry and its details open to public scrutiny.

There have been a handful of more or less rigorous efforts to estimate a 'total' number of Iraqi deaths, including a few that briefly captured the headlines despite their shortcomings but, as Lily Hamourtziadou reminds us, these provided only snapshots rather than the continuous monitoring and updating that a long war requires. The true number therefore remains unknown, not least because the nations that rushed to war on the flimsiest of pretexts remain incurious about, and have done very little to discover, the scale of its human toll.

There is another problem with only aiming for numbers. When it comes to recording people killed, the only appropriate question is *who* died, not merely how many (the latter is important too, but easily enough derived from the former). Each of those 200,000 people had a name; each was as individual as you or I; and it follows that each should be remembered as an individual whose life was violently ended, not as part of a statistic. The Iraq Body Count project records the names and demographic details of civilian victims whenever possible but despite our best efforts, less than 7% can yet be listed by name and little more than a third by age or gender. 'Counting' is therefore what we must do when we lack the means to properly record individual lives lost: we resort to it only to ensure that it is at least never forgotten that on this day, in that place, as a result of some specified form of armed violence, this many people were killed.

There are however other, much more detailed public lists of the killed in Iraq: those that list the names (and often photos and brief biographies) of the dead who served in the militaries of the invading nations. These lists are also important, for the public record as well as for their families and friends. Should the same considerations not also apply to the Iraqis killed (civilian and combatant), to *their* friends and families? In this, the 'information age', should their loss not form an equally individual, person-by-person record of the war in Iraq, rather than remain forever known to us only in the purest of abstractions – as numbers? And should this not be a universal norm, everywhere, while armed conflicts continue to plague our species?

The history of war is too often the history as seen from the top down, analyzing the dilemmas and crises facing presidents and prime ministers (whose names we are all too familiar with), and charting the strategies and tactics of the huge military forces they command. Yet the one ineluctable and therefore entirely predictable consequence all wars is the deliberate and abrupt ending of life on en masse, predominantly in these times the lives of civilians.

It has been the intention of Iraq Body Count, and many similar organizations (mainly NGOs) around the world, to tell a story of war from the bottom up, detailing one by one the men, women and children who paid the ultimate price of decisions taken, often far away and over which they had little or no influence. Since 2006, Lily Hamourtziadou has been at the front line of telling this story for Iraq, scouring the world's media on a daily basis for details of those who were killed, not only in headline-grabbing big events, killing tens or hundreds in high-profile locations, but also in the far more frequent, but often barely noticed, killings of ones and twos – locally recorded on one day and often forgotten the next. Our other longest-serving colleagues, Kay Williams and Josh Dougherty (a full list is on our website), worked to the same ethos: engaging tenaciously with each case, large or small, to glean as much detail and truth for posterity as possible.

When we founded Iraq Body Count in 2003, the internet had just established its credentials as the universal and freely accessible medium for information storage and exchange it has now become. Recently available tools such as search engines made it easier to discover and save relevant information than ever before in human history. At the same time, the capacity to store vast quantities of information (both locally on personal computers, but also globally in the cloud) had grown exponentially and continues to do so. In 2003, few organizations were systematically documenting civilian deaths on a daily basis. Now there is an entire field of endeavour, to which the name 'casualty recording' has been given, involving many organizations across the world, some of which have elected to collaborate on a long-term basis through an international casualty recorders' network (http://everycasualty.org/practice), sharing good practice, and developing agreed standards for the field (http://everycasualty.org/newsandviews/casualty-standards-published).

We touched earlier on the importance of memorializing the dead as individuals. But with that as the right and proper goal of our work, we have also become increasingly aware of the multiple beneficial consequences that flow from the use of aggregate casualty data when subjected to careful analysis. Such data allows humanitarian (including medical) aid to be more precisely targeted to areas and types of need. It allows the uncovering of patterns of harm, lending unassailable weight to advocacy against the use of certain weapons or tactics when they have a disproportionate effect on the civilian population. They assist those assessing asylum cases to make better judgements concerning which areas it remains unsafe to send refugees back to. In short, detailed and robustly compiled casualty records bring clearer recognition of the human costs of war, and those who want to reduce – or end – this toll will find ways to use it accordingly.

The international community has committed itself to do better in the protection of civilians. Despite the fact that deliberate targeting of civilians is a war crime, progress among governments towards the reduction of harm to civilians in war goes far too slowly. It remains a vital responsibility of global citizenry, individually and collectively, to speak truth to power in whatever ways are available to them. Illustrating, as Lily Hamourtziadou does with passion and commitment in this book, how the decisions and acts of the powerful have affected the powerless, remains a continuing necessity.

Hamit Dardagan and John Sloboda

Introduction: Human Security and the Emergence of Body Counts

In the 15th century, Renaissance mathematician and astronomer Nikolaus Copernicus formulated a model of the universe that put the sun, rather than the earth, at the centre of the solar system. That was a paradigm shift that led to a transformation in the way we view the universe. In a similar way, the 'human security' approach puts the individual, the citizen, the civilian, at the centre of understanding security, rather than the state and its borders.

The Commission on Human Security was established in January 2001, in response to the UN Secretary-General's call at the 2000 Millennium Summit for a world 'free of want' and 'free of fear'. On 1 May 2003, co-chairs of the Commission on Human Security, Sadako Ogata and Amartya Sen, presented the Commission's Final Report, 'Human Security Now', to the United Nations Secretary-General, Kofi Annan (Commission on Human Security, 2003).

According to the United Nations Commission on Human Security (CHS), human security is

> to protect the vital core of all human lives in ways that enhance human freedoms and human fulfilment. Human security means protecting fundamental freedoms – freedoms that are the essence of life. It means protecting people from critical (severe) and pervasive (widespread) threats and situations. It means using processes that build on people's strengths and aspirations. It means creating political, social, environmental, economic, military and cultural systems that together give people the building blocks of survival,

livelihood and dignity. (Human Security Unit Office for the Coordination of Humanitarian Affairs United Nations, 2003)

Overall, the definition proposed by the CHS reconceptualizes security by:

- moving away from traditional, state-centric conceptions of security that focused primarily on the safety of states from military aggression, to one that concentrates on the security of the individuals, their protection and empowerment;
- drawing attention to a multitude of threats that cut across different aspects of human life and thus highlighting the interface between security, development and human rights; and
- promoting a new integrated, coordinated and people-centred approach to advancing peace, security and development within and across nations.

As the shift was made from state to person, so the need to account for the human casualties of armed conflict grew. In 2002, Iraq Body Count (IBC), a human security project, was co-founded by Hamit Dardagan and John Sloboda, to document civilian deaths in Iraq following the US-led invasion in 2003. The UN started a body count of its own in 2006, to record violent deaths in Iraq. Other projects, such as Airwars, a collaborative project aimed at tracking and archiving the international air war against Islamic State and other groups, in both Iraq and Syria, and the Syrian Observatory for Human Rights, an information office documenting human rights abuses in Syria since 2011, followed a few years later.

According to Bulent Gokay, Professor in International Relations and founding member of Iraq Body Count,

'The original logic of the Iraq Body Count was based on the understanding that the warring parties in Iraq, the US authorities and their allies, as well as the Iraqi regime, were not interested in civilian casualties and therefore there was a real human security need to assess the level of damage to civilian life in the conflict. On the basis of this premise, Iraq Body Count emerged as an ongoing human security project which records violent deaths of Iraq civilians stemming from the 2003 military intervention. The count includes civilian deaths caused by coalition military action and by

military or paramilitary responses to the coalition presence
(e.g. insurgent and terrorist attacks). It also includes excess
civilian deaths caused by criminal action resulting from the
breakdown in law and order, which followed the coalition
invasion.' (Interviewed 22 June 2019)

The need to secure the civilian and holder of fundamental rights has led
to the moral imperative to track, record, document and memorialize the
killing and the suffering of those who find themselves in the midst of
violent conflict. The need for documenting the effects of military action
on civilians was underlined by John Chilcot in his report, published on 6
July 2016. It is the government's responsibility, he stated, to identify and
understand the likely and actual effects of its military action. Referring
to the Iraq war, he wrote that greater efforts should have been made 'to
determine the number of civilian casualties and the broader effects of
military operations on civilians' (The Iraq Inquiry, 2016, p 170). Among
his recommendations was that the government should be ready 'to work
with others, in particular NGOs and academic institutions, to develop
such assessments and estimates over time' (The Iraq Inquiry, 2016, p 219).
Section 17 points out that in 2006 the UK government

signed the Geneva Declaration on Armed Violence and
Development. Signatories resolved to take action to reduce
armed violence and its negative impact on socio-economic
and human development, including by supporting initiatives
'to measure the human, social and economic costs of armed
violence, to assess risks and vulnerabilities, to evaluate the
effectiveness of armed violence reduction programmes,
and to disseminate knowledge of best practices'. (The Iraq
Inquiry, 2016, p 207)

How then do we understand human security and casualty recording in
the 21st century, our fundamental human rights, and the importance
of bearing witness to a life and to a death?

International humanitarian law and human rights law

'Human security and human rights are mutually reinforcing, as they
identify the rights that need to be protected and recognize the ethical and
political importance of securing the holders of those rights. Protecting
human rights and upholding humanitarian law are essential to human
security' (Hamourtziadou, 2017, p 58). According to the Universal

Declaration of Human Rights, proclaimed by the United Nations General Assembly in Paris on 10 December 1948, human beings have the right to life, freedom and security. The first three articles set these out, with Article 1 stating that all human beings are born free and equal in dignity and rights; Article 2 stating that everyone is entitled to all the rights and freedoms set out in the declaration, without distinction of any kind, such as race, colour, sex, language, religion, political or other opinion, national or social origin, property, birth or other status. Furthermore, no distinction shall be made on the basis of the political, jurisdictional or international status of the country or territory to which a person belongs, whether it be independent, trust, non-self-governing or under any other limitation of sovereignty; and Article 3 stating that everyone has the right to life, liberty and security of person.

In August 1949, the Geneva Convention relative to the Protection of Civilian Persons in Time of War defined humanitarian protections for civilians in a war zone. In the General Provisions, Article 3 states that even where there is not a conflict of international character, the parties must at a minimum adhere to the protections described as: non-combatants, members of armed forces who have laid down their arms, and combatants who are *hors de combat* (out of the fight) due to wounds, detention, or any other cause *shall in all circumstances be treated humanely*, with the following prohibitions:

- violence to life and person, in particular murder of all kinds, mutilation, cruel treatment and torture;
- taking of hostages;
- outrages upon personal dignity, in particular humiliating and degrading treatment;
- the passing of sentences and the carrying out of executions without previous judgment pronounced by a regularly constituted court, affording all the judicial guarantees which are recognized as indispensable by civilized peoples. (Geneva Convention relative to the Protection of Civilian Persons in Time of War, 12 August 1949, Diplomatic Conference for the Establishment of International Conventions for the Protection of Victims of War)

Article 4 defines who is a protected person: 'Persons protected by the Convention are those who, at a given moment and in any manner whatsoever, find themselves, in case of a conflict or occupation, in the hands of a Party to the conflict or Occupying Power of which they are not nationals.' Those persons are to be protected regardless of race, nationality, religion or political opinion.

Article 32 states that a protected person/s shall not have anything done to them of such a character as to cause physical suffering or extermination.

Collective punishments are also prohibited:

> Article 33 stipulates that no persons may be punished for an offence they have not personally committed. Collective penalties and likewise all measures of intimidation or of terrorism are prohibited. Pillage is prohibited. Reprisals against persons and their property are prohibited.

Under the 1949 Geneva Conventions, collective punishment is a war crime:

> International humanitarian law seeks to limit the effects of armed conflict, by protecting those who are not or are no longer participating in the hostilities, and by restricting the means and methods of warfare. International humanitarian law is also known as the law of war or the law of armed conflict. Starting in the nineteenth century, an increasing number of states have contributed to its development and today it forms a universal body of law. (Hamourtziadou, 2017, p 59)

The four Geneva Conventions of 1949 have been developed and supplemented by two further agreements: the Additional Protocols of 1977 relating to the protection of victims of armed conflicts.

Other agreements prohibit the use of certain weapons and military tactics and protect certain categories of people and goods. These agreements include the 1954 Convention for the Protection of Cultural Property in the Event of Armed Conflict, plus its two protocols; the 1972 Biological Weapons Convention; the 1980 Conventional Weapons Convention and its five protocols; the 1993 Chemical Weapons Convention; the 1997 Ottawa Convention on anti-personnel mines; the 2000 Optional Protocol to the Convention on the Rights of the Child on the involvement of children in armed conflict (Advisory Service on International Humanitarian Law, 2004).

The aim of international humanitarian law is to protect those who do not take part in the fighting, such as civilians and medical personnel, and those who have ceased to take part, such as wounded, shipwrecked and sick combatants, and prisoners of war, all of which are entitled to respect for their lives and for their physical and mental integrity. In addition, medical personnel, supplies, hospitals and ambulances must all be protected. International humanitarian law also prohibits all means and methods of warfare which fail to discriminate between those who are taking part in the fighting and those who are not, so as to protect the civilian population, individual civilians and civilian property. International tribunals have been created to punish the breaking of those laws. An international criminal court, with the responsibility of repressing inter alia war crimes, was created by the 1998 Rome Statute (Hamourtziadou, 2017).

Just War theory is closely related to the international law of war crimes. 'Was the decision to wage war morally justified (*jus ad bellum*), and were the tactics employed in war morally justified (*jus in bello*)?' (May, 2007, p 4). The violation of a person's rights and of rules of humanitarian law is subject to prosecution as a war crime. *Jus in bello* carries the requirement of discrimination, or distinction. The Institute of International Law adopted a resolution at its 1969 Edinburgh meeting concerning the principle of distinction. The resolution declared:

- The obligation to respect the distinction between military objectives and non-military objectives, as well as between persons participating in the hostilities and members of the civilian population, remains a fundamental principle of international law.
- Existing international law prohibits all armed attacks on the civilian population.
- Existing international law prohibits the use of all weapons which, by their nature, affect indiscriminately both military objectives and nonmilitary objects, or both armed forces and civilian populations. (May, 2007, p 169)

Ingrid Detter, in *The Law of War*, writes: 'The protection of civilians is, from the humanitarian point of view, the most important task of any legislative effort on warfare as such persons include the weakest members of the community most in need of protection, such as women, children and the aged' (Detter, 2000, p 317). The status of being vulnerable is key to the principle of discrimination or 'distinction'.

The value of human life and the importance of its protection are evident in all this modern legislation. The case for the protection of human life and security is made on many levels and from many aspects: moral, legal, political and religious. Through the centuries 'we see a slow but steady development of the idea that each person is deserving of respect and protection as a free-thinking being equal to all others. The right to life is paramount and this is reflected by the abolition of the death penalty in many western countries in the last 100 years' (Hamourtziadou, 2017, p 60).

The doctrines of individualism and liberalism, doctrines on which much of Western society and culture has been constructed, dictate that all values and rights originate in the individual. According to individualism, each person's needs are more important than those of the group (society, nation and so on), and each person's interests are ethically paramount. Each self in the collective is autonomous and equal to all others, and the beliefs and aspirations of each are to be respected. Individual rights and liberties ought to be maximized, for the political and moral agency of the individual are at the heart of the development of the concept of universal human rights, that is, the rights of each individual regardless of the collective in which they find themselves and regardless of gender, age or physical ability (Hamourtziadou, 2017).

In the 20th century, liberalism led to the recognition and establishment of universal suffrage and civil rights. Liberals sought and established a constitutional order that prized important individual freedoms, racial and gender equality. Liberal internationalism was the driving force behind the establishment of the League of Nations after World War I and the United Nations after World War II. The recognition of the importance of human rights and the right of each individual to life, security and liberty has placed great demands on governments and organizations to closely monitor and record human deaths from armed violence. 'In the final analysis, human security is a child who did not die, a disease that did not spread, a job that was not cut, an ethnic tension that did not explode in violence, a dissident who was not silenced' (UNDP, 1994, p 22).

Casualty recording

Only five days before the publication of the Chilcot report, which stressed the importance of documenting civilian deaths and the effects of military operations on civilians, the White House released an executive order to address civilian casualties in US operations involving the use of force. President Obama emphasized the commitment of the USA to comply with its obligations under the law of armed conflict, including those that address the protection of civilians. The protection of civilians, he said, is consistent with the use of force in pursuit of US national interests. Minimizing civilian casualties can maintain the support of partner governments and vulnerable populations, especially in the conduct of counterterrorism and counterinsurgency operations;

and enhance the legitimacy and sustainability of US operations critical to national security.

He promised that his government would 'maintain and promote best practices that reduce the likelihood of civilian casualties, take appropriate steps when such casualties occur, and draw lessons from our operations to further enhance the protection of civilians' (Obama, 2016). In terms of policy, he resolved to train personnel to comply with legal obligations and policy guidance that address the protection of civilians; to develop, acquire and field intelligence, surveillance and reconnaissance systems that enable more accurate battlespace awareness, thus contributing to the protection of civilians; to develop technological capabilities that further enable the discriminate use of force in different operational contexts; to take precautions in conducting attacks to reduce the likelihood of civilian casualties; and to conduct assessments that assist in the reduction of civilian casualties.

There was also an expressed commitment to

- review or investigate incidents involving civilian casualties, including by considering relevant and credible information from all available sources, such as other agencies, partner governments, and nongovernmental organizations (NGOs), and take measures to mitigate the likelihood of future incidents of civilian casualties;
- acknowledge US government responsibility for civilian casualties and offer condolences, including ex gratia payments, to civilians who are injured or to the families of civilians who are killed.

In order to fulfil the above, the US president was prepared to obtain and use

> information about the number of strikes undertaken by the U.S. Government against terrorist targets outside areas of active hostilities from January 1, 2016, through December 31, 2016, as well as assessments of combatant and non-combatant deaths resulting from those strikes, and publicly release an unclassified summary of such information no later than May 1, 2017. (Obama, 2016)

Reports would then be written that would include the sources of information and methodology used to conduct these assessments and 'address the reasons for discrepancies between post-strike assessments from the U.S. Government and credible reporting from nongovernmental organizations regarding non-combatant deaths resulting from strikes undertaken by the U.S. Government against terrorist targets outside areas of active hostilities' (Obama, 2016).

Just days apart, there was official recognition by the US and the UK of the importance of casualty recording in war and armed conflict. By then, a number of bodies were painstakingly recording the violent deaths of people on a daily basis. The Every Casualty project was initiated in 2007 as a project at the Oxford Research Group, by Hamit Dardagan and John Sloboda, who together had co-founded Iraq Body Count in 2002. 'The Every Casualty Campaign refers to the civil society organisations who endorse a call on states to agree an international framework on casualty recording, building on the Charter for the recognition of every casualty of armed violence' (Every Casualty, 2011b).

The Charter for the recognition of every casualty of armed violence is founded on the principle that no person should die unrecorded, and calls on states to uphold this principle for the victims of armed violence. The charter applies equally to every person and encompasses every party to armed violence. All casualties of armed conflicts must be promptly recorded, correctly identified and publicly acknowledged. Any personal details must be verifiably established and be made accessible to all.

States and their military bear particular responsibility for populations under their control or jurisdiction, or who are endangered by their actions. For this reason, they must:

- ensure that the information produced is adequate and accessible as a basis for addressing the rights and needs of victims;
- take all relevant actions at the national level;
- work with others to develop an international framework for casualty recording.

Such an initiative will enable timely, transparent, reliable and comprehensive monitoring of armed violence, including its impact on specific groups, give a human face to the many nameless victims of armed violence, provide information for all parties to take steps to protect civilians from armed violence, and bring states and parties to armed violence into better compliance with international humanitarian, human rights and refugee law.

Every Casualty contributes to the Reclaiming the Protection of Civilians initiative, first published 13 June 2013, after a Global Conference on Reclaiming the Protection of Civilians under International Humanitarian Law in Oslo. The roughly 300 participants from 94 states discussed how to strengthen the protection of civilians under international humanitarian law. Casualty recording was recognized as an essential means to identify specific patterns of harm, enhance compliance with the law, inform effective missions to protect civilians and influence military practices in conflict.

As the foreign minister of Norway highlighted in his opening speech, 'Another key factor in improving the protection of civilians is ensuring that military operations and their effects on civilians are documented properly' (Eide, 2013).

Casualty recording plays a central role in the better understanding of failures in civilian protection, in order to prevent future failures. States needed to do much more to fulfil their share of responsibility in ensuring that every casualty is promptly recorded, correctly identified and publicly acknowledged – the three core demands around which the Every Casualty campaign is built.

The Oxford Research Group (ORG) has researched the work of 40 organizations and individuals that record the casualties of different conflicts across the globe, conducting the largest study of casualty recording practice ever carried out. They have provided some reasons why this practice is important *during* and *following* an armed conflict or war. According to them, casualty recording can support the rights and recognition of victims and their families; fuller knowledge of the trends and consequences of conflict, which can help inform humanitarian response planning and violence reduction policies; and processes to uphold the law. Casualty recorders provide information that may counteract misinformation or ignorance about casualties. Collecting and sharing knowledge about human losses could achieve positive changes in policy, humanitarian response or planning and could contribute to the on-going assessment of a conflict.

Some recorders working during conflict reported that the information they collected was used by local communities, by UN agencies, international NGOs and others for their assessment of the conflict situation, and to inform response planning through the indications given about areas of danger and need. Some of these recorders used mapping software to display their casualty data in a way that was dynamic and relevant to those seeking 'what, where, when' information about conflict incidents.

Casualty recording can be used for policy evaluation and conflict analysis, by governments, international organizations such as the World Health Organization (WHO), United Nations Development Programme (UNDP), the World Bank and the EU for research and assessment of conflict dynamics, media organizations, NGOs and university researchers. Identifying patterns and trends in deaths and violence can help assess the impact of strategy. Casualty recording by nongovernmental groups like Iraq Body Count has contributed to official records or counts of the dead, the allocation of war benefits by the state to the families of people who died, the seeking of compensation, criminal investigations and prosecutions by regional and international courts. Casualty recorders have provided information to courts about individuals and about patterns of harm or victimization in conflict. The information can also be used to seek asylum, or to assess asylum-seeking claims. The latest project Iraq Body Count conducted was a report it produced for the European Asylum Support Office (EASO) in 2019, on Iraq's security situation (EASO, 2019).

Casualty recording provides a body of evidence of how violence has affected particular communities or groups, such as the Yazidi or the Kurds. Such evidence is useful for political transition and future conflict prevention.

> By knowing and understanding who died and why, we can address and redress harm done, and prevent its recurrence. Any such historical record centred on the victims of war is valuable for both living and future generations. It is valuable for the families and communities of the victims, for policymakers and governments, for humanitarian and legal bodies, NGOs, researchers and the general public. (Hamourtziadou, 2017, p 63)

Casualty recording means building detailed knowledge of victims, perpetrators and incidents for every case. Casualty recording means collecting and confirming information about deaths thoroughly, and with a consistent methodology.

There are many ways the recording of casualties can be done, using a range of sources of information and methodologies, either during or after a conflict, which will give different levels of accuracy, certainty or confirmation, and different levels of detail about victims and incidents. Casualty recording usually involves the documenting of the deaths of individual people or groups of people, giving (where possible) details such as names, dates, locations, number of people killed and the type of violence used.

This book tracks and explores civilian deaths in Iraq following the 2003 invasion by the US-led coalition. It is a *recounting* of the conflict through the *counting* of its victims. It highlights the importance and the challenges of casualty recording. It maps the insurgency in Iraq and the ensuing civilian deaths, the struggle between military power and ideology, the increasing radicalization in failed states like Iraq, the seeking of security through hegemony, and the cycle of violence following the destruction and reconstruction of Iraq. It offers an understanding of war through a recording and comprehension of its casualties, central to our assessment of the costs of war; of whether the force used has been proportionate to the threat that prompted it; and it shows our concern for human welfare. It is important for any conflict to be understood not only in terms of the perpetrators of violence, or of the political and economic reasons behind it, but also in terms of its impact on the civilian population.

That the war in Iraq is part of the War on Terror is relevant in a number of ways. The war is still ongoing. This is not so much a historical account, but an examination and analysis of ongoing violence that needs to be addressed. People are being killed and injured on a daily basis, so any questions about this war and why it is happening are questions about why these civilians are being killed and what can be done about it. Has the latest strategy had the desirable impact? Have previous strategies? Any actions, reactions and their consequences need to be looked at, and this is what this book provides: an insight into those actions, any reactions to them, and the consequences for civilian life. In other words, it is important in both understanding the conflict and in developing strategies.

The originality of this book lies in its approach to conflict, in its angle on the still ongoing War on Terror and on the fact that it offers an account of the war in Iraq as it happened. As it will be composed of the recording and analysis of security as the conflict developed, it will trace, map and recount the violence documented by a casualty recorder. The work the NGO Iraq Body Count, twice nominated for the Nobel Peace Prize, will form the basis for this volume, as the author has been its principal researcher for the past 14 years. The aim is to disseminate research to scholars, policy advisers, national and international organizations and the public, but also to develop a new human security approach to war.

The IBC database is used not only for the numbers (which are only a fraction of IBC's work), but also to discuss and analyse Iraq's security and politics. IBC not only provides figures, although there is a daily count provided, but uses those figures to assess the security situation in Iraq through articles and annual reports. Those reports examine the violence in terms of location, incidents, demographics, perpetrators and weapons used. They will be part of this book.

The structure of the book is largely chronological, narrating the war as it happened, with the first chapter exploring the journey to the War on Terror, debates surrounding it and explanations provided: the question of clashing civilizations, the battle between good and evil, the politics of a hegemon and a hegemonic shift. The securitization of Iraq is traced back to the Gulf War, where it originated, and links are made between the two wars, in terms of both how issues around Iraq became part of America's, or the West's, security agenda and how 'speaking security' resulted in the deaths of thousands. The chapter concludes by introducing the first publication of Iraq Body Count, the Dossier on Civilian Casualties, compiled by IBC in the 2003–2005 period, starting from the night of the invasion. The Dossier was to provide the world with an initial assessment of the War on Terror, by revealing the recorded impact of the invasion and the violence it triggered on civilians.

The second chapter covers the 2006–2007 period, Iraq's most violent, presenting security and political developments partly through the weekly column 'A week in Iraq'. The chapter contains editorials with information about weekly deaths and the author's commentary, written as the violence occurred. They are a small selection out of about 100 the author has written for IBC, and provide a 'live' narrative of the human devastation in its context. The chapter discusses the 'price' of civilian life in Iraq, through compensation claims that reveal the monetary value of a human life lost as 'collateral damage', notions of 'victory' and the legal obligation of states to record the casualties of armed conflict. It examines regime security in weak states and its role in growing insecurity and in contributing to the creation of sectarian identities. It also addresses the impact of the war and occupation on children, the growing phenomenon of suicide and the inability of the government to provide basic security to the population. As it was during this period that Iraq become 'democratic', the chapter traces the roots of Iraq's current bloody anti-government protests and general discontent, and even a 'Saddam nostalgia', in the events of those early years of democracy under the control of a foreign power. The chapter ends by assessing the American surge of 2007 as part of a Western security culture where force is the solution or method of control, by applying Paul Rogers' control paradigm that centres on the military-industrial complex and the use of military force in responding to threats. In Iraq this strategy has been proven to be, at times, insufficient in ensuring peace and stability, and, at times, the cause of further insurgency and insecurity.

The third chapter covers the 2008–2009 period through editorials and annual security analysis. The narrative continues as both 'live', with events being recounted through the editorials, and reflective. It looks at the consequences of state collapse, at the impact of enforcing a neoliberal system on Iraq, in terms of exploitation and economic insecurity, but also in terms of leading to deepening socioeconomic divisions which have marginalized, alienated and angered millions of people, thus increasing instability and insecurity, nationally and regionally. Iraq's economic transformation that has led to low standards of living, dismal economic and employment conditions, energy and food shortages, all of which plague Iraq today, is discussed within the context of power, leadership and hegemony. Causes and weapons of war, nation-building 'military style', community trauma, energy security and state vulnerability are also discussed within the framework of a discussion on threats, risks and impact.

The fourth chapter narrates the 2010–2013 period. The chapter discusses the new American presidency and the use of drones; the release of the Iraq War Logs by WikiLeaks, which enabled IBC to conduct further research into civilian deaths and add thousands more victims to its database; the Human Terrain System, a strategy to manage the 'far enemy'; finally, it provides the context in which we can understand the emergence of the 'Awakening Councils', which appeared to change the course of the war, by reducing the casualties and by reflecting the power and the influence of a true hegemon, one that rules not through coercion, but through persuasion.

The fifth chapter provides records of civilian deaths in the 2014–2017 period, in the context of political and security developments, raising questions regarding the nature and role of the Islamic State of Iraq and Syria (ISIS), and the impact of the way the coalition has countered the terror. 'Precision bombing', the Arab Spring, ISIS and the rise in civilian deaths are explored as factors contributing to the state of human security in Iraq.

The book exemplifies and analyses human security using the 2003 invasion of Iraq by following in the footsteps of IBC's casualty recording work. It concludes with a discussion on the challenges and contributions of IBC as a casualty recording body of an ongoing conflict. The War on Terror is revisited in how it simultaneously relates to (a) Iraq, (b) civilians and (c) security. As Western publics are becoming ever more desensitized to Iraqi suffering, after 16 years of never-ending bloodshed, how do we understand, explain and justify the violent deaths of over 200,000 Iraqi civilians as they try to manage their day-to-day existence? Were they necessary, and, if so, to whom? Were they inevitable? And how does our understanding/explanation/justification of those killings relate to our understanding of the War on Terror?

1

The Long Journey to the War on Terror

The War on Terror was officially declared on 12 September 2001, by US President George W. Bush, and the invasion of Iraq 18 months later took place as part of that war. Since then, other states have joined the US-led coalition in fighting that now global war in Afghanistan, Iraq and Syria, but also in many other parts of Asia, Africa, Europe, Australia and the Americas, in terms of training, conducting military exercises, combat and air/drone strikes. Seventeen years after the first invasion, of Afghanistan, the US was actively engaged in countering terrorism in 80 nations on six continents, including Pakistan, Iraq, Syria, Libya, India, Bangladesh, Sri Lanka, Turkey, Bulgaria, Albania, Serbia, Philippines, Australia, Colombia, Argentina, Mexico, Yemen and South Africa (Savell, 2019).

'Our war on terror begins with al Qaeda, but it does not end there. It will not end until every terrorist group of global reach has been found, stopped and defeated' Bush promised in his State of the Union address on 21 September 2001 (Bush, 2001c). That promise was made on the back of 2,977 deaths ten days earlier, but since that clear day on 11 September 2001, hundreds of thousands of civilians have lost their lives in unimaginable violence, over 200,000 in Iraq alone. And with such devastating loss of life in a war not only still fought, but also grown in size, comes the question: what is this War on Terror? Other than to 'find, stop and defeat' terrorist groups, why are men, women and children killed daily, or live in poverty and fear, without home or country? How can we come to understand this human insecurity, its context and its consequences?

This chapter aims to provide an understanding of the context/s of those deaths, an understanding of the importance of recording them and, finally, an understanding of war not through military deaths or victories, not through states and borders, but through the security of the civilians whose lives have been impacted.

The wars

'The 1991 war against Iraq never ended. The United States and Iraq agreed to a ceasefire on February 28, 1991, but this agreement did not signify the coming of peace. Rather, the war was transformed into an eleven-year-long siege. US military forces enforced the tightest economic blockade against an entire country in human history.' The US and Iraq agreed to a ceasefire on February 28, 1991, but the war was far from over. Eleven years of economic sanctions followed, an economic siege that was to further cripple a defeated country, a civilian population suffering the effects of a bombardment that had resulted in thousands of deaths.

In fact, the conquest of the Middle East and complete regional domination by the West, especially of the oil-rich areas of the Persian/Arabian Gulf, was a century-old foreign policy by the start of the 21st century. Iraq, much like Iran, Turkey, Palestine, Egypt, Afghanistan and Syria, had enjoyed periods of alliance and cooperation with the West, and suffered periods of enmity and war, as regimes changed and interests were threatened. Since 1991 Iraq was a clear threat to US interests in the Middle East and a new war to 'finish the job' was needed. 'Using the post-September 11, 2001 opening, the Bush White House has pushed the so-called doctrine of pre-emptive war. That is, Washington will select a designated enemy and attack regardless of whether the "enemy" has attacked the United States, or anyone for that matter' (Clark, 1992, p xx).

The broad rubric of the War on Terror would be used to redefine the threat of terrorism to include governments-as-sponsors, to fight a limitless number of wars of aggression and to justify acts of mass destruction.

When Bush spoke of the threat of states that had or were developing weapons of mass destruction or non-conventional weapons, he did not mean the US, Britain, France, Russia or Israel, all of which possess them. 'Presumably the threat to humanity came from Iraq, Iran, North Korea, Cuba, Libya and Syria – all formerly colonised countries located in strategic, resource-rich areas. Countries that have pursued their own independent political and development policies rather than follow the dictates of Washington or the International Monetary Fund' (Clark, 2005, p xx).

On 17 January 1991, the US began its bombing campaign across Iraq, starting with 2,000 aerial sorties a day; in the 42-day assault US overflights would exceed 109,000, with more than 88,500 tons of explosives dropped on Iraq (Gellman, 1991, p A1). In this war against civilian life, 'the bombing was a deadly, calculated, and deeply immoral strategy to bring Iraq to its knees by destroying the essential facilities and support systems of the entire society' (Clark, 2005, p 59).

The bombing of Iraq had little to do with driving Iraq from Kuwait, or with punishing a brutal dictator, who had previously, though just as brutal, been an ally of the West. It was intended to cripple a developing country, rich in oil, that wanted to be politically independent.

As early as August 1990, Pentagon plans to conduct air strikes against civilian sites, such as industrial sites, power and water treatment plants, had appeared in the press. What was bombed were 'homes, electrical plants, fuel storage facilities, civilian factories, hospitals, churches, civilian airports, vehicles, transportation facilities, food storage and food testing laboratories, grain silos, animal vaccination centres, schools, communication towers, civilian government office buildings, and stores' (Clark, 1994, p 6).

The bombing of all of those was illegal, according to Protocol 1, Additional to the Geneva Conventions, 1977, as stated by Articles 52, 53 and 54:

Article 52. General Protection of Civilian Objects.
Article 53. Protection of Cultural Objects and Places of Worship.
Article 54. Protection of Objects Indispensable to the Survival of the
    Civilian Population.

There were thousands of direct civilian casualties from the bombings, but, with the sanctions that followed, the damage to life-support systems meant that thousands more died. There was no systematic casualty recording by any organization like the Iraq Body Count back then, but it was estimated that the six-week bombing killed around 50,000 civilians, while twice as many died in the post-war period, according to Iraq's health minister, Doctor Umaid Midhat Mubarak. Other estimates were higher; based on infant mortality rates, UNICEF (United Nations International Children's Fund) estimated in December 1991 that 87,000 children alone would have died by the war's anniversary (Clark, 2005, p 83). The destruction, devastation and sanctions that followed meant that Iraq could not recover its vital services, nor could it restore or rebuild its economy and infrastructure. 'Together, bombing and sanctions reduced Iraq to a pre-industrial state' (Clark, 2005, p 75). It was this state the US and Britain invaded in March 2003. This time, Iraq Body Count was ready to record the casualties.

US security policy: neoconservatism and empire

Notwithstanding the destruction and devastation, Iraq was not invaded, occupied or dismantled in the 1990s. George H.W. Bush and his administration wanted Iraq to remain a counterweight to Iran. The US did not want a Shiite regime in southern Iraq or a Kurdish regime in northern Iraq (Dorrien, 2004). Yet by the mid-1990s there were calls for a change in policy: to declare Saddam Hussain a war criminal, cut off his access to oil money and secure northern Iraq. Paul Wolfowitz exhorted that 'Iraq is not a sideshow; it is about vital American interests. We have lost a lot of ground. The US has virtually abandoned its commitment to protect a besieged people from a bloodthirsty dictator'. Instead of sitting by, 'with our passive containment policy and our inept covert operations', the United States needed to 'take concerted action to get rid of Saddam' (Wolfowitz, 1996).

Moreover, America's pursuit of exporting democracy to the rest of the world, a mission that had started during the Cold War, when it protected 'freedom' from communism, was now possible. Having 'won' the Cold War, having made parts of the world safe and ready for democracy, the call to spread American values, while simultaneously serving American interests, compelled a new crusade. In this crusade the United States was to strive for universal freedom, but also for universal dominion, a world order described by Francis Fukuyama in *The End of History*, which proclaimed that the Hegelian end of history was occurring in a world at such a stage of sociocultural evolution that perfect civil society was possible. Liberal democracy would be the final form of human government, bringing with it the end of war, the West's ideological debates and a common marketization of the world (Fukuyama, 1989). America's vision now was to steer the world away from a multipolar system to a unipolar world, where a strong West would dominate, guided by the greatness and power of America, a 'super-sovereign West economically, culturally, and politically hegemonic in the world' (Krauthammer, 1989, p 49).

Attacks must be on terrorist-harbouring countries, not terrorist networks. It was important to capture bin Laden and to defeat al-Qaeda, but the overriding aim of the War on Terror was to change regimes, as neither universal freedom nor universal dominion could be achieved without regime change. When Colin Powell demanded the Taliban give up bin Laden and al-Qaeda, journalist and political columnist Charles Krauthammer replied that the Taliban had to pay even if it delivered both: 'If the administration goes wobbly on the

Taliban, it might as well give up the war on terrorism before it starts … The take-home lesson must be: Harbor terrorists – and your regime dies.' Krauthammer wanted the United States to overthrow Syria's Assad regime, a 'low-hanging fruit' that harboured terrorist groups. After Syria, the United States would have to remove the regimes in Iran and Iraq. 'The war on terrorism will conclude in Baghdad', he predicted. 'If this president wants victory in the war he has declared, he will have to achieve it on the very spot where his own father, 10 years ago, let victory slip away' (Krauthammer, 2001b).

What the war and the end of history required was nothing less than complete regional transformation. Of the 22 Arab states, none was a democracy, while nearly all were hostile to Israel. The war against terrorism was a war against Arab-grown radical Islamism, and the key to changing the Middle East was to overthrow the Baathist regime in Iraq: 'A de-Saddamized Iraq with a decent government could revolutionize the region (Krauthammer, 2003). Upon overthrowing Saddam Hussain, America would have a base 'for the outward projection of American power' and the dissemination of 'democratic and modernizing ideas'. Global subordination to American power was to be America's imperial burden.

This was imperial realism: '9/11 was a wake-up call for the United States to unambiguously embrace its imperial responsibilities' (Dorrien, 2004, p 155). The call was to consolidate American power in the Middle East by changing political culture in the region.

Iraq was a prize bigger than Taliban-controlled Afghanistan. 'Saddam Hussein, because of his strategic position in the Persian Gulf and the Middle East, surely represents a more potent challenge to the United States and its interests and principles than the weak, isolated and, we trust, soon to be crushed Taliban' (Kagan and Kristol, 2001). The attacks of 9/11 opened the door to a worldwide American war against terrorism; 'The war on anti-American terrorism must target Hezbollah, the terrorist group backed by Iran and Syria, as well as the Taliban. And it must include a determined effort to remove Saddam Hussein from power' (Kagan and Kristol, 2001). Regime change in Afghanistan and Iraq was by no means sufficient, but it was a necessary condition, if political, economic and cultural transformation/domination were to begin.

European Kantians and American Hobbesians

Much of Europe opposed a lot of what the War on Terror would entail, back in 2001–2003. With the exception of Britain, Europe did not support the long and bloody military campaign commenced by the US. Neoconservative American historian Robert Kagan explained that this opposition to employing military force was to be understood within the historical and political world the Europeans inhabited, a world very different from the one in which Americans lived. According to Kagan, at the start of the 21st century, Europeans lived in a 'post-historical paradise' of international law and cooperation, in which power was not the determinative reality in higher forms of civilization. They lived in the social contract world of 'perpetual peace' that Kant had envisioned. Americans, on the other hand, 'lived in the Hobbesian world of history and power, where international rules were unreliable and social order depended upon and was shaped by military might' (Kagan, 2002a, p 1).

The Europeans, having little power, no longer believed in it. After World War II, in a state of post-historical moralism, they became averse to employing military force, seeking a world 'where strength doesn't matter so much, where unilateral action by powerful states is forbidden, where all nations regardless of their strength are protected by commonly agreed rules of behavior' (Kagan, 2002a, p 5). The Kantian world of perpetual peace was more important than the slaying of a tyrant, but Americans were powerful enough not to be frightened of the Hobbesian state of nature (Kagan, 2002b, 2003). Weak nations like those in Europe seek security through rules, but great powers rely on their own power to provide security. Those who lack power seek to restrain those who have it, and those who have it, want to keep and maximize it. The US emerges as a benevolent but also a hectoring hegemon, liberating and democratizing through force, aggression and the unlimited exercise of its power.

The War on Terror: four narratives

Debates on the War on Terror have been ongoing since 2001, with views ranging from American domination in a New World Order, to the battle of freedom against the enemies of freedom. The debates can roughly be arranged into four categories, each providing an explanation of the nature of this war. According to each explanation, the War on Terror is:

- A clash of civilizations (cultural);
- A battle between good and evil (moral);
- Imperialism by a (benevolent?) hegemon (political);
- A cluster of morbid symptoms (structural).

A clash of civilizations

Samuel Huntington argued in 1993 that 'the fault lines of civilizations would be the battle lines of the future' (Huntington, 1993, p 22. Huntington's theory, which predates 9/11 and the War on Terror, maintains that nations will become more divided culturally, as identity politics become more important in global relations:

> It is my hypothesis that the fundamental source of conflict in the new world will not be primarily ideological or primarily economic. The great divisions among humankind and the dominating source of conflict will be cultural. Nation states will remain the most powerful actors in global affairs, but the principal conflicts of global politics will occur between nations and groups of different civilizations. The clash of civilizations will dominate global politics. (Huntington, 1993, p 22)

Huntington argued that the most troublesome civilization in the world was the Islamic, because, he claimed, it encourages a loyalty to the religion that supplants the nation state, while it is hostile towards ideas such as democracy, liberty, individualism and universal human rights. This makes it incompatible with Western values.

Huntington's clash of civilizations argument had partly been prompted by Francis Fukuyama's end of history thesis. Fukuyama argued that the fall of the Soviet Union signalled the triumph of liberal democracy and capitalism, which signalled the end of history, because history is the progress of society towards an ideal form of government. This government is democracy, for democracy equals peace, order and prosperity.

The incompatibility of values between Islam and the West was certainly highlighted by both President Bush and Osama bin Laden, leader of al-Qaeda. Osama bin Laden's rhetoric, when he said 'These events have divided the whole world into two sides. The side of believers and the side of infidels', fully supported the idea of a clash of civilizations and he often portrayed Islam as being at war with the West, as he wanted the Muslim world to see it that way (Bin Laden, 2001). Continuing from al-Qaeda, ISIS has been more successful in promoting this view and has convinced large numbers of Muslims in the West (foreign fighters) and the East (local support), many of whom have been persuaded to join the fight against the Western enemy in Iraq and in Syria. Indeed the clash of civilizations argument that presents the West as being at war with Islam can be a powerful tool for radicalization. 'Every Muslim has to rush to make his religion victorious. The winds of faith have come', urged bin Laden (2001).

In 'The War on Terrorism: A Cultural Perspective', Fawaz Gerges writes,

> Bin Laden claims that targeting American civilians is a legitimate defensive act, because 'Muslims believe that the Jews and America have overplayed their hand in humiliating, degrading, and punishing Muslims'. Moreover, 'these attacks on American targets are legitimate public reactions by the Muslim youth, who are willing to sacrifice their lives to defend their people and Islam'. (Gerges, 2002, p 18)

'Bin Laden has stated that his goal is to destroy the very foundation of international relations and overhaul the system of power politics that punishes Muslims and keeps them down. This is a revolt against secular history and heritage and what he terms Western hegemony over the lands of Islam', he continues (Gerges, 2002, p 19). 'This humiliation and atheism has ruined and blinded Muslims', Bin Laden claims. 'The only way to destroy this atheism is by Jihad, fighting, bombings that bring martyrdom. Only blood will wipe out the shame and dishonor inflicted on Muslims' (Rubin and Colp Rubin, 2002, p 181).

George W. Bush defined the 9/11 attacks as attacks on 'our freedom' and 'our way of life'. The 9/11 attacks were not simply an attack on America, but an attack on Western values and civilization, one that all freedom-loving Western countries would need to defend themselves from. 'Today, our fellow citizens, our way of life, our very freedom came under attack in a series of deliberate and deadly terrorist acts' was how he started his address to the nation (Bush, 2001b). 'Civilized people everywhere have recognized that terrorists threaten every nation that loves liberty and cherishes the protection of individual rights. Respect for human dignity and individual freedoms reaffirms a core tenet of civilized people everywhere', he proclaimed on 9 December 2001. Those Middle Eastern groups like al-Qaeda and the Taliban were promoting inequality, oppression and the glorification of violence, all of which were not only incompatible with Western values, but, on this basis, morally unacceptable. This was evident in Bush's Proclamation 7513:

> The terrible tragedies of September 11 served as a grievous reminder that the enemies of freedom do not respect or

value individual human rights. Their brutal attacks were an attack on these very rights. When our essential rights are attacked, they must and will be defended.

Americans stand united with those who love democracy, justice, and individual liberty. We are committed to upholding these principles, embodied in our Constitution's Bill of Rights, that have safeguarded us throughout our history and that continue to provide the foundation of our strength and prosperity.

The heinous acts of terrorism committed on September 11 were an attack against civilization itself, and they have caused the world to join together in a coalition that is now waging war on terrorism and defending international human rights. Americans have looked beyond our borders and found encouragement as the world has rallied to join the American-led coalition. Civilized people everywhere have recognized that terrorists threaten every nation that loves liberty and cherishes the protection of individual rights.

Respect for human dignity and individual freedoms reaffirms a core tenet of civilized people everywhere. This important observance honoring our Bill of Rights and advocating human rights around the world allows all Americans to celebrate the universal principles of liberty and justice that define our dreams and shape our hopes as we face the challenges of a new era. (Bush, 2001f)

It was also evident in Laura Bush's 18 November 2001 radio address urging condemnation of the Taliban, which mirrored her husband's speeches, in an attempt to justify the invasion of Afghanistan:

Afghan women know, through hard experience, what the rest of the world is discovering: the brutal oppression of women is a central goal of the terrorists. Civilized people throughout the world are speaking out in horror – not only because our hearts break for the women and children in Afghanistan, but also because in Afghanistan, we see the world the terrorists would like to impose on the rest of us. (Bush, Laura, 2001)

It appears that the Taliban's cruel regime and values, which had been in existence in Afghanistan for years, only became a real concern, one that justified an invasion, in late 2001.

The two civilizations that were clashing then were one that promoted democracy, freedom, tolerance, justice and equality, at least from a Western perspective, and one that espoused intolerance, oppression, tyranny, injustice and dictatorship. From the opposite perspective, it was the West that stood for oppression, intolerance, brutality, exploitation and injustice; the West that showed hypocrisy in first setting up and then not respecting all human rights, but only the rights of its own people, while Islam was the protector of truth and virtue, of justice and peace and of all those that have been the victims of Western oppression in the Middle East.

Deepa Kumar, in 'Imperialist Feminism', questions this distinction between 'good culture' and 'bad culture', as well as the concern shown by the West, for 'female oppression elsewhere'. The message is that female oppression takes place

> in the Global South, in cultures that the West considers backward and barbaric, and not only is it not a problem here, but it is the responsibility of women in the West to wage a moral crusade to rescue their Brown and Black sisters. This then is the logic of imperialist feminism in the twenty-first century, shaped by the deeply racist framework of the 'clash of civilizations', which is based on the idea that the West is a superior culture because it believes in democracy, human rights, secularism, women's rights, gay rights, freedom of speech, and a whole host of other liberal values, whereas the Global South is barbaric, misogynistic, driven by religion, and illiberal. From this follows the 'white man's burden' and the 'white woman's burden' to intervene through any means necessary, including wars of colonization, to 'liberate' less fortunate women in other parts of the world. (Kumar, 2015)

In the launching of the War on Terror, old orientalist tropes are being used to serve imperial aims, and Western nation states are being recreated in line with the 'clash of civilizations' framework. The origins of imperial feminism can actually be traced to the 19th century, when 'Brown and Black women were constructed within the dominant colonial logic', and 'white women were implicated within colonial politics'. Some middle- and upper-class women supported colonialism, seeing it as a means to win rights for women, she argues, yet 'empire does not liberate women either in the colonies or in the metropole. I argue that women in imperial centers, particularly working-class women, have little to gain from empire. In reality, the liberation of Eastern women has never been on the agenda for colonial powers' (Kumar, 2015). She describes the imperialist feminist narrative as 'a false feminism' for two reasons. First, it fails to address or 'liberate' Eastern women, and, secondly, it does a disservice to Western women, in presenting them as being already liberated because they are a part of a 'superior civilization'. This rhetoric 'further drives a wedge between Eastern and Western women that is predicated on racism, nationalism, and the logic of civilizational superiority' (Kumar, 2015).

Having seen his 'end of history' argument serve as the basis for a series of wars based on civilizational/cultural superiority and the imperative to spread good Western values, Fukuyama wrote a rather defensive piece in *The New York Times* in 2006, where he claimed his argument had been misunderstood.

In 'After neoconservatism' Fukuyama wrote,

> The so-called Bush Doctrine, elaborated in the 2002 National Security Strategy of the United States, argued that 'America would have to launch periodic preventive wars to defend itself against rogue states and terrorists with weapons of mass destruction; that it would do this alone, if necessary; and that it would work to democratize the greater Middle East as a long-term solution to the terrorist problem'. (Fukuyama, 2006)

The principles of this doctrine were a concern with democracy and human rights; a belief that American power can be used for moral purposes; and a belief that international institutions cannot solve security problems.

However, he argued, the end of history was not about enforcing values or political systems. It was not about using American or any other power. The end of history was

> an argument about modernization. What is initially universal is not the desire for liberal democracy but rather the desire to live in a modern – that is, technologically advanced and prosperous – society, which, if satisfied, tends to drive demands for political participation. Liberal democracy is one of the byproducts of this modernization process, something that becomes a universal aspiration only in the course of historical time. (Fukuyama, 2006)

The end of history was 'A Marxist argument for the existence of a long-term process of social evolution, but one that terminates in liberal democracy'. The neoconservative position, on the other hand, was Leninist, believing that 'history can be pushed along with the right application of power and will' (Fukuyama, 2006).

Good versus evil

In 'World War IV: how it started, what it means and why we have to win', Norman Podhoretz defines the War on Terror as World War IV (World War III having been the Cold War), 'a global battle to preserve liberty' (Podhoretz, 2004).

The Bush doctrine, he writes, has four pillars:

- terrorists and the regimes that sponsor them are members of an 'irregular' army that must be dealt with through war and regime change;
- it is America's right to pre-empt those who would attack it;
- commitment to help friendly nations and oppose the unfriendly;
- moral clarity and the right to call regimes 'evil'.

If Bush's World War IV doctrine is of regime change and pre-emption, it is so for the purpose of spreading freedom and other good values, and for the purpose of fighting evil, which includes all that is against those good values. We see that the language chosen to explain the 9/11 attacks worked to enforce a particular understanding of their political, military and cultural meaning. It justified and normalized a military response. Writing the War on Terror entails writing identity: the evil terrorists versus the good Americans. The social construction of all war requires an 'othering' process. When he addressed the nation, Bush described the attackers/hijackers as 'evil, 'despicable', 'the very worst of human nature' (Bush, 2001a). They are 'enemies of freedom', 'the heirs of all the murderous ideologies of the 20th century' (Bush, 2001d), 'parasites that hide' (Bush, 2001e) and 'faceless enemies of human dignity' (Bush, 2003). While Americans were described as 'moms and dads, friends and neighbors', 'strong', a 'great people has been moved to defend a great nation', 'the brightest beacon for freedom and opportunity in the world', 'daring' and 'caring' (Bush, 2001a), 'a loving and giving people' (Bush, 2001d), and America 'loves peace, America will always work and sacrifice for the expansion of freedom' (Bush, 2003).

This was echoed by others. 'Has there ever been a time when the distinction between good and evil was more clear?' asked

Krauthammer shortly after the attacks (Krauthammer, 2001a). It was not a distinction that could easily be dismissed or discredited, when we witnessed, live, the murder of thousands of people going about their day, working, or travelling; when we watched men and women jumping off burning towers and crashing on the road below; when we heard the terror in the voices of those calling from the planes and the buildings, some asking for help, others sending their last messages of love. How could those men who inflicted such pain, such devastation and death, not be *evil*? And how could we, in fighting against them, not be *good*?

Foucault wrote that language is the force that creates and maintains the world. It is through language, the terms we use to give meaning to events and behaviours, that meaning is created. It is through language that 'evil' and 'good' are defined, 'self' and 'other' are constructed, meaning is bestowed and knowledge is established. Moreover, this knowledge, this set of 'truths' we accept, is produced by power, it relies on power and it reinforces power. Truth and knowledge are simply and inextricably part of social settings. What is 'true' is so within specific discourses, some of which dominate others, so that some truths dominate others.

When the planes hit the twin towers, what we witnessed was metal hitting concrete. What this meant, in terms of it being a good act or a bad act, was not inherent in the event itself, but was given, thus creating a truth and knowledge. One narrative, that became the dominant Western narrative, used terms such as 'act of war', 'evil' and 'mass murder'. This then became the truth that dominated other truths in narratives that described the same events as part of a holy war 'against the friends of Satan' (Bin Laden, 2002). Which side was good and which side was bad, as clear as we took it to be, was not at all contained within the act, but was decided by a number of parties, all holders of power, users of speech and moral agents.

When American air strikes hit civilian homes in Iraq, killing thousands of people, much like those in the twin towers or on the planes, we again had metal hitting concrete and we again had to ask if those were good acts or evil acts. Those events could once again be described as 'murder', as 'collateral damage', as 'necessary sacrifice', or as something else. The 'grand narratives', those stories a culture tells itself about its practices and beliefs (for example, that democracy is the most enlightened and rational form of government), define and contain the values, truths, meanings and knowledge created by power, which in turn maintain that power. Moreover, it is through those grand narratives and constructed meanings that we understand the world.

Sharing in that power that produces knowledge is the media. Stuart Hall wrote that 'the media play a part in the formation, in the constitution, of the things that they reflect. It is not that there is a world outside, "out there", which exists free of the discourses of representation. What is "out there" is, in part, constituted by how it is represented'. What is 'out there' is 'media-mediated' (Hall, 2011, p 15), in 'a world that absolutely insists on dividing everything it says into good and bad' (Hall, 2011, p 16).

> Our histories actually intertwine and interpenetrate; how necessary 'the Other' is to our own sense of identity; how even the dominant, colonizing, imperializing, power only knows who and what it is and can only experience the pleasure of its own power of domination in and through the construction of the Other. The two are the two sides of the same coin. And the Other is not *out there*, but *in here*. It is not outside, but inside. (Hall, 2011, p 16)

Imperialism by a (benevolent?) hegemon

Consistent with the realist position, the War on Terror has been described as a neo-imperial programme, designed to further American political interests. It is a struggle for power. By invading the Middle East, America gains physical and strategic control over energy supplies, as it transforms regimes, brings peace, liberty and democracy. It is the perfect marriage of *might* and *right*.

As the US is an economic superpower, dollar hegemony is strategic to US global dominance of the economic marketplace. The dollar is deeply rooted in the geopolitical role of the US. America's hegemonic position rests on its ability to control the sources and transport routes for crucial energy and other material supplies needed by leading industrial states. For this it needs strategic positioning so as to achieve and maintain sea, air and land dominance, especially in the Middle East, the eastern Mediterranean, the Atlantic, Pacific and Indian oceans. The 9/11 attacks gave the US the opportunity to try to monopolize energy resources, to increase its grip on the Middle East and to demonstrate that it had an important role to play in the post-Cold War world, one that combined military force and political and economic control.

The 9/11 attacks were an opportunity for America to declare its (Western) values universal and to start to enforce them, which was consistent with its neo-imperial ideology. Thus it was going to dominate by making its ideas and values the dominant ideas and values:

> This is an era of 'tremendous opportunity' for America, inasmuch as America can present its national values as universal ones and impose them on the globe, also by means of violence. Again, this is not a new ingredient of imperialism: It is an ages-old and enduring ideological principle that conditions the political attempt by a group of people to become dominant either nationally or internationally. To dominate others, one's ideas must become dominant over other people's ideas. The events of 9/11 are presented as an opportunity opening the way for America to achieve just that. (Fouskas and Gokay, 2005, p 126)

Again, we see how truth and knowledge, meaning and morality, are produced through narratives that become dominant, that is, through power. As a global hegemon, America would have that power, thus defining what is true and what is right, as well as gaining control of resources, the global economy, land and sea. For that, it would need to apply military force, with as much loss of life as was necessary. 'America must strike constantly, incessantly, and where necessary unilaterally and preemptively', according to the 'National Strategy for Combating Terrorism' (Fouskas and Gokay, 2005, p 126). The War on Terror may be infinite; it would last as long as necessary for America to achieve full dominance and imposition of its values of liberal democracy and free market economy on the globe.

It has now become almost a cliché to say that the War on Terror was declared by the US so it could gain access to Iraq's oil. Yet plans to take control of the oil were made a few months before the events of 11 September 2001, by Dick Cheney's Energy Task Force, which discussed the 'capture' of Iraqi oil from February 2001. 'By May 2001 it had already set out, urgently and in some detail, plans for taking control over Iraqi oil' (Scott, 2007, p 187).

A National Security Council document, dated February 2001, directed NSC staff to cooperate fully with Cheney's task force. The document, reported in *The New Yorker* magazine, noted that the task force would be considering the 'melding' of two policy areas: the review of operational policies towards 'rogue states' and 'actions regarding the capture of new and existing oil and gas fields'. So Cheney's Energy Task Force was considering the capture of oil and gas reserves in 'rogue' states, including presumably Iraq (McQuaig, 2004a, 2004b).

The Energy Task Force's concerns are illustrated by two documents, released after a fierce court battle. The first is a map of Iraq whose 'detail is all about Iraq's oil. The south-west is neatly divided, for instance, into nine "Exploration Blocks". Stripped of political trappings, this map shows a naked Iraq, with only its ample natural assets in view. It's like a supermarket meat chart, which identifies the various parts of a slab of beef' (Scott, 2007, p 189). The second document is a chart titled 'Foreign Suitors for Iraqi Oil Fields'. 'It identifies 63 oil companies from 30 countries and specifies which Iraqi oil fields each company is interested in and the status of the company's negotiations with Saddam Hussein's regime.' Among them was France's Total Elf Aquitaine, interested in the 25-billion-barrel Majnoon oil field. Baghdad had agreed to the French plans to develop this 'succulent slab of Iraq. There goes the filet mignon to the mouths of the French!' (Scott, 2007, p 189).

A strategy to deal with Middle East oil, at the centre of which was Iraq, had started to develop a few years earlier. In 1997 a report from the James A. Baker Institute of Public Policy at Rice University had addressed America's energy security problem, noting that Saddam Hussein was still a threat to Middle Eastern security. A second report from the same institute followed in 2001, co-sponsored by the Council on Foreign Relations in New York. The report, 'Strategic Energy Policy: Challenges for the Twenty-first Century', advised that 'the US should conduct an immediate policy review toward Iraq including military, energy, economic and political/diplomatic assessments' (Morse and Myers Jaffe, 2001, p 40).

The strategy involved dominating the oil, but also defending the dollar. The dollar's current strength is supported by the requirement of the Organization of the Petroleum Exporting Countries (OPEC), secured originally by a secret agreement between the United States and Saudi Arabia, that all OPEC oil sales be denominated in dollars. This was threatened by some OPEC countries that followed the lead of Iraq in 2000 'to allow some OPEC sales to be paid in euros' (Scott, 2007, p 190). The *Financial Times*, on 5 June 2003, confirmed that Iraqi oil sales were now switched back from euros to dollars: 'Iraq stepped back into the international oil market yesterday for the first time since the war, offering 10m barrels of oil from its storage tanks for sale to the highest bidder ... The tender, for which bids are due by June 10, switches the transaction back to dollars' (Hoyos and Morrison, 2003).

The Project for the New American Century (PNAC), a neo-imperialist project of the mid-1990s, provided a model for attaining global primacy. The 11 September 2001 attacks may have accelerated but did not alter the course the US was already on. The PNAC was created as an answer to post-Cold War conditions, but served just as well as an answer to post-9/11 conditions. Here we see the parallels between the Clinton and the Bush administrations. Clinton's neo-imperial administration was not identical to the neocon programme, but the differences were subtle, as Gokay and Fouskas point out, for example,

> neocons demanded, first from the first President Bush and then from Clinton, that US forces should overthrow Saddam unilaterally, thus overruling the UN mandate that the war must end once Iraqi forces were driven out of Kuwait. Clinton followed a halfway approach: He periodically authorized bombing raids against Iraqi targets throughout the 1990s – the most serious being that of December 1998 on the pretext that Saddam was blocking the work of US inspectors in their search for weapons of mass destruction … At best, therefore, this is a difference between reformist neo-imperialism and radical neo-imperialism. At worst, there is no difference. (Fouskas and Gokay, 2005, pp 60–61)

More than combating terrorism, the priority was to open up opportunities for US banks and corporations. *Economic* security was at the top of the security agenda. For the American public to support a war on Iraq, however, they had to be convinced they had been attacked. Iraq had to be securitized, so that extraordinary means, such as an invasion, could be justified in the name of national – even global – security. So 9/11 immediately became the opportunity the planned war depended on.

This political and economic predominance or control of the US over other states, their resources and systems, is a mark of hegemony, suggesting that the US is indeed a hegemon. A concept of control represents a bid for hegemony: a project for the conduct of public affairs and social control that aspires to be a legitimate approximation of the general interest in the eyes of the ruling class and, at the same time, the majority of the population (Van der Pijl, 1984, p 7). Those who accept and support America's hegemonic position, however, claim that America, as a defender and promoter of freedom and democracy, is in fact a 'benevolent hegemon', whose foreign policy is the marriage of might and right. America has power and it exerts it, in the Hobbesian world it inhabits, but only in order to do good. Kristol and Kagan, back in 2000, argued that the US was a 'benevolent hegemon', fixing problems like rogue states with weapons of mass destruction (WMD), terrorism and human rights abuses. The rest of the world would accept this, because America and its foreign policy are infused with an unusually high degree of morality (Kristol and Kagan, 2000). America's benevolent hegemony has been premised on American exceptionalism, 'the idea that America could use its power in instances where others could not, because it was more virtuous than other countries' (Fukuyama, 2007, p 123).

In a world order, a situation of hegemony may prevail 'based on a coherent conjunction or fit between a configuration of material power, the prevalent collective image of world order (including certain norms) and a set of institutions which administer the order with a certain semblance of universality' (Cox, 1981, p 139). This suggests that hegemony, in any case, is more than state dominance. Dismissing America's 'virtue' or strong sense of 'morality' does not reduce its authority to brute force and ruthless exploitation. Hegemony appears as an expression of broadly based consent, involving the acceptance of ideas, supported by material resources and institutions. This may start within the state, and then be projected out to the world, as with democracy and neoliberalism. Hegemony may be a form of dominance, but it is a consensual one, involving the exporting of ideas regarded as universally good, so that 'dominance by a powerful state may be a necessary but not a sufficient condition of hegemony' (Cox, 1981, p 139). There may be at least an appearance of acquiescence, treated as natural, a product perhaps of the end of history, no matter how imposed or enforced the norms are.

Michael Doyle writes that a hegemon is the 'controlling leadership of the international system as a whole' (Doyle, 1986, p 40). Michael Mastanduno argues that hegemony is when a political unit has the power to shape the rules of international politics according to its own interests (Mastanduno, 2005). Stuart Kaufam, Richard Little and William Wohlforth equate it with hierarchy, the political-military domination of a unit 'over most of the international system' (Kaufman, Little and Wohlforth, 2007, p 7). John Ikenberry and Charles Kupchan place the emphasis on material power, most effectively exercised when a hegemon is able to establish a set of norms that others willingly embrace (Ikenberry and Kupchan, 1990).

In a way, a hegemon shapes reality, if hegemony is more than brute force of dominance. Its values, its intersubjective meanings – shared notions about social relations – create a reality, a moral and ideological context, supported by institutions, that shapes desirable and acceptable thoughts and actions. Hegemony filters through economy, culture, gender, ethnicity, class and ideology, so 'there can be dominance without hegemony; [and] hegemony is one possible form dominance may take' (Cox, 1981, p 153).

THE LONG JOURNEY TO THE WAR ON TERROR

Whether or not America is a benevolent or any other type of 'reality-shaping' hegemon may be a subject of debate; , there is a more fundamental question: Is America a hegemon at all? Is it, perhaps, a dying hegemon? This question and its answer lead us to the next narrative and possible explanation of America's actions and of those of other parties to the War on Terror.

A cluster of morbid symptoms

In *Good-bye Hegemony: Power and Influence in the Global System*, Lebow and Reich write that America's hegemony was partial and short-lived, and that 'American efforts to maintain order (e.g., in Vietnam, Afghanistan and Iraq) were a primary source of disorder in the international system' (Lebow and Reich, 2014, p xi). Charles Kindleberger posits that American hegemony had run its course by the 1970s, as American-assisted economic development and success in Western Europe and Japan made hegemony superfluous (Kindleberger, 1981).

> Americans nevertheless convinced themselves that their hegemony was alive and well – and benign. Given the Soviet threat ... American hegemony was also described in the common Western interest. Following the Cold War and the collapse of the Soviet Union, the United States remained 'the indispensable nation', in the words of former secretary of state Madeleine Albright. (Dobbs and Goshko, 1996, p 25)

As other nations regained their economic strength and political stability, American hegemony eroded, leaving it with little or no control over Third World nationalism and the rise of China.

Despite this erosion, or maybe due to an awareness of this erosion, America continues to embrace hegemony through its foreign policy. 'The glaring discrepancy between America's self-image and goals on the one hand, and the others' perception of them, may explain one of the principal anomalies of contemporary international relations: *the extraordinary military and economic power of the United States and its increasing inability to get other states to do what it wants*' (Lebow and Reich, 2014, p 3).

The greatest concern regarding this erosion of hegemonic power is that a global system without a hegemon would become unstable, insecure and more prone to war, as both power and the capability to influence decline, leading to an increase in conflict and anarchy.

'Effective influence rests on persuasion' and 'persuasion depends on shared values and acceptable practice, and, when it works, helps to build common identities that can make cooperation and persuasion more likely in the future. Influence of this kind also benefits from material capabilities but is not a function of them' (Lebow and Reich, 2014, p 6).

Lebow and Reich describe three functions of hegemony, all of which require influence rather than the blunt exercise of power.

- *Leadership* (normative): 'the capacity to shape the policy agenda of global institutions or ad-hoc coalitions. It requires knowledge and manipulation of appropriate discourses', 'appeal to shared norms' and 'persuasion over coercion'.
- *Economic management* (custodial): 'to stabilise and undergird the functions of the economic system'.
- *Sponsorship*: enforcement of global initiatives. 'Sponsorship ultimately depends on capabilities. They may be military, economic, or knowledge-based.' Material resources are insufficient; 'sponsorship requires dialogue, negotiation, and the use of regional or global institutions as venues'. Sponsorship requires the implementation of consensual goals that are consistent with self-interest (Lebow and Reich, 2014, pp 6–8).

In all of these functions – leadership, economic management and sponsorship – the US has been losing influence, increasingly resorting to the blunt exercise of power, militarily imposing its leadership. At the end of the Cold War and with the collapse of the Soviet Union, the US became the global hegemon, as bipolarity gave way to unipolarity; but as its power and influence had already been declining, its need to reassert its power and influence, and carve out a new, bigger role for itself in world affairs, led to a number of morbid symptoms. What we see now is primarily the *material* dominance of one state, a dominance that is also declining. The US accounts for over 40% of the world's military spending and is the source of one quarter of its economic activity, while 65% of the world's currency reserve is held in US dollars (Norrlof, 2010).

The claim of hegemony is false, according to Lebow and Reich.

> Imperial overstretch was evident in the interventions in Afghanistan and Iraq. In each instance, America's capacity was found wanting and its strategic objectives were frustrated. The supposed 'unipolar moment' of US power in the early 1990s was accompanied by an unprecedented number of intrastate wars, with the United States unable

to impose solutions consistent with hegemony. (Lebow and Reich, 2014, p 23)

In other words, American leadership has eroded in terms of both power and legitimacy. It is argued that, for the time being, the global economic system functions without a hegemon. Leadership, economic management and security provisions are no longer interrelated. 'Key management functions – providing market liquidity, reinforcing open trading patterns, market and currency stability, and reinforcing patterns of economic development – take place without a hegemon' (Lebow and Reich, 2014, p 42).

Michelle Fine writes, in the introduction to Maxine Greene's reissue of *The Dialectic of Freedom*, that today we live 'in the echoes of old struggles and the fresh sprouts and thorns of new inequities and violences' (Fine, 2018, p xii). It is a time of crisis, of transformation. Gramsci, in the famous *Prison Notebooks* (1929–1935), wrote that a crisis consists in that the old is dying and the new cannot be born, and in this interregnum a great variety of morbid symptoms appear (Hoare, 2005). The global shift from bipolar, to unipolar, to hegemonic decline has caused the appearance of morbid symptoms like Islamic terrorism, the uprisings of the Arab Spring and America's War on Terror. Emerging powers China, India, Russia and the European Union have challenged America's already weakened hegemony, creating a crisis whereby the old order has died, but the new one is not *yet* born. In this period of change, we see both (a) a peoplehood challenging the postcolonial authoritarian order through activism, moral protest, insurgency and/or terrorism, and (b) the expiring hegemon clinging to its power.

This structural explanation of the War on Terror goes a long way towards providing a morals-free narrative, in which there is neither 'good' nor 'evil', neither 'oppressor' nor 'oppressed', neither a 'better' nor a 'worse' act or actor, but rather a phenomenon we can observe and understand as the outcome of a historical and political global shift that has altered the international power structure.

Which narrative is the correct one? As the narratives are interrelated – the cultural and the moral (with one culture having the good values and the other having the bad ones), the political and the structural (with the declining hegemon trying to maintain its power) – how does the narrative or narratives we choose to believe affect how we read or think about the deaths of thousands of people? Do we think of those deaths as caused by political decisions? Or as caused by the inevitable clash of two very different civilizations? Or perhaps it is a morally imperative fight between good and evil? Or are those deaths a result of a structural change, a shift of power?

The reader may want to keep in mind those narratives or explanations, while reading the reports, articles and body counts in this book, as the names, figures and mental images appear, as they learn of perpetrators of horrific violence, of executions, of the blowing up of women shopping at open markets, and of the flattening of entire neighbourhoods.

Knowledge of the impact of war on human security and an understanding of war through human security, both require the recording of the impact of war, through the counting and documenting of its victims. To even begin to address the issue of why those people die, we need to know who has died, how they have died, when they have died and who has caused their death. It has been the painstaking daily job of casualty recorders like those at Iraq Body Count to read reports and extract and disseminate the data, so as to both enable this understanding of war and to honour the vulnerable that should have been protected.

Iraq Body Count

Iraq Body Count records the violent deaths that have resulted from the 2003 military intervention in Iraq, civilian deaths caused by the US-led coalition, Iraqi government forces and paramilitary or criminal attacks by others. IBC uses media reports of violence leading to deaths, or of bodies being found, and is supplemented by the careful review and integration of hospital, morgue, NGO and official figures or records. Each deadly incident is stored in the database, including (where possible) the names, ages and occupations of those killed, when and how, and by whom. As the site explains:

- IBC's figures are not statistical 'estimates' but a record of actual, documented deaths.
- IBC records solely violent deaths.
- IBC's detailed database records solely civilian (strictly, 'non-combatant') deaths. A separate total that includes combatant deaths is provided on the homepage.
- IBC's figures are constantly updated and revised as new data comes in, and frequent consultation is advised (Iraq Body Count, nd-a).

The IBC project was founded in January 2003 by volunteers from the UK and the USA who wanted to ensure that the human consequences of military intervention in Iraq were not neglected. They believed that our common humanity demanded the recording of the deaths resulting from that invasion and wanted to promote a more human-centred approach to conflict. For this reason, they wished to make the recording of civilian deaths a priority, rather than a side effect of the 'War on Terror'.

The project collects and analyses media reports written or published in the English language, but also in Arabic. Almost all data in the IBC database is derived from information acquired by journalists from 'primary' human sources, including injured survivors, family members and other eyewitnesses, as well as emergency department medics, local police and other officials. IBC also includes specific information from non-political NGOs in Iraq, such as the Iraqi Red Crescent. Official cumulative figures are obtained from reports by the Medico-Legal Institutes (morgues) and the Ministry of Health, for corroborating purposes.

In all, IBC systematically extracts 18 pieces of information in relation to each incident and/or person killed.

For each incident: date, time, place, target, minimum deaths, maximum deaths, minimum injuries, maximum injuries, weapons, killers, media sources and primary witnesses.

For each person/victim: name, age, gender, marital status, parental status, occupation.

However, the above information is not always available in the reports collected. The availability of incident and victim details is as follows:

Incident

Date 94%
Time 85%
Town 99%
Target 98%
Weapon 94%
Aggressor 27%

Victim

Sex 38%
Age 41%
Occupation 19%
Identification 7.6%

Parental status 1.4%
Marital status 1.2%

Information on incidents far exceeds information on victims; almost
every report gives date, time and location of violent incidents, as
well as weapon/s used. What is less frequent is identification of the
perpetrator; even in the case of airstrikes, reports identify the aggressor
as 'coalition', rather than British or American. The one exception is
Turkish airstrikes, which are always identified as such. Other aggressors
are simply described as 'gunmen', or 'militia', or 'terrorists'. In many
cases, only the weapon is given, such as 'IED' (Improvised Explosive
Device) or 'car bomb', with no information or clue as to who may
have planted it.

It is more common in small incidents (with fewer than five victims)
to have some of the dead identified as 'women', or to give the ages of
those killed, however in larger incidents this information on gender
and age is very rarely given. This is also the case with the victim's
occupation. Gathering as many reports and documents as possible,
from as many sources as possible, is crucial in ensuring more of those
'blank spaces' are filled. However, this is still a limitation of this type
of casualty recording, as we were to discover.

Each new data entry is reviewed and checked by at least two data
checkers prior to publication. All past data entries are kept under review
and, if necessary modified when new information becomes available,
as when mass graves are found.

IBC documents civilian deaths, on a case-by-case basis. Who is a
'civilian' and who is not is carefully examined and determined for
each incident by the team, through systematic scrutiny of the data
sources. As the site states, the boundary between civilians and others
is not always clear-cut. The following distinctions are those the team
routinely applies for the purposes of the project:

> Excluded from IBC are those aged 18 and over who, at the
> point of death, were reported as initiating deadly violence
> or being active members of a military or paramilitary
> organisation. We also exclude overseas 'contractors' providing
> security and other private services related to the occupation
> of Iraq. Included are all others killed violently, including
> regular local police forces. However we do not include police
> 'commando' units who work under the Interior Ministry
> and are best described as paramilitary. Under one special
> circumstance we also include members of Iraqi military or

paramilitary/militia forces in our database, namely when they are killed – i.e. summarily executed – after capture. Under those conditions even military personnel automatically acquire 'protected person' (effectively, POW) status under International Humanitarian Law, and this distinction is respected by IBC. (Iraq Body Count, nd-b)

The IBC database identifies thousands of civilians, as shown in Table 1.1.

A named victim is a recognized victim, a remembered life, witness to what is lost. Dignifying and memorializing those lost not only recognizes the right of every person to be remembered. It also gives victim communities a voice.

IBC researchers strive to record the deaths of individuals to the greatest level of detail possible. They have defined and developed inclusion/exclusion criteria regarding who has died, how they have died, in what time period and in which region, in which specific conflict, and involving which actors. Categories and definitions have been applied consistently from the invasion to the present day. It has been vital to always work towards avoiding bias and to acknowledge the types of data used and their limitations. It has also been useful and revealing to compare types of data, for example official reports and data (produced by state agencies or by intergovernmental organizations), civil society reports and data (press and media reports, NGO reports, human rights organizations, social media) and reports and data provided by individuals (family members of a victim, witnesses or people providing local information). Corroboration is always sought, so as to evaluate the data collected.

Recording casualties based on reports is not easy or straightforward. When the daily research involves the collection and reading of over 100 reports, it becomes apparent that there is often disagreement between sources and the question arises of how to manage the disagreement in numbers or in other details of an incident. One solution is to adopt a range, as IBC has done. Another is to prioritize certain sources, say reports from medics. Cases can be kept as 'pending', while more information is sought. A strict checking system also helps confirm some details, question others, and even debate whether an incident should be included at all.

Above all, transparency has been very important, especially concerning rationale, mission and objectives; but also transparency in the data collection process and the sources used, and transparency on funders.

Table 1.1: Individual named victims

IBC page	Date	Name or personal identifier	Age	Sex	Location	Occupation
a5872–dc3693	17 Nov 2016	Sajid Sulaiman Al-Jubouri	Adult	Male	Near the Pepsi Factory, Canal 14, south-east of Balad	Electricity department employee
a5939–xh3515	16 Nov 2016	Dr Safwan Imad	Adult	Male	al-Zuhoor, al-Tahrir and al-Zahraa areas, east Mosul	University professor
a5939–dc3453	16 Nov 2016	Children of dead female	Child	Unknown	al-Zuhoor, al-Tahrir and al-Zahraa areas, east Mosul	
a5939–ur3638	16 Nov 2016	Mother of dead children	Unrecorded	Female	al-Zuhoor, al-Tahrir and al-Zahraa areas, east Mosul	
a5865–ed3676	16 Nov 2016	Family members	Unrecorded	Unknown	Hay Al-Wahda, east Mosul	
a5865–zu3490	16 Nov 2016	Family members	Child	Unknown	Hay Al-Wahda, east Mosul	
a5856–nz3518	14 Nov 2016	Laila Raed Saad	4	Female	Hay Aden, central Kirkuk	
a5933–ka3548	13 Nov 2016	Mohammed	12	Male	Hay Al-Samah, east Mosul	
a5933–nf3487	13 Nov 2016	Shafiq	15	Male	Hay Al-Samah, east Mosul	

IBC was first to set in place a running body count with a public database. Within a year or two, other bodies started investigations into Iraqi casualties, as counts or as estimates. Some of those, when released, became added sources for IBC. Despite the statement by General Tommy R. Franks that the US army 'don't do body counts', it turned out that they did. There are two US army sources of data that IBC has used:

- Documents received from the Department of the Army in response to American Civil Liberties Union (ACLU) Freedom of Information Act Request: 13,000 pages of records accounting for over 800 claims for compensation relating either to the Foreign Claims Act or to the Commander's Emergency Response Program (CERP Condolence) payments.
- Significant Actions (SIGACTs) secret documents leaked by WikiLeaks containing incidents where civilians were killed, which are still being processed by IBC.

Another count was started in 2012 by the United Nations Assistance Mission for Iraq (UNAMI), which included civilians, security forces and militias.

Estimates have been given by Opinion Research Business (ORB) – based on survey responses from 1,499 adults – and the *Lancet* – estimating 'excess deaths' from any and all causes, of combatants and civilians, based on surveys of random households, to compare mortality in the months before the invasion with the months after it. The comparison was made using death certificates provided. The estimates were criticized as being too high and improbable, while the methodology of the two *Lancet* studies was seen as fundamentally flawed by 'main street bias' (Gourley, Johnson and Spagat, 2006).

IBC has been criticized for having a limited approach that provides a serious underestimation of casualties. The IBC researchers never claimed to have a complete record of violent deaths and were always clear about the methodology used and its limitations. Other casualty recording – as done by UN bodies and the US army, for example – has added over 15,000 civilian deaths to the IBC database, deaths that IBC, using its methods of data collection, had no information on. Mass graves are continuously being discovered, some containing as many as 100 bodies and going back several years – deaths that were unknown, but when known, have been added to the IBC database.

The casualties controversy is still sparked by talk of Iraqi deaths. It is not the subject of this volume. Rather, the book is about how the data IBC has collected has enabled us to construct and narrate the story of the Iraq war, in terms of its impact on the Iraqis. How it further enabled us to narrate the War on Terror and chart its course through collective and individual experiences.

2003–2005 shock, awe and the dossier of civilian casualties

How to manage the occupation? As soon as the invasion commenced, violent crime erupted, looting, destruction of electrical substations, no power or clean water for thousands and daily anti-occupation demonstrations and Shia insurgency. Soon civil war followed. The civilian death toll of the first three years is shown in Table 1.2.

> Rumsfeld, Wolfowitz and Cheney wanted a secular, pro-American transitional government that would eventually give way to a secular, pro-American government. They believed it was more important to quickly get the right people in place than to worry about the appearance of American imperialism, and they opposed any substantive role for the United Nations besides humanitarian missions. The Pentagon and White House, like the State Department, were very nervous about the rise of a vocally anti-American, Islamic movement in Iraq; Rumsfeld was emphatic that the Bush administration would not tolerate a government that was led or shaped by Shiite clerics. (Dorrien, 2004, p 176)

Key players were Chalabi, Allawi, Barzani and Talabani. Allawi (Iraqi National Accord) wanted a secular democracy; Barzani (Kurdistan Democratic Party) and Talabani (Patriotic Union of Kurdistan) a federal system with Kurdish autonomy. American diplomat Paul Bremer, who led the Coalition Provisional Authority following the invasion, disbanded the Iraqi army and called for disarmament of all militias, except Kurdish militias, and banned up to 30,000 former Baath Party members from employment in the public sector.

As those plans were being made and policies put in place, Iraq Body Count was following security developments, collecting its findings in a dossier for the 2003–2005 period.

A Dossier on Civilian Casualties in Iraq, 2003–2005 was the first detailed account of all non–combatants reported killed or wounded during the first two years of the continuing conflict. The report, published by Iraq Body Count in association with Oxford Research Group, is based on

Table 1.2: Civilian deaths by month 2003–2005

	Jan	Feb	Mar	Apr	May	Jun	Jul	Aug	Sep	Oct	Nov	Dec	Total
2003			3,977	3,438	545	597	646	833	566	515	487	524	**12,133**
2004	610	663	1,004	1,303	655	910	834	878	1,042	1,033	1676	1,129	**11,737**
2005	1,222	1,297	905	1,145	1,396	1,347	1,536	2,352	1,444	1,311	1,487	1,141	**16,583**

comprehensive analysis of over 10,000 media reports published between March 2003 and March 2005 (Iraq Body Count, 2005a).

Findings included:

Who was killed?
- *24,865 civilians were reported killed in the first two years.*
- *Women and children accounted for almost 20% of all civilian deaths.*
- *Baghdad alone recorded almost half of all deaths.*

When did they die?
- *30% of civilian deaths occurred during the invasion phase before 1 May 2003.*
- *Post-invasion, the number of civilians killed was almost twice as high in year two (11,351) as in year one (6,215).*

Where did they live?
- *77% of civilian deaths occurred in 12 cities:*
  Baghdad 11,264 killed, 45.3% of national deaths
  Al Fallujah 1,874 killed, 7.5% of national deaths
  Nassriya 984 killed, 4.0% of national deaths
  Karbala 929 killed, 3.7% of national deaths
  Najaf 784 killed, 3.2% of national deaths
  Mosul 735 killed, 3.0% of national deaths
  Basra 704 killed, 2.8% of national deaths
  Kirkuk 613 killed, 2.5% of national deaths
  Hilla 456 killed, 1.8% of national deaths
  Tikrit 312 killed, 1.3% of national deaths
  Baquba 304 killed, 1.2% of national deaths
  Samarra 256 killed, 1.0% of national deaths

Who did the killing?
- *US-led forces killed 37% of civilian victims.*
- *Anti-occupation forces/insurgents killed 9% of civilian victims.*
- *Post-invasion criminal violence accounted for 36% of all deaths.*
- *Killings by anti-occupation forces, crime and unknown agents have shown a steady rise over the entire period.*

What was the most lethal weaponry?
- *Over half (53%) of all civilian deaths involved explosive devices.*
- *Air strikes caused most (64%) of the explosives deaths.*
- *Children were disproportionately affected by all explosive devices but most severely by air strikes and unexploded ordnance (including cluster bomblets).*

How many were injured?
- *At least 42,500 civilians were reported wounded.*
- *The invasion phase caused 41% of all reported injuries.*
- *Explosive weaponry caused a higher ratio of injuries to deaths than small arms.*
- *The highest wounded-to-death ratio incidents occurred during the invasion phase.*

Who provided the information?
- *Mortuary officials and medics were the most frequently cited witnesses.*
- *Three press agencies provided over one third of the reports used.*
- *Iraqi journalists, increasingly central to the reporting work.*

In 2003, from April 14th to 31st August, 2,846 violent deaths were recorded by the Baghdad city morgue. When corrected for pre-war death rates in the city a total of at least 1,519 excess violent deaths in Baghdad emerges from reports based on the morgue's records.

IBC's study is the first comprehensive count to adjust for the comparable 'background level' of deaths in Baghdad in recent pre-war times. It is therefore an estimate of additional deaths in the city directly attributable to the breakdown of law and order following the US takeover and occupation of Baghdad. The study confirms the widespread anecdotal evidence that violence on the streets of Baghdad has skyrocketed, with the average daily death rate almost tripling since mid April from around 10 per day to over 28 per day during August.

Another worrying development is that during the pre-war period deaths from gunshot wounds accounted for approximately 10% of bodies brought to the morgue, but now account for over 60% of those killed. The small number of reports available for other cities indicate that these trends are being mirrored elsewhere in the country.

Although the majority of deaths are the result of Iraqi on Iraqi violence, some were directly caused by US military fire. There is evidence that these deaths, often from indiscriminate use of firepower, increasingly fail to be reported or remain unacknowledged by occupation forces. But responsibility for the current mayhem in Baghdad and elsewhere in Iraq is not diffused at the bottom – at the level of ordinary soldiers ill-suited for police-work in a hostile environment – but is concentrated at the top, in the air-conditioned corridors of power in Washington and London.

The Geneva Conventions and Hague Regulations, to which the US and UK are signatories, place the responsibility for ensuring public order and protecting the civilian population from violence on the occupying powers. UN Resolution 1483, which recognized the US/UK as the de facto occupying authority in Iraq, clearly bound them to these duties. But the US/UK are manifestly failing to fulfil them, compounding the death and destruction already unleashed by their invasion of Iraq. At the same time the US, in particular, resists any multilateral initiatives which would lead to an early end to its dominance over the country. (Iraq Body Count, 2005a)

Speaking at the launch of the report in London, Professor John Sloboda, FBA, one of the report's authors said:

> 'The ever-mounting Iraqi death toll is the forgotten cost of the decision to go to war in Iraq. On average, 34 ordinary Iraqis have met violent deaths every day since the invasion of March 2003. Our data show that no sector of Iraqi society has escaped. We sincerely hope that this research will help to inform decision-makers around the world about the real needs of the Iraqi people as they struggle to rebuild their country. It remains a matter of the gravest concern that, nearly two and half years on, neither the US nor the UK governments have begun to systematically measure the impact of their actions in terms of human lives destroyed.' (Iraq Body Count, 2005b)

Meanwhile reports from Baghdad showed that the city's daily death toll continued to rise.

IBC cofounder and researcher Hamit Dardagan said, in an IBC press release,

> 'The US may be effective at waging war but the descent of Iraq's capital city into lawlessness under US occupation shows that it is incompetent at maintaining public order and providing security for the civilian population. The US has toppled Saddam and discovered that it won't be discovering any weapons of mass destruction in Iraq. So why is it still there? And if the US military can't ensure the safety of Iraqi civilians and itself poses a danger to them, what is its role in that country?
>
> It is high time for the occupying authority to take serious steps towards an orderly hand-over of power and jurisdiction to Iraqis instead of making them junior partners in running their own country, and for the US/UK to stop requiring the international community to act as nothing more than a fig-leaf for US control of Iraq.

Until they do, ordinary Iraqis may justifiably feel ungrateful for a 'liberation' that has removed the fear of Saddam but left them under military occupation and living in terror of their own streets.' (Iraq Body Count, 2003)

The 12 cities where most deaths occurred during this period (Baghdad, Fallujah, Nassriyah, Karbala, Najaf, Mosul, Basra, Kirkuk, Hilla, Tikrit, Baqubah and Samarra) were to feature in daily reports of violence and killings for the next 15 years, with many other cities and villages added, such as Ramadi, Tal Afar, Rutbah, Sulaymaniya, Haditha, Baiji, Kut, Tuz Khurmatu, Al Mukhisa, Shirkat. As a researcher into the daily violence I became acquainted with all those places where innocent people were dying in bombings, explosions and shootings. The maps of Iraq and Baghdad I got accustomed to using in my daily work were no longer maps of political boundaries, of geography, of terrain, of topography, or of roads; they were death maps, mapping the murders of people like Hamoodi's seven grandchildren, of the father, mother, siblings and uncle of 15-year-old Omar, the boy who lost his family when their vehicle was shot at by US forces at a checkpoint, five miles from Baghdad (James Meek, *Observer*, 6 April 2003). The death maps were complemented by my own daily records, which began to grow in volume the following year.

2

The Rising Violence: Writing
the War 2006–2007

In June 2006 I started working for Iraq Body Count as a news collector and writer. The year was remarkable in a number of ways. It was the year Nuri Al-Maliki was elected prime minister of Iraq. It was also the year Saddam Hussein was tried, convicted and executed. It was the worst year in terms of civilian deaths, with over 29,000 people losing their lives in violence. With over 55,000 civilian deaths, 2006 and 2007 marked what came to be known as Iraq's 'sectarian violence', or, more controversially, 'civil war'.

The following two chapters focus on the period 2006–2009, a time when over 71,000 civilians died in bombings and shootings, when Iraq was for the first time a 'democratic' state, when the civil war raged, when the US President George W. Bush announced 'the surge', employing more American troops in Iraq in order to crush the insurgency (2007), when British troops withdrew (2009), followed by American troops in 2011, and the rise of Sunni discontent in Shia-ruled Iraq.

By the end of this period, end of 2009, it seemed as though the violence had decreased, as Table 2.1 shows, enough for an external observer to be optimistic.

As a new researcher, I was given the task of recording the violence and monitoring the security and the political developments. What followed was a few years of keeping and publishing a weekly record of incidents, 'The Week in Iraq', as well as working with the rest of the team on annual reports. This chapter includes some of those editorials and reports, so as to shed light on developments and themes arising from the occupation of Iraq, terrorism and the effects of both on the lives of Iraqi civilians. It highlights the nature and frequency of the violence in Iraq, which was and still is daily.

Table 2.1 Civilian deaths by month 2006–2009

	Jan	Feb	Mar	Apr	May	Jun	Jul	Aug	Sep	Oct	Nov	Dec	Total
2006	1,546	1,579	1,957	1,805	2,279	2,594	3,298	2,865	2,567	3,041	3,095	2,900	**29,526**
2007	3,035	2,680	2,728	2,573	2,854	2,219	2,702	2,483	1,391	1,326	1,124	997	**26,112**
2008	861	1,093	1,669	1,317	915	755	640	704	612	594	540	586	**10,286**
2009	372	409	438	590	428	564	431	653	352	441	226	478	**5,382**

My first publication on the IBC website that was read by thousands and filled my inbox with messages from all over the world was 'The Price of Loss', which was based on US army records involving Iraqi compensation claims for deaths caused by US troops.

The price of loss: how the West values civilian lives in Iraq

12 November 2007

The American military has expressed regret 'that civilians are hurt or killed while coalition forces search to rid Iraq of terrorism', after the 11 October killing of 15 women (one pregnant) and children in an air raid near lake Thar Thar (BBC, 12 Oct 2007; IBC record k7704). The civilian death toll by US fire was 96 in October, with 23 children among them, while in September US forces and contractors killed 108 Iraqi civilians, including 7 children. In August US troops killed 103 civilians, 16 of them children, and in July they killed 196. In fact, during the last five months US forces in Iraq have killed over 600 Iraqi civilians. Regrettably, as always.

It is the 'price to pay', the 'sacrifice' that has to be made as we fight terrorism, the 'cost' of this war against evil forces. That is what we say to justify these killings. But those of us who speak of this price to be paid, this sacrifice to be made, do not pay this price, do not make this sacrifice. Our own country is not being destroyed, attacked, occupied. Our own children are not being blown up, our civilians are not becoming homeless by the millions. Those who speak of the necessity of this sacrifice, would they be prepared to pay such a price? In their own country? With the blood of their own families?

How much easier it is to sacrifice others, to let others pay with their lives. The value of those lives is hardly high enough to trouble us. It is nothing our military cannot afford. Here is an example:

'A fisherman was fishing in the Tigris river in the early morning, when a Coalition Forces (CF) helicopter flew over and shone a spotlight on him. The fisherman began to shout in English, "Fish! Fish!" while pointing to his catch. A patrol of Humvees arrived, and as the deceased bent down to turn off the boat's motor, CF shot and killed him. CF did not secure the boat, which drifted off and was never retrieved.' Compensation for death denied due to combat exemption; compensation for boat granted: $3,500 US (IBC record d1910).

The US Army paid $7,500 to two children whose mother they killed inside a taxi that ran a checkpoint – both children were also in the taxi, and were shot and injured (IBC record d1908); they also paid $6,000 for killing a child looking out of the window, while a raid was on-going in the house across the street (IBC record d1904). They refused, as they do in the majority of cases, to compensate the child whose father they killed as he drove home,

53

but agreed to make a 'condolence payment' of $1,500 (IBC record d1905). More recently, the US military is reported to have paid $2,500 to each family of the three men they killed near Abu Lukah, as they guarded their village (IBC record k7615).

There are more:

Al Matasan Street, Samarra, Iraq

Claim on behalf of Iraqi [Redacted] by son. [Redacted], who was deaf, was shot and killed by US forces near the Samarra museum. Two eyewitnesses corroborated the story. Finding: denied for lack of evidence and combat exception. Condolence payment granted: $500 US (IBC record d3353).

Samarra, Iraq

Claim on behalf of Iraqi [Redacted] by parent. [Redacted], a four year-old girl, was playing in her front yard when she was killed by Coalition Forces' (CF) fire. The CF and a Humvee were trying to cross the road and they shot to clear the traffic. A bullet ricocheted off of a wall and hit [Redacted]. Army memo: 'A SIGACTS investigation revealed no activity meeting' the incident's description, and 'the claim is too old to verify'. Finding: denied due to lack of evidence. Condolence payment of $2,500 US granted (IBC record d3352)

Tikrit, Iraq

Claim on behalf of Iraqi [Redacted], an ambulance driver. [Redacted] was on his way to the scene of an accident with an IED when he was shot and killed by a US soldier. Finding: negligent fire; Compensation: $2,500 US (IBC record d3348).

Reading through the Army compensation reports, it is fairly clear just what the value of an Iraqi life is, of how the loss of a beloved child, parent and sibling is valued, priced. A few thousand dollars (if that) is how much they are worth, and no more. Their loss covered by a shockingly low monetary compensation. No further consequences, punishment, no further accountability.

Those of us who opposed this war and the long occupation that followed hold our political leaders responsible for the horrors of Iraq. We sometimes blame our soldiers. We always blame the terrorists. But we are reluctant to blame our nation or ourselves. 'We can continue to blame the Bush administration', writes Frank Rich, 'but we must also examine our own responsibility for the hideous acts committed in our name in a war where we have now fought longer than we did in the one that put Verschärfte Vernehmung on the map.' We cannot simply 'look the other way' (Rich, 2007).

We, who have lost very little, who have sacrificed very little, who have paid very little, we 'turn the page', to use Rich's phrase, and we continue to speak of 'our' war, of 'our' fight against the terrorists, 'our' ideals, 'our' kindness, 'our' courage; things that we value far more than *the lives of millions of others, people whose deaths do not hurt us, whose loss does not affect us, and whose sacrifice we do not see bloodying our own hands.* (Hamourtziadou, 2007d)

Many were disturbed by the revelation that to those who were fighting this war 'for the Iraqis' the lives of Iraqi were, in fact, worth very little.

However, by 2007 thousands were reading the weekly column 'The Week in Iraq' and were keeping up to date with the developments in the country, realizing the nature and frequency of attacks, becoming aware of the scale of civilian suffering and finding out who the perpetrators of those daily crimes were. The column started in the summer of 2006 and ended in the winter of 2009. What follows is a selection of editorials from that period, 'writing the war' as it happened.

The price they pay for our humanity

8 Oct 2006

How sad that Iraqis are suffering so much as a result of our 'humanitarian' war. In all wars there are civilian casualties, but in this case the deaths of Iraqi civilians are particularly tragic, because one of the main justifications for this war was humanitarian, especially after the Weapons of Mass Destruction threat proved to have been unfounded. Indeed, at first glance this reasoning seems fair: nations intervene to end massive suffering at little cost to themselves, and rescue civilians from a tyrant. However, what at first appeared to be a humanitarian intervention has ended up being a humanitarian disaster. What Iraq's 'liberators' are facing more and more is hostility and violence, rather than gratitude, as the new Iraq is facing a civil war and hundreds of civilians are murdered every week. It comes almost as a joke when the Iraqi Foreign Minister declares that the situation in Iraq 'is not as desperate as people think'. Is it not? Let's see what happened in Iraq this past week.

At least 400 civilian deaths were reported between Monday 2 and Sunday 8 October.

Monday 2 October was declared a 'tragic day' by the US military, because on this day 8 US soldiers were killed in Baghdad. How tragic then for the Iraqis who lost nearly 70 of their people. Some of Monday's victims were workers abducted from a meat factory the previous day. Another kidnapping: 14 engineers are abducted from computer stores (their fate is still unknown). Also 2 children are blown up by a bomb hidden in a rubbish bag. It is announced that Martial Law, which has been in force since November 2004, is to be extended at least until 1 November. Which means that the curfews, raids and arrests without warrants, the army and police patrols will continue.

On Tuesday 3 October gunmen kill 4 members of the same family as they are moving to another house in Baquba, after receiving threats, while 7 bodies from another family are found. In Baghdad hundreds of Iraqis participate in a protest demanding the removal of Iraqi and US troops from their districts.

On Wednesday 4 October 16 are killed in a triple bombing in Baghdad, dozens of bodies are found in the streets, and a horrific killing takes place in Samarra: gunmen storm a house, shoot dead 3 women and slit the throat of a baby girl.

On Thursday 5 October Condoleezza Rice arrives in Baghdad. Her arrival is delayed for nearly an hour, as her plane cannot land due to 'indirect fire' around the airport. She urges Iraqis to reconcile. A Kurdish lawmaker is assassinated together with his driver, becoming the first Member of this Parliament to be killed. In Falluja US forces kill a woman when their vehicle patrol, trying to make its way, opens fire over people's heads. This is apparently common practice.

Friday 6 October is the most peaceful day this week: only about 20 people die... but unfortunately it is followed by a very bloody Saturday 7, during which at least 90 people lose their lives. One of them is Nasir Shamel, former captain of the national volleyball team, found shot to death outside his shop. Another is a woman gunned down as she walks with her 5-year-old son down the street in Mosul. British soldiers open fire and kill an Iraqi customs policeman, after the British military base in Basra comes under attack. On the same day, Iraqi Police Major General Jamal Taher announces that a 15-km-long and 2m-deep trench has been dug south of Kirkuk to prevent car bombs and insurgents from entering.

On Sunday 8 October heavy fighting is reported between US and Iraqi forces and insurgents in Diwaniyah. A policeman and his 8-year-old son are shot and killed as they walk through a market in Samarra, while hundreds of policemen appear to have been poisoned. Late on Sunday reports come in that 11 policemen have so far died, while up to 700 are seriously ill, bleeding from their ears and noses, after breaking their fast on Sunday evening.

Is this situation desperate? This is clearly a disastrous result. Saddam Hussein was the easiest target to eliminate; allies are now fighting so many. Rowan Scarborough, writing for the Washington Times, *mentions some of them: Al-Qaida in Iraq, suicide bombers, Shiite militias, and at least 4 Sunni groups – Ansar al Sunna, Islamic Army in Iraq, Mujahedeen Army in Iraq, Iraq National Islamic Resistance (*World Peace Herald 7 October).

Yes, it is a desperate situation when the human cost is so high and rising daily, and when all the allies can boast of is the creation of a police state. Iraqis are paying a very high price for our humanity. A price they should not have been expected to pay. (Hamourtziadou, 2006a)

It was in the autumn of 2006 that Salam al-Zawba'i, then deputy prime minister for security, said that this government was the Iraqi people's only option. However, what that actually meant was that there was no option; the Iraqis had to live and cope with the daily killings, foreign control and, in Zawba'i's words, 'paralysis in all sectors of life'. They had no choice. Yet others have had options, and still do. Other options were available to the young men and women who joined the army and were sent to fight in Iraq. The army was not their only option. Their governments too had other options, other than to 'kick the door in', as Sir Richard Dannatt put it, in Iraq in 2003. They can still opt to withdraw from Iraq, or they could stay for several more years.

Helena Cobban, writing for *The Christian Science Monitor*, echoed Dannatt when she counted the military cost of this war. 'Mr Bush's quite voluntary decision to invade and occupy Iraq has cost the United States dearly. We're now paying $7 billion per month to maintain the troop presence there – and the nonfinancial costs have also been huge. More than 2,740 US service members and scores of thousands of Iraqi citizens have been killed' (Cobban, 2006). It is time, she wrote, to hold those who made such 'disastrous decisions' accountable, for the deaths of soldiers and civilians.

The civilian cost the week starting 9 October 2006 was high: nearly 500 of them were killed in violence around the country, starting with the assassination of the vice president's brother, Amir al-Hashimi, outside his home. His death, on Monday 9 October, came five months after his sister and another brother were shot dead. His death was one of around 80 that Monday.

Clashes dominated that week, when shelling and fighting broke out in Baghdad's Sadr City, in Diwaniya, Al-Jadiriyah, Al-Karradah, Al-Sayidiyah, Al-Jami'ah, Al-Khadrah, and a rocket and mortar attack was launched at a US military base in southern Baghdad, causing dozens of explosions and fires burning for several hours. Overall, nearly 120 people were killed on Tuesday 10 October, including 11 civilians blown up outside a bakery.

It was that week it was announced that the US army would maintain its current level of soldiers in Iraq until 2010. The parliament approved a law creating autonomous regions, despite vehement opposition by Sunnis. The headless corpse of a Christian priest was found in the outskirts of Mosul.

Sir Richard Dannatt, head of the British army in Iraq, admitted that the presence of the armed forces in Iraq exacerbated the security problems there and worldwide. It was also revealed that attacks on

US troops had increased by 43% since midsummer. On the same day, Thursday 12 October, gunmen broke into the offices of Al-Shaabia TV station and killed 11 employees; in Balad, gunmen broke into a house and shot dead 7 members of the same family. The dead that day exceeded 100.

One of the most shocking incidents of that week in October was the murder of 6 women and 2 little girls, killed as they picked crops in a field, on Friday 13 October. The gunmen then abducted 2 teenage girls. The headless corpses of 14 construction workers, abducted the previous evening, were found, while 2 British contractors were killed on the road to Karbala. The killing of the 14 construction workers sparked off the revenge killing of 26 Sunnis, on Saturday 14 October. A family of 10 was murdered in Safiya, while a family of 4 was murdered in Wahda. A family of 5 was killed in Mosul the following day, Sunday 15 October, and a family of 8 was killed in Latifiya. Hala Shaker, deputy to interior minister, survived an assassination attempt, in which 7 civilians were killed, and in Kirkuk bombs killed 12.

It was generally admitted that by the end of 2006 that 'we' were not winning the war in Iraq. The Iraq Study Group report, published on 5 December, confirmed what many had already admitted and many more already realized: 'Current US policy is not working.' The situation in Iraq was 'grave and deteriorating', the report explained, as Iraq was 'sliding toward chaos'. The government could collapse and a 'humanitarian catastrophe' may result, it warned. Moreover, 'there is no path that can guarantee success'. It looked like Iraq may have gone past the point of no return. Success looked unlikely, because 'the Iraqi people and their leaders have been slow to demonstrate the capacity or will to act'. 'The United States should work closely with Iraq's leaders to support the achievement of specific objectives – or milestones – on national reconciliation, security, and governance' (The Iraq Study Group Report, 2006).

Though disappointed by the findings of the ISG, President Bush remained optimistic and confident he would be 'vindicated by history', insisting that America would still achieve victory in the Iraq war. 'It is a noble mission, and it's the right mission', echoed Mr Blair, 'and it's important for the world that it succeeds' (The White House, 2006). It is not only his 'idealism' (to use his own term) that drives President Bush, but also his belief that 'the only realistic path to security is by ensuring the spread of liberty'. As if the free, liberal and democratic USA were not the most aggressive state in the world. The 'other side' was also confident of victory. Shiite politicians, such as radical clerics

Moqtada al-Sadr and Abdel-al-Hakim, were happy with the report's findings and could see victory within their reach after the American withdrawal from Iraq. Al-Qaeda in Iraq could also claim 'victory' in their jihad. To them, and to the American and British governments, it was all defined and explained in terms of 'winning' and 'losing'.

Reports of clashes in Baghdad dominated the news. Militiamen stormed houses and opened fire on residents, issued death threats and forced thousands from their homes. Dozens were killed in the process. Employing another familiar tactic, US forces, 'firing randomly', shot dead civilians after a US soldier was shot by a sniper. Who valued these lives? Not the militiamen. Not the Americans. Not the British. Not even the Iraqi prime minister, the 'national leader' who expected loyalty from Iraqi people. He also wanted to be counted among the winners, whatever the cost. But the human cost was so great it surpassed concerns over 'victory' or 'defeat'. Assessment of war that does not take into account the civilians killed makes us lose sight of the real losses.

With the end of 2006 approaching, the ISG admitted,

> Saddam Hussein has been removed from power and the Iraqi people have a democratically elected government that is broadly representative of Iraq's population, yet the government is not adequately advancing national reconciliation, providing basic security, or delivering essential services. The level of violence is high and growing. There is great suffering, and the daily lives of many Iraqis show little or no improvement. (The Iraq Study Group Report, 2006, p 9)

Tragically, this could have been written in December 2019, since, to this day, no democratically elected government in Iraq has advanced national reconciliation, provided basic security, or delivered essential services.

The report also warned that Iraqis were 'embracing sectarian identities' and that 'lack of security impedes economic development'; but, most tellingly, it stressed that 'Iraq is critical to US interests'. It mentioned attacks against US, coalition and Iraqi security forces, pointing out that October 2006 was the deadliest month for US forces since January 2005, with 102 Americans killed. Attacks against civilians, the report stated, were increasing, with 'some 3,000 Iraqi civilians killed every month' (The Iraq Study Group Report, 2006, p 10).

The report did not give a source for this figure of 'some 3,000 civilians killed every month', however, one look at Iraq Body Count's figures for the second part of 2006, when the report was written, makes it clear what the source was:

Civilian deaths in 2006 as recorded by Iraq Body Count:

- July 3,298
- August 2,865
- September 2,567
- October 3,041
- November 3,095
- December 2,900

Despite keeping very detailed records of US military deaths, neither the group, nor the army, nor the Iraqi government were keeping track of the daily killing of civilians, despite the fact that states are legally obliged to undertake casualty recording – that is, to record individual casualties, whether combatant or civilian. 'The burden lies on states to make sure that this work is done, but it has largely been left to civil society organisations' (Breau and Joyce, 2011, p 3). Breau and Joyce outline the content of the international legal obligation to record every civilian casualty of armed conflict:

1 There are binding international legal obligations upon parties to armed conflict to:
    - search for all missing civilians as a result of hostilities, occupation or detention;
    - collect all of the casualties of armed conflict from the area of hostilities as soon as circumstances permit;
    - if at all possible, the remains of those killed are to be returned to their relatives;
    - the remains of the dead are not to be despoiled;
    - any property found with the bodies of the dead is to be returned to the relatives of the deceased;
    - the dead are to be buried with dignity and in accordance with their religious or cultural beliefs;
    - the dead are to be buried individually and not in mass graves;
    - the graves are to be maintained and protected;
    - exhumation of dead bodies is only to be permitted in circumstances of public necessity which will include identifying cause of death;
    - the location of the place of burial is to be recorded by the party to the conflict in control of that territory;
    - there should be established in the case of civilian casualties an official graves registration service.

2 These international legal obligations taken together constitute a binding international legal obligation upon every party to an armed conflict to record every civilian casualty of armed conflict whether in an international or non-international armed conflict. (Breau and Joyce, 2011, pp 1–2)

Article 3 of the Geneva Conventions of 1949 provides criteria on human rights that are non-derogable – that is, rights protected at all times: in peace, in war and in national emergencies. These relate to the protection of civilians in international armed conflicts (between two or more states) and in non-international armed conflicts (between the armed forces of a state and armed non-state groups, or between such groups). For some non-international armed conflicts, some scholars use the term 'internationalized armed conflict', when there is an international dimension. 'The term "internationalized armed conflict" describes internal hostilities that are rendered international. The factual circumstances that can achieve that internationalization are numerous and often complex: the term "internationalized armed conflict" includes … war involving a foreign intervention in support of an insurgent group fighting against an established government' (Stewart, 2003, p 315).

As much as talk of a 'civil war' in Iraq was starting to become popular, the wars being fought in Iraq never lost their 'international' dimension. Since 2003, conflict in Iraq has been 'internationalized'. As such, it has placed the legal and moral responsibility to record casualties on those international actors, as well as the state of Iraq. Both combatant and civilian.

For casualty recorders, the distinction between combatants and non-combatants is not unproblematic, as the careful examination of each incident is required in order to reach a consensus on who had participated in hostilities and who had not. Civilians lose their immunity from attack when they directly participate in an armed conflict. Children are automatically classified as civilians by IBC, even when recruited as combatants.

Terrorists

26 Nov 2006

'The president and his team, in and out of the White House, believed that the Iraqis were just like us, that they were a reasonable people, yearning to be free' writes Llewellyn King (Columbia Tribune, November 21 2006). Unlike the Western Europeans and Americans, *though, Iraqis 'harbored an enormous desire to settle ancient scores', showing a savagery equal to 'anything that was seen in the Balkans or in Africa'. The execution of the war, a war full of president Bush's 'romanticized dreams of democracy', has nothing to do with this violence, according to King, which is 'the Iraqis' affair'. It then follows that 'some resolution has to be found among the Iraqis'.*

Joan Smith, writing for The Independent, *also places the 'moral responsibility' for the 'slaughter of their fellow citizens' on Iraqi shoulders. The correct term for such people, she exclaims, 'isn't fighters or insurgents; people who carry out indiscriminate attacks on civilians are terrorists' (*Independent on Sunday, *26 November 2006).*

*And those are people found in the Middle East, the Balkans, Africa... or are they? 'The world's first global terrorists', Walter Davis calls them. He is not referring to anyone in the Middle East, or in the Balkans, or in Africa, or in any other savage, uncivilised nation, state or region. He is referring to the Americans. 'Hiroshima', he writes, 'was the first act of global terrorism ... an act that abrogated all distinctions between combatant and non-combatant, the object of military action now being an entire city, of no military significance, its inhabitants indifferently identified as a single mass delivered to death in an effort to inflict the maximum moral and psychological damage on the enemy' (*Death's Dream Kingdom, *2006). The US is still committing acts of global terrorism, according to Davis, when it unleashes 'a weapon of mass destruction, depleted uranium, on a country, people, race, and religion that deserve that fate for being the non-cause of 9-11'. The 'American/Western European/civilised/romantic/idealistic/freedom-loving' versus the 'Eastern/African/uncivilised/savage/terrorist' dichotomy is not as clear as some would like us to believe.*

Perhaps the US had good reasons to exterminate those innocents. Perhaps not. Perhaps the perpetrators (US forces included) of those acts that killed over 900 people this week also had good reasons for their violence. Perhaps not. Either way, it makes no difference to the 900+ victims.

On Monday 20 November more than 160 lose their lives. Among the dead are 2 professors, a comedian, as well as around 140 unidentified bodies discovered in Baghdad, Mosul, Tikrit and Falluja. The Iraqi Minister of State and an Iraqi Deputy Health Minister survive an assassination attempt. The Associated Press announces that 'more civilians have been killed in Iraq in the first 20 days of November than in any other month since the AP began tracking the figure in April 2005'.

Over 80 die on Tuesday 21 November, including the Dean of Education Faculty at Tikrit University, a mother and her baby, while 40 unclaimed bodies are buried in Tikrit.

The dead exceed 100 on Wednesday 22 November. Another journalist is killed and over 80 bodies are found.

Thursday 23 November is a truly tragic day, as over 300 people die in violence around the country. Out of 320 dead, 215 die in a series of explosions in Sadr City, and over 30 more in retaliatory attacks. In addition, dead bodies litter the streets of Baghdad, Falluja, Baquba and Latifiya. Other victims include a doctor, policemen, guards, a 10-year-old boy, 2 gasoline sellers, and 4 people in a minivan killed by US forces when they refused to stop. A 3-day curfew is declared in Baghdad. The US celebrates Thanksgiving.

More than 100 are killed again on Friday 24 November, most of them in reprisals. More than 90 Sunni families receive death threats, others are forced out of their homes at gunpoint. In the Amiriyah neighbourhood of Baghdad, Sunnis start to form neighbourhood militias under the guidance of local clerics, to protect themselves. By Friday evening, 25 volunteers sign up, and those without weapons are handed AK-47 rifles.

On Saturday 25 November the 80 or so dead include 21 men and boys from an extended family killed by unknown gunmen. Also 2 children killed at a checkpoint. US bombs kill 7 family members in their house near Falluja, while another US air raid kills 4 women in Baquba.

Around 70 die on Sunday 26 November. An angry crowd throws stones at the Iraqi Prime Minister at a ceremony of mourning for Thursday's victims. Some shout 'coward' and 'collaborator'. As the curfew nears its end, the Iraqis fear more violence in the coming days. In the coming weeks, months or years. Until Iraq is a stable, possibly democratic country, and bodies no longer litter the streets. How this can be achieved is not clear – one thing is clear though: it will not be achieved by American militarism. Or terrorism.
(Hamourtziadou, 2006b)

The democratically elected government of Iraq, not even a year old, was already in trouble. From its first year Iraq's democracy has produced an insecure regime inside a weak state. Highly developed nations face no real threat of major war and enjoy economic prosperity, comparatively low levels of crime, and enduring political and social stability. Despite warnings to the contrary by our security services, even the threat of terrorism is minor. Iraq, on the other hand, was and still is a weak state. Between 2003 and 2020 the only constants have been the following: communal violence, terrorism, poverty, weapons proliferation, crime, political instability, social breakdown, riots, disorder and economic failure. In Iraq we observe the lack of basic security that exists in 'zones of instability', where Iraq, after 16 years of 'reconstruction', remains.

As in all weak states, the primary security threats facing the Iraqi population originate primarily from internal, domestic sources. In such states, the more the ruling elites try to establish effective state rule, the more they provoke insurgency. Despite it being declared a democracy, Iraq lacks regime security. 'Regime security – the condition where governing elites are secure from violent challenges to their rule – becomes indistinguishable from state security – the condition where the institutions, processes and structures of the state are able to continue functioning effectively' (Jackson, 2013, p 201). In Iraq and other 'liberated and democratized' states those internal/domestic security threats have gone hand in hand with the external threat posed by a collaborative external actor.

It was thought – even promised – that an Iraq free of its dictator would become a strong state. A democratic, liberal state, much like those in the developed world. However, Iraq has become a state even weaker than it was under Saddam Hussein's iron rule. Buzan argues that state strength/weakness rests mainly on the 'idea of the state' and the extent to which society forms a consensus on and identifies with the state. Weak states 'either do not have, or have failed to create, a domestic political and social consensus of sufficient strength to eliminate the large-scale use of force as a major and continuing element in the domestic political life of the nation' (Buzan, 1983, p 67). The continuing protests in Iraq and the killing of protesters in their hundreds by government forces, combined with a persisting insurgency, demonstrate the lack of identification of the population with 'the state'.

In Iraq we see several of the threats weak states face: warlords and strongmen, ethnic rebellions, insurgencies and protest movements, leading to a sustained intra-state war. Weak states, writes Jackson, face internal and external security challenges. Internally, they face the continual threat of violent interventions in politics by the armed forces, such as coup d'état, mutiny and rebellion (Jackson, 2013). They face threats from

> individuals or groups who exercise a degree of coercive and/or infrastructural power in their own right and who challenge the authority of the state. They may be semi-legitimate actors such as politicians or traditional and religious leaders who nonetheless command large followings and private access to weaponry. Alternatively, they may be criminal gangs or warlords. (Jackson, 2013, p 204)

Weak states also face challenges from protestors, ethnic groups or local militias. Increasing lawlessness can create a power vacuum in which 'the ruling elite simply becomes one of several factions struggling to fill the void and claim the formal mantle of statehood' (Jackson, 2013, p 204). Weak states are threatened by the uncontrollable spread of arms, weapons that can be used both to challenge the authority of the state and to kill civilians. 'An estimated $5 billion worth of light weapons are traded illegally every year to the world's conflict zones, killing an estimated half a million people per year in criminal activity and civil violence' (Jackson, 2013, p 205). Due to their fragility and vulnerability, weak states also face external threats. They can be invaded by powerful states, or have their sovereignty violated by them. In Iraq, the sovereignty of the state has so far been violated by several regional states, including Turkey and Iran.

Jackson argues that the inability of the state to meet internal threats and to provide order and security creates an environment of competition between each component of society, including the regime, to protect its own well-being. By trying to improve their own security, they create regime insecurity. Such an insecure regime is able to meet neither internal nor external threats.

Winning was said to come at a cost. What is the cost exactly? In the words of James Baker, former US secretary of state, 'a helluva mess'. By the end of 2006, Iraq was not a functioning state. More Iraqis were seeking asylum abroad than any other nation and UN monitors reported that 2,000 a day were crossing the Syrian border. The United Nations High Commissioner for Refugees (UNHCR) estimated 365,000 internal refugees in Iraq in 2006. A third of Iraq's professional class was reported to have fled to Jordan, while over 100 lecturers at Baghdad University alone had been murdered. Electricity supply was down to four hours a day and the arrival anywhere of an army unit could be prelude to a mass killing.

'The Iraq war', wrote Ximena Ortiz, 'has been portrayed in such principled terms – bringing democracy to the Iraqi people – that it has taken an abstract quality and, indeed, is often discussed in abstract terms. But there is nothing abstract about a corpse' (Ortiz, 2006). Images of war necessarily include blood, corpses, often dismembered; they are images of poverty, of terror, of flight, of despair, when law and order have completely broken down; when women are killed for wearing trousers, men for wearing shorts; when soldiers shoot indiscriminately. War does not look like its heroes as much as it looks like its victims. War looks less like its winners than its losers. Hans Blix, during an interview with the Danish newspaper *Politiken*, concluded that Iraq was 'a pure failure' (*New York Times*, 2006).

Inside Pandora's Box

17 Dec 2006

Tribal leaders and political groups in Diyala are turning to terrorists and insurgents for protection, rather than trust Iraqi soldiers and police, according to the commander of US forces in the area, Col. David Sutherland. 'This sort of unity only worsens the sectarian divide and encourages further violence', he said, adding that 'these are not new problems in Iraq'. Indeed, they are not. The level of violence we have seen since the invasion may be something new, but sectarianism was already there, contained to a large extent by Saddam Hussein's autocratic regime. As though inside a box. After the fall of Saddam Hussein, what has come to triumph in Iraq is a sort of religious nationalism, not unlike the nationalisms of the former Yugoslavia. Following the official end of the war on May 1 2003, the US realised that they were not engaged in a mopping-up operation, but were fighting a new war, with new enemies, whose purpose was to prevent the American government, the America-friendly Iraqi government, and their allies in Iraq (Kurds and Shiites, initially at least) establishing control of the country. 'While the new elected government had more legitimacy than the old, this did not change the balance of power on the ground', and 'communities were becoming more not less fearful of each other' (Patrick Cockburn, The Occupation: war and resistance in Iraq, 2006, p. 188). They had good reason to be more fearful now, since some of the groups had made new and powerful friends, allies they were to use against others, outside their own group. With the invasion and occupation of Iraq, those ethno-religious groups came to represent new threats: political, societal and military.

The dead this week again exceeded 600.

On Monday 11 December nearly 100 die, 4 of them young children. In Tuz Khurmato 6 members of the same family are shot dead; in Salaja, near Kirkuk, a pregnant mother is killed along with her 3 children; 5 die in a restaurant, 4 in a vegetable market, while 60 bodies are found in the streets of Baghdad.

On Tuesday 12 December the dead reach 168, about half of whom are labourers blown up by a suicide bomber pretending to offer them work. In this attack 3 children also die. Another mother is killed with her children and over 60 bodies are found in 4 cities.

More labourers die in 2 bombing incidents on Wednesday 13 December. A family of 9 is shot dead in al-Hesna, 3 of them children, while 4 more children are killed by mortars in al-Hawija. Another child is killed by an Iraqi soldier in Falluja, and bombs kill 9 Palestinians in Baghdad. Altogether around 100 people lose their lives.

Around 90 die on Thursday 14 December, most of whom are bodies found bound and tortured in Baghdad, Al-Lij, Khallisa, Mosul, Suwayra and Wahda.

On Friday 15 December more than 30 bodies are found in Baghdad and Baquba, while 4 civilians are killed in Ramadi by US fire. Altogether around 60 are killed around the country, and the Karbala Health Department receives 50 unidentified bodies for burial.

On Saturday 16 December Tony Blair pays a 'surprise' visit to Iraq, on a day when the Iraqi Prime Minister is holding a reconciliation meeting with leaders of various political groups. Around 150 people are killed during Saturday and Sunday, a child among them. Near Falluja 4 are killed when a US air raid destroys 3 houses on Sunday, and more than 100 bound and tortured bodies are found in 5 cities.

In this climate of fear and violence, it was a good idea on Al-Maliki's part, though perhaps unrealistic at this point, to have a reconciliation conference in Baghdad. The Prime Minister convened leaders from various communities across the country, including members of the Baath Party, but not members of armed groups, as he did not want to include those 'who committed crimes against Iraqis and continue today to shed the blood of innocents' (New York Times, *17 December). He clearly does not hold himself or his foreign allies responsible for the shedding of innocent blood in Iraq. Still, the purpose of the conference seemed noble enough: to attempt to form an Iraq based on national unity and not individual sects.*

Is this possible? Reconciliation necessarily requires mutual respect, tolerance and trust. At present Iraqis have not, and cannot be expected to have, any of the above for each other or for their leaders. But at least they have democracy, as Tony Blair triumphantly declared during his Sunday visit: 'The first time I arrived in this country there was no proper functioning democracy. Today there is.' What he omitted to say was that the first time he arrived in Iraq there were no daily killings of dozens and no mass abductions. There was no chaos.

A joke was circulating among Iraqis shortly before al-Maliki met George Bush in Amman recently, Jonathan Steele reports. 'What would the US be demanding? Answer: a timetable for Iraqis to withdraw from Iraq' (The Guardian, *15 December 2006). The only way to save Iraq is to remove the Iraqis. It is their fault that their country is in this mess. They seem to be incapable of the 'tolerance and moderation' Tony Blair was preaching on Sunday in Basra.*

This post-modern view of tolerance and respect as the instant solution to all conflict cannot be applied to the Iraqis, as it could not apply to Bosnians 15 years previously. At this point Iraqis would have to be mad to feel respect, to trust each other or to be tolerant. How can you trust, respect or tolerate those who are killing you? You cannot and should not. When the US and British armies attacked and invaded Iraq in 2003 they hoped to find weapons of mass destruction in Iraq. Instead, what they found was that Pandora's Box contained a different kind of weapon: humans capable of mass destruction. And those angry humans were not simply unleashed or let out of the box by them. They were violently kicked out of it. (Hamourtziadou, 2006c)

Violence in Iraq was rising at an 'unbelievably rapid pace', according to the Pentagon's assessment of the security situation. It was now higher than at any time since the overthrow of Saddam Hussein's regime. The quarterly 'Measuring Stability and Security in Iraq' reported to Congress in November 2006 that the level of violence in Iraq 'in all specific measurable categories' had reached 'the highest level on record' and posed a 'grave threat' to the Iraqi government:

> In the past three months, the total number of attacks increased 22%. Some of this increase is attributable to a seasonal spike in violence during Ramadan. Coalition forces remained the target of the majority of attacks (68%), but the overwhelming majority of casualties were suffered by Iraqis. Total civilian casualties increased by 2% over the previous reporting period. Fifty-four percent of all attacks occurred in only 2 of Iraq's 18 provinces (Baghdad and Anbar). Violence in Iraq was divided along ethnic, religious, and tribal lines, and political factions within these groups, and was often localized to specific communities. (Report to Congress, 2006)

Iraqi civilians were indeed paying the heaviest price. The number of attacks on US and Iraqi troops, as well as civilians, had risen to almost 1,000 a week between 12 August and 10 November. Most casualties were Iraqi, despite the fact that 68% of the attacks targeted US-led coalition troops. The report further said that that Shia cleric Moqtada al-Sadr's Mahdi Army militia had replaced al-Qaeda in Iraq as the single largest threat to the country's security. As the violence and the casualties were rising, the number of American troops was also rising, shooting up to 142,000, with plans to send an additional 20,000–30,000 troops to Iraq in the new year. Consequently, the financial cost of this war was on the rise too, with the US spending $8 billion per month in Iraq, according to the Iraq Study Group.

'We simply cannot afford to fail in the Middle East', Robert Gates, new defense secretary, warned hours before the Pentagon report was released. 'Failure in Iraq at this juncture would be a calamity that would haunt our nation, impair our credibility, and endanger Americans for decades to come' (Breaking News, 2006).

It may have already been too late. As the violence rose in Iraq, it fed the global jihadi network with recruits, propaganda and extremist ideology. Al-Qaeda followers took full advantage of the chaotic security situation left by the invasion and the decision to disband the Iraqi army. In Iraq, nowhere outside the fortified Green Zone was safe. In the Western world, we had not been less safe in a long time.

'The end of a dark period in Iraq', was how President Bush described Saddam Hussein's execution on Saturday 30 December 2006, as if Saddam Hussein's deeds had been the only factor contributing to Iraq's 'dark period'. Yes, it was at least a 'dark year', possibly the worst year in Iraq's recent history and a year in which Saddam Hussein was in custody. The year had now come to an end, yet Iraq's 'dark period' was far from over. It was a truly violent year, as over 29,500 civilians lost their lives in Iraq. This was a massive rise in violence. In December 2006 alone IBC recorded 2,900 civilian deaths.

December 2006 was a bad month for US troops in Iraq as well: it was the deadliest month in two years, with as many as 111 American soldiers reported killed. Reports suggested that more than 700 US troops were killed in Iraq during 2006. Overall, it seemed US military deaths had reached the 3,000 mark since the start of the war.

During 2006, we saw two reports outline the terrible, and worsening, situation in Iraq: the Iraq Study Group and the Pentagon quarterly report. Both painted a picture of violence, despair and pessimism. George W. Bush was forced to admit that the US was 'not winning' the war in Iraq. For the first time, that year the conflict in Iraq was described as a 'civil war' in the media. The warring parties, the Shia and the Sunni, appeared to be fighting for, among other things, control of Baghdad. The Shia in particular were increasingly hostile to the occupation, with 62% of them approving of armed attacks on US-led forces. The militias all grew stronger during the year, as the army and police forces seemed unable to provide security. A total of 1.6 million Iraqis had now fled from Iraq, to escape the violence and the poverty. In a country rich in oil, supplies of electricity, water, gasoline and kerosene remained inadequate.

It was also noted that 2006 was the worst year for reporters in over a decade, with Iraq once again proving the most dangerous place in the world for the media to work. According to Reporters without Borders (RSF), 113 reporters and media staff were killed in Iraq in 2006, the highest death toll since 1994, when scores of reporters died in the Rwandan genocide. Twenty-five media assistants also died in Iraq in 2006. Almost 90% of the journalists killed were Iraqi.

The number of suicides also increased in Iraq. Suicide, a rare phenomenon in Iraq, was now ten times more common than it was in previous years. Based on statistics from the Baghdad mortuary and hospitals in five regions, the Ministry of Health said that about 20 people had been committing suicide each month since January. 'The numbers are high when compared to those during Saddam Hussein's regime when we used to have one or two suicide cases a month', said Ahmed Fatah, member of the suicide investigation department at the Ministry of Health (Relief Web, 2006). The country's continuing violence had more psychological effect on the less privileged: the poor and the uneducated. If to those 20 suicide cases per month we add another 20 suicide bombers, we come up with a very depressing 40 suicides each month.

Perhaps the most alarming report of 2006 was the one concerning Iraqi youngsters. 'Children are the most affected by the tragic events', Dr Khalil al-Kubaissi, a psychotherapist in Falluja, told Inter Press Service. 'Their fragile personalities cannot face the loss of a parent or the family house along with the horror that surrounds them. The result is catastrophic, and Iraqi children are in danger of lapsing into loneliness or violence' (Jamail, 2006).

The difficulties of children became particularly noticeable this year, as children suffered the psychological effects of the insecurity around them, especially with the fear of kidnapping and explosions. Three wars since 1980, a refugee crisis, loss of family members, poverty, suicide attacks, bombings, raids by soldiers and death squads, have shattered young Iraqis both physically and mentally. As early as April 2003, the UN Children's Fund had estimated that half a million Iraqi children had been traumatized by the US-led invasion. Since then, the situation has degenerated. The vast majority of deaths recorded by IBC in 2006 were, as every year, direct deaths from conflict violence, that is, deaths that resulted directly from the violent actions of participants to the conflict. As in other countries of conflict, conflict parties were also involved in criminal activities that caused deaths, such as robberies, kidnappings for extortion, or trade in narcotics. The resulting deaths from those were also recorded, as the perpetrators were committing criminal acts and associated violence in order to finance or otherwise support their conflict activities. These criminal activities were committed in order to advance the conflict objectives of the perpetrators. Therefore, these activities were part of the conflict violence and evidence that the breakdown in security the conflict caused made those crimes not only possible, but tragically also very common. One of those criminal activities then on the rise, the kidnapping of children, plagues Iraq to this day.

Iraq's dark period was far from over. And its end has not yet come, as the voices of Iraqi people have so far been largely ignored, by their elected politicians and by their occupiers/liberators. Responsibility for the breakdown of the state has not been accepted by anyone. There has been no accountability for crimes committed and no reparations have been paid by states with a deeply rooted imperial mentality. Such thoughts are generally beyond the consideration of those ruling the Iraqi people, who are content to let Iraq fall deeper and deeper into its darkness, while they themselves sit within their own dim light.

Iraq 2007: the surge as America fights back

The year started with the news that the Iraqi Defence Ministry was going to receive a gift of 4,000 armoured personnel carriers (APCs), 1,800 Humvee vehicles and 16 helicopter gunships from the Pentagon in March, according to a ministry spokesman. There was of course the added gift of thousands of troops, some already in Iraq, others due to arrive in the next few weeks, to provide more security. In January 2007 President George W. Bush announced the 'new way forward in Iraq' would involve the deployment of 30,000 additional troops and a new counterinsurgency strategy. The surge aimed to, ultimately, reduce the violence enough so that 'daily life will improve, Iraqis will gain confidence in their leaders, and the government will have the breathing space it needs to make progress in other critical areas' (CNN, 2007).

Meanwhile, health and security authorities in Karbala were put on high alert, in case of major attacks during a very important upcoming religious festival: the day of Ashura. The 'most religious event in the Shiite Muslim calendar' draws millions of pilgrims every year, who march, chant and flagellate themselves in ritualistic processions. The processions mourn the 7th century killing of Imam Hussein, grandson of the Prophet Mohammed, murdered in the Battle of Karbala in 680 AD on the day of Ashura. His martyrdom is widely interpreted by Shiites as a symbol of the struggle against injustice, tyranny and oppression. Attacks blamed on Sunni extremists had killed hundreds of pilgrims over the past two years during Ashura ceremonies.

Karbala was not the only city bracing itself for more violence. Baghdad was a city paralysed by fear, full of checkpoints and heavily armed men, daily mortar attacks and a civilian population caught between the hammer of insurgency and the anvil of the military.

The long-awaited Baghdad conference yielded little. The meeting was largely cordial, but delegates from Syria, Iran, Jordan, Kuwait, Saudi Arabia, Turkey, the five permanent members of the UN Security Council, the Arab League and the Organization of the Islamic Conference did not set a date for a second, higher-level gathering of foreign ministers. They agreed only to establish working groups to focus on various issues. During the conference, Iraqi Prime Minister Nuri al-Maliki demanded that states 'do not seek to have a quota or influence in Iraq through influencing a certain sect or ethnic community or a party' (Radio Free Europe/Radio Liberty, 2007). Iran's chief delegate, Abbas Araghchi, a deputy foreign minister, openly criticized US actions in Iraq, for making mistakes, because of the false information and intelligence they had at the beginning.

In 2007, the daily violence, everyday terrorism, remained Iraq's greatest problem. As the Iraqis say, 'the mud was getting wetter', meaning that things were getting worse. Iran's warnings that the vicious circle of violence – where the presence of foreign troops is fuelling attacks and leading to high levels of violence, which is then used to justify the necessity of the troops – cannot be broken until foreign armies withdraw from Iraq, rather than increase, went unheeded. With more American soldiers arriving in Iraq and with ineffective attempts to reach some international consensus on political and security matters, the mud was going to get wetter still.

The Hero

18 Mar 2007

As those around him fled in panic, Ahmed Draiwel ran with the bomb in his arms toward a rubbish pile, where he planned to hurl the explosive parcel. When he realised he wouldn't make it, he began praying, and then the parcel bomb blew up in his arms, killing him. A vendor in a Sadr City market, 18-year-old Ahmed Draiwel sold vegetables from his stall, and was not armed or on a mission to save anybody. Disposing of bombs was not his job, yet he saved everyone at that market on 15 March, when he spotted a suspicious parcel, picked it up and shouted to everyone to get away. He saved everyone but himself.

Ahmed was one among 450 people who died this week, people whose stories cannot all be known or told. As the 4-year anniversary of the invasion of Iraq approaches, the number of civilians killed in this war has now exceeded 65,000, of which 26,500 died in the fourth year alone.

During this year, two reports outlined the terrible, and worsening, situation in Iraq: the Iraq Study Group and the Pentagon quarterly report. Both painted a picture of violence, despair and pessimism. George W. Bush was forced to admit that the US was 'not winning' the war in Iraq.

Violence in Iraq is rising at an 'unbelievably rapid pace', according to the Pentagon's latest assessment of the security situation. It is now higher than at any time since the overthrow of Saddam Hussein's regime. The quarterly report 'Measuring Stability and Security in Iraq' said the level of violence in Iraq 'in all specific measurable categories' has reached 'the highest level on record' and poses a 'grave threat' to the Iraqi government. Iraqi civilians have paid the heaviest price, as their casualty rate has remained 60% higher than in February, when the Golden Mosque was bombed. The number of attacks on US and Iraqi troops, as well as civilians, has risen to almost 1,000 a week, in recent months, between 12 August and 10 November. This constitutes a 22% increase in attacks and a 2% jump in civilian casualties, compared to the three previous months. Most casualties were Iraqi, despite the fact that 68% of the attacks targeted US-led coalition troops. The report further said that that Shia cleric Moqtada al-Sadr's Mahdi Army militia has replaced al-Qaeda in Iraq as the single largest threat to the country's security. It was generally admitted in December that 'we' are not winning the war in Iraq. The Iraq Study Group report, published on December 5, confirmed what many had already admitted and many more already realised: 'Current US policy is not working.' The situation in Iraq is 'grave and deteriorating', the report explains, as Iraq is 'sliding toward chaos'. The government could collapse and a 'humanitarian catastrophe' may result, they warned. Moreover, 'there is no path that can guarantee success'.

The conflict in Iraq is now regularly described as a 'civil war' in the media. The warring parties, the Shia and the Sunni, appear to be fighting for, among other things, control of Baghdad. The Shia in particular are increasingly hostile to the occupation, with 62% of them approving of armed attacks on US-led forces. The militias have all grown stronger during the year, as the army and police forces seem unable to provide security. 1.6 million Iraqis have now fled from Iraq, to escape the violence and the poverty. In a country rich in oil, supplies of electricity, water, gasoline and kerosene remain inadequate.

It was also reported that 2006 was the worst year for reporters in over a decade, with Iraq once again proving the most dangerous place in the world for the media to work. According to Reporters without Borders (RSF), 113 reporters and media staff were killed in Iraq in 2006, the highest death toll since 1994, when scores of reporters died in the Rwandan genocide. RSF also says that 25 media assistants also died in Iraq in 2006. Almost 90% of the journalists killed were Iraqi.

In an attempt to calm Iraq's sectarian violence and begin a process of reconciliation, Iraqi Prime Minister Nuri al-Maliki visited Ramadi, the capital of Anbar province, one of the least stable regions in the country, to meet tribal Sunni leaders and local officials last week.

It was a good idea. Not such a good idea was to go there accompanied by top US Gen. David Petraeus and his troops. 'Maliki and Petraeus flew together from Baghdad in a convoy of Black Hawk helicopters … While Petraeus met his soldiers and ventured into the centre of Ramadi, Maliki stayed under heavy security on the US military base, Camp Blue Diamond, and held meetings inside a palace built by Saddam Hussein' (Washington Post, 14 March 2007). This 'symbolic' visit, the Washington Post reports, was not even al-Maliki's idea, but happened after Gen Petraeus urged him to 'come and visit your folks'. In one neighbourhood, Petraeus walked through the streets, speaking with residents, and as he headed back to the convoy stopped at a house, spoke a few words in Arabic and, looking at his soldiers, told the family: 'Meet your new neighbour.' If al-Maliki wants to reconcile the Sunnis and the Shias in Iraq, under his rule as a strong leader of all Iraqi groups, within a sovereign Iraq, he is certainly not going about it the right way. All he has achieved so far, in this now barely functioning state, is to show himself allied to the occupying forces, which are trusted just by 18% of the population, according to the latest polls.

Just three days after the Prime Minister's visit to Ramadi, Shiite cleric Moqtada Al-Sadr called upon followers inside his stronghold of Sadr City to resist US forces in the capital. In a message to them distributed at the Kufa mosque in southern Iraq, he urged them raise their voices and shout 'No America, no Israel, no, no Satan.' His statement continued: 'And here you are standing up for the support of your beloved city; this city which the occupier wanted to harm, and tarnish its reputation by spreading false propaganda and rumours and claiming that there are negotiation and collaboration between you and them. But I'm sure that you consider them as your enemies' (Washington Post 17 March 2007). On Friday 16 March thousands of his followers demonstrated in several parts of Iraq.

Meanwhile insurgent attacks continue, despite the dispatch of more than 20,000 additional US troops. Insurgents are confronting the surge strategy head-on, killing civilians daily; over 2,500 civilians were killed in the past month, since the launch of the surge on 14 February, by insurgents, US troops, death squads, al-Qaeda and various unknown attackers. This summer troop levels will top 160,000, compared with the 150,000 at the time of the invasion.

In the words of James Baker, former US Secretary of State, Iraq is in 'a helluva mess', and has been in a State of Emergency for more than a year. With no sign of any significant improvement in terms of its security or its political situation, Iraq will need a lot more heroes.
(Hamourtziadou, 2007a)

'Jesus called the children to him and said "Let the little children come to me, and do not hinder them, for the kingdom of God belongs to such as these"' (Luke 18:16). As we in the West celebrated Easter in April 2007, an increasing number of Iraqi children were going to 'the kingdom of God' or simply into the ground. Others lost their families. Throughout 2007, childhood, the most important, the most precious and most innocent time in a person's life, continued to be systematically destroyed, defiled and devalued by the daily violence, the daily attackers that did not take them into account when selecting their intended target. The insurgents would bomb the patrol/government building/politician even if there was a school/child nearby; US planes/tanks would attack the homes of suspected insurgents, even though there were children inside; soldiers would shoot at a suspected terrorist, even when he was holding a child.

As the world marked another anniversary of Orphan's Day on 5 April, orphans were increasing in Iraq, as violence claimed more lives every day. The acts of violence that swept Iraq after the US-led invasion in 2003 have left scores of Iraqi orphans, but the same number of orphanages.

In Mosul Orphanage, on 5 April 2007, children gathered to mark the anniversary by remembering their parents who were killed in the acts of violence. According to Nahla Zannun, an orphanage teacher, some blamed the world for their lost parents and others envied the rest of the world's children because they lived with their families. Some screamed at night, others could not speak, a number of them were the only survivors from their families. Then there were those that tried to imagine their families were still alive and would come to get them, even though they had seen them die.

There were fears that these children would start to hate society and would join armed groups, as soon as they were old enough to do so. A few years later, when the Islamic State entered Iraq and established 'The Cubs', such children would be recruited and trained to fight to the death, or be executed if they became too frightened.

During our Holy Week of Easter, our 'week of the passions', around 550 civilians were killed in Iraq; at least 32 of them were children. On Monday 2 April, our first day of the Holy Week, around 120 died. A suicide truck bomb killed 14 civilians in Kirkuk, when it exploded outside a government building during a visit by American troops, which may have been the bomber's target. In the event, 9 young girls died as they left their classroom – their school was next to the government building – as well as 5 more people, including mothers. A roadside bomb killed 10 in Khalis, US forces killed 6 (3 of them brothers) in Mosul, and 45 bodies were found in Baghdad, Baquba, Mosul and Falluja. There were reports that 30 civilians died in a US bombing of the houses of two brothers in Al-Bu-Aytha, 14 children among them.

On Tuesday nearly 60 died, including 2 university students killed in Baghdad, a teenager killed by mortars while playing football, and 30 bodies found in Baghdad, Ramadi and Diyala. One body, found with its throat cut in Sab al Bor, was that of an 11-year-old boy.

Wednesday 4 April was the quietest day of the week, as there were only 49 civilian deaths reported. Of the 49, 11 were employees of an electricity station shot dead near Hawija and 5 were policemen. A further 20 bodies were found, while US troops attacked 5 buildings in Ramadi and killed, among others, a man, a woman and a child. In Karbala, 93 unidentified bodies were buried.

On Thursday 5 April 80 were reported to have died, 54 of them found bound, tortured and executed in 6 cities, 2 of them just heads. Among the dead a journalist, an interpreter, killed alongside 4 British soldiers blown up in Basra, and a 3-year-old child, little Ali, shot dead as he sat on his grandfather's lap.

On Good Friday 6 April over 80 died, 9 of them university students ambushed and shot dead in the minibus they were riding in Hawija. A suicide truck bomber targeting a police checkpoint killed 35 in Ramadi, while a family of 7, 3 children among them, was blown up by a roadside bomb near Falluja. Clashes between US troops, Iraqi soldiers and insurgents killed 7 civilians in Diwaniya.

Ninety died on Saturday 7 April. Clashes continued for a second day in Diwaniya, where 6 more civilians were reported killed. A judge was murdered in Qara Taba, while US air strikes of two villages, Al-Nay and Al-Dohma, killed 8. Mortars killed a teacher in Baquba, and police found 64 bodies in 8 cities. Among the bodies, 6 herdsmen who had been abducted the day before, dumped in Karbala.

On Easter Sunday 8 April 70 civilians were reported dead in Iraq. A car bomb killed 7 in Baghdad, while another car bomb killed 18 in Mahmudiya. Clashes in Diwaniya killed a further 2 civilians, while clashes in Diyala killed another 3. Police found 35 bodies in Baghdad, Falluja, Baquba and the Missan province. Thousands of Iraqis flocked to the holy city of Najaf for a big demonstration scheduled for Monday, and called by Moqtada al-Sadr against the US presence in Iraq, on the fourth anniversary of the fall of Baghdad. A new dispatch of US forces, 3,000 of them, arrived in Baghdad to 'assist in law enforcement'.

Who cared for the children of Iraq? Who cared enough not to take away their parents? Who cared enough not to sacrifice them to their cause? As the fighting continued, there were no places left for the children to hide.

Fighting terrorism in a free Iraq

15 Apr 2007

We are 'fighting terrorism' in Iraq, that is why we are there, said Tony Blair this week. This story has changed so many times: first we were removing the WMD threat, then we were removing a dictator, then we were bringing democracy and free elections, and now we are fighting terrorism. 'It is a worthy cause', echoed Dick Cheney.

Well, it is not strictly true that we are in Iraq to fight terrorism. We may be fighting terrorism there now, but it is terrorism we have brought to the country. We, outside Iraq, have brought terror to Iraqi homes, streets and cities. We have brought terror to their schools, markets and mosques, to their old and young, to their men and women. To their poor children.

Terror claimed another 500 civilian lives this week, at least 21 of them children.

On Monday 9 April 45 lose their lives. Tens of thousands of peaceful protesters waving Iraqi flags and calling for US forces to leave Iraq march into Najaf, marking the fourth anniversary of the fall of Baghdad. Torching American flags, Shiites and Sunnis voice their anger and frustration over the US government's record in Iraq since it led the invasion in 2003. The march comes as a response to a call by Shia cleric Moqtada al-Sadr, who has demanded that US forces leave the country.

Sadr's statement to the crowds read: 'So far 48 months of anxiety, oppression and occupational tyranny have passed, four years which have only brought us more death, destruction and humiliation ... Every day tens are martyred, tens are crippled, and every day we see and hear US interference in every aspect of our lives, which means that we are not sovereign, not independent and therefore not free. This is what Iraq has harvested from the US invasion' (Los Angeles Times, *April 10 2007). The speech, delivered by cleric Abdelhadi al-Mohammadawi, was interrupted by chants of 'Leave, leave occupier' and 'No, no, to the occupation.'*

On Tuesday 10 April 85 civilians are reported dead, 19 of them police recruits blown up by a suicide bomber at a police station in Muqdadiya. A shocking 34 are reported dead in a US/Iraqi raid in Baghdad, while 16 are found bound, tortured and executed in Baghdad, Falluja, Mahaweel and Kirkuk.

On the most peaceful day of the week, 42 die on Wednesday 11 April. The dead include 5 policemen, a mother and her son killed in Mosul, a teacher shot dead in Baghdad, a radio journalist and her husband. Over 30 more bodies are found, while 18 unidentified bodies are buried in Kut.

Over 50 are killed on Thursday 12 April. A suicide truck bomber kills 11 and blows up al-Sarafiya bridge in Baghdad. Up to 8 are reported killed when a bomb explodes in the Iraqi Parliament, inside the Green Zone. Among the dead on Thursday, 3 people killed during a US raid in Haditha and 13 bodies discovered in Baghdad and Kut.

Around 70 more are killed on Friday 13 April. Among the dead, an imam killed with his brother on their way to the mosque in Mosul, a woman and her child blown up by a roadside bomb in Baghdad, 2 interpreters killed in an attack on US soldiers, and over 20 bodies found in Baghdad and Mosul.

Saturday 14 April is the worst day of the week, when around 110 die. A suicide bomber blows up a car at a busy bus station in Karbala, killing 47 civilians, 16 of them children. A further 4 are killed in clashes with the police after the bombing. Another car bomb kills 10 at Jadriya bridge in Baghdad, while police find 28 bodies in Baghdad, Kirkuk, Kut and Mosul.

The week ends with nearly 100 victims of violence on Sunday 15 April, 80 of them in Baghdad. Among the victims 3 children, blown up by car bombs that kill 18 in the Shurta al-Rabia area of Baghdad.

In a statement to the Iraqi Prime Minister, Moqtada al-Sadr has criticised him for refusing to set a timetable for the withdrawal of the occupation forces. 'Your statements have nothing to do with the millions who flocked to Najaf', his statement reads. 'Can you not hear their voices urging the pullout of the occupier or setting a timetable for its withdrawal? Where do you stand vis-à-vis the people who made you assume this post?' (Al-Sharqiya 12 April 2007).

Following his statement, al-Sadr announced that he would be withdrawing from the Iraqi government, due to Baghdad's close ties to Washington and its 'policy of appeasement for the occupation'. Sadr's movement holds a quarter of parliamentary seats in Prime Minister Nuri al-Maliki's Shiite Alliance.

Meanwhile, the threat of a Turkish invasion seems to be moving closer to Kurdish-dominated northern Iraq. The head of Turkey's armed forces said publicly on Thursday that he was prepared to conduct operations to crush Kurdish rebels hiding there. 'Should there be an operation into northern Iraq?' asked Gen. Yasar Buyukanit, Turkey's chief of staff. 'If I look at it from an exclusively military point of view, yes, there should be. Would it be profitable? Yes, it would' (New York Times, *April 13 2007*).

This is a very sensitive issue, as the Kurds remain the United States' strongest allies in Iraq. Yet the United States is also an ally of Turkey, an unhappy ally, as the Turkish government is growing increasingly frustrated that it cannot use its leverage in a country occupied by fellow NATO members. When entering northern Iraq today 'you are met by Kurdish flags, not Iraqi ones', complained Gen. Buyukanit, surely the fault of the US. Not many would disagree with him.

It seems Iraq is facing a variety of threats, internal and external, as well as an indefinite period of occupation. The International Red Cross has declared the situation for civilians in Iraq 'ever worsening'.

Letters sent by the US military to Iraqi families, to notify denial of a compensation claim, conclude 'I wish you well in a Free Iraq.'

Indeed, good luck. In 'free' Iraq. (Hamourtziadou, 2007b)

The US led a war against Iraq in March 2003. As a result of that war, bombings, invasion and continuing occupation of Iraq, terrorism has skyrocketed. Of the 14,338 reported terrorist attacks worldwide in 2006, 45% took place in Iraq, and 65% of the global fatalities stemming from terrorism occurred in Iraq.

The US-led actions resulted in violent reactions from those opposed to them, creating an insurgency and terrorism in the country. The main armed groups operating in Iraq in 2007, apart from the US and British military, were: al-Qaeda in Iraq, Mujahideen Shura Council, Sunni nationalists, Ansar al-Islam, Mahdi Army and Badr Brigade.

The daily killings are one of the consequences of the invasion and subsequent reaction of armed groups; another is poverty. According to an Iraqi government survey (conducted by the Central Statistical Bureau), 43% of Iraqis suffered from 'absolute poverty', lacking the necessary food, clothing or shelter to survive, while 11% lived in 'abject poverty', lacking a minimum income or consumption level necessary to meet basic needs.

The reactions and consequences of this invasion should not surprise us. Our armies did not go to war for the sake of Iraq, or the Iraqis. A 'friendly' regime was the desired end, a seemingly legitimate government that would allow the West to control Iraq. The security of the Iraqis was never a consideration. The feelings of the Iraqis, their beliefs, their attitudes, their view of the invading Westerners, were not important in this. The British and American public were simply told that the oppressed Iraqis would be grateful. Or should be grateful. But this war was not a response to a humanitarian crisis. Rather, it led to a humanitarian crisis.

Iraqi civilians were paying daily with their lives: 2,573 were killed in April of that year.

The second international conference on Iraq, in the Egyptian resort of Sharm al-Sheikh, produced very little. At the conference, Arab nations committed to stop foreign fighters from crossing their borders to join Iraq's insurgency. The Iraqis, in turn, vowed to do more to include Iraq's Sunni Arabs in the political process. Many Arab papers ranked this conference as one of many that achieved nothing.

This was not surprising. The Iraqis are nobody's priority. Just like the Americans and the British, the Iraqi government is interested largely in securing its own objectives. The insurgents, reacting, are interested in achieving theirs.

Tony Blair's legacy

13 May 2007

Two wars and a decade of sanctions have led to a huge rise in the mortality rate among young children in Iraq, leaving statistics that were once the envy of the Arab world now comparable with those of sub-Saharan Africa. A new report shows that in the years since 1990, Iraq has seen its child mortality rate soar by 125%, the highest increase of any country in the world (Independent 8 May). Years of UN sanctions, followed by the US and Britain-led invasion, devastated Iraq's infrastructure and health services. Figures show that in 1990 Iraq's mortality rate for under-fives was 50 per 1,000 live births; in 2005 it was 125.

Those that survive face a life of poverty, fear, struggle and loss. Baghdad has thousands of orphans – no one knows the exact number. The orphans are too many for the 8 orphanages in Baghdad, yet other than the orphanages no one will take these children, as in Iraqi culture orphans are mostly scorned, and seldom adopted. As a result, they end up in the streets. Scared, angry, violent, trying to survive by selling incense, gum, they are barely more than beggars.

Poverty drives others to work for armed groups. 11-year-old Seif and his brothers make bombs for Sunni insurgents who are fighting US troops. 'The bombs are used to fight American soldiers. I was really afraid in the beginning, but then my parents told me that it was for two good causes: the first is to help our family eat; and the second is to fight occupation forces', he says (IRIN 10 May). Thousands of poor children in Iraq are forced to work to help their families, many by helping insurgents. In Seif's words, 'hunger is worse than anything'.

Violence killed another 580 civilians last week, and there was another major attack (with 50 or more deaths), the 15th so far this year (in 2006 there were 12 altogether).

Around 140 die on Monday 7 May. Among the dead 13 killed by a suicide bomber in Ramadi, 61 killed or found dead in Baghdad, and 40 more bodies found in Hilla, Kharma, Tikrit, and Diyala.

Over 60 die on Tuesday 8 May. In Baghdad, police find 25 bodies, tortured and executed, a suicide bomber kills 16 in a market in Kufa, while a US helicopter reportedly kills 7 children while shelling a primary school in Al-Nedawat village. Not included in the day's count, but worth mentioning, are the 2 new-borns in incubators that die due to power shortage, and because they could not be transferred to another hospital, as security measures prevent ambulances from entering and leaving the city, Samarra.

Nearly 90 die on Wednesday 9 May, 19 of them in Arbil, victims of a suicide bomber. Gunmen kill 11 people inside a bus, 2 of them children, and 3 journalists are shot dead with their driver near Kirkuk. Among the dead a construction worker and a university professor. 34 bodies are found in Baghdad, Falluja and Baquba, 4 of them headless.

On Thursday 10 May 50 lose their lives. In Baghdad's Sadr City 8 civilians are reported dead during a US raid, and another civilian is shot dead in Basra by British troops. A further 29 bodies are found in Baghdad, Mosul and Mahaweel.

Another 60 civilians are killed on Friday 11 May, including 22 blown up by suicide bombings on two bridges in Baghdad. Another university professor is shot dead with his brother in Baghdad, 3 women are shot dead inside their car near Balad, a young girl is slaughtered in front of her policeman father in Samarra, and 25 bodies are found dumped in Baghdad, Hawija and Falluja.

On the most peaceful day of this week, Saturday 12 May, only 45 are killed. Among them a doctor shot dead in Mosul, an interpreter and 24 bodies found in Baghdad, Baquba, Latifiya and Mosul.

The violence is up again on Sunday 13 May, when around 140 are killed. In another major attack, the 15th this year, a suicide bomber blows up a truck and kills 50 near the Kurdistan Democratic Party (KDP) headquarters in Makhmour. A car bomb kills a further 17 people in Baghdad's al-Wathba square, gunmen shoot dead 5 at a flour mill, a former university dean is shot dead in Mosul, and a US plane kills a woman and a child sleeping on the roof of their house in Sadr City. Police find 40 bodies in Baghdad, Mosul and Diyala.

Over the past four years tens of thousands have been killed, and thousands more are missing. There is no accurate number of the missing: human rights groups put the figure at 15,000 or more, while government officials estimate that 40–60 disappeared daily for much of last year, a rate equal to at least 14,600 in one year. What happened to them is a mystery that 'compounds Iraq's overwhelming sense of chaos and anarchy' (McClatchy, 2007). They may be dead, kidnapped, or held prisoner by the US, which is holding 19,000 Iraqis at its two main detention centres, Camp Cropper and Camp Bucca.

Thousands dead, thousands missing, in this country of poor and starving children, orphaned and begging in the streets, dying daily, increasingly joining in terrorist activities to survive. Yet the British Prime Minister Tony Blair, as he is about to step down, still defends his decision to invade and occupy this country. Still accepting none of the responsibility.

Tony Blair, who made his nation complicit in the destruction of so many lives, who sent British soldiers, young men and women, to die and kill 'in the name' of the British public, who made Britain a target for terrorists... he must never be forgiven by the British. No, the British must never forgive him for disgracing them, for endangering them, for involving them in the killings, the poverty, the loss of so much.

'There is no future for any Iraqi people', Quammer al-Janni, coordinator of orphan programmes for the Red Crescent, observes sadly. 'Not just for the orphan babies, for all the Iraqi people. We don't have any future.' (Hamourtziadou, 2007c)

The fourth year of the war was the worst since the invasion for violence against civilians. Almost half of all violent civilian deaths since March 2003 took place during the fourth year of the conflict, March 2006–March 2007. Large explosions (killing over 50 people) nearly doubled in that period, from 9 to 17, while mortar attacks that killed civilians quadrupled (from 73 to 289). Fatal suicide attacks, car bombs, and IED attacks doubled in that period (from 712 to 1476). Baghdad residents were hit the hardest. By 2007 1 in 160 of Baghdad's 6.5 million population had been violently killed since the beginning of the war, representing 64% of deaths recorded. By the fourth anniversary of the invasion in March 2007 70,000 Iraqi civilians had been killed.

Following the six-week 'Shock and Awe' invasion phase (19 March–1 May 2003), which alone caused the deaths of some 7,400 civilians, the violent death toll had steadily risen year on year. There were 6,332 reported civilian deaths in the 10.5 months following the initial invasion in year one, or 20 per day; 11,312 in year two, 55% up on year one's daily rate; 14,910 in year three (32% up on year two); and a staggering 26,540 in year four (78% up on year three, and averaging 74 per day). Not counting the 7,400 invasion-phase deaths, four times as many people were killed in the last year as in the first. And from the invasion to the fourth anniversary, at least 110,000 civilians were wounded, 38,000 of them during year four.

IBC's monthly figures showed an upward trend in violence, which peaked in July and remained elevated at around 2,500 or higher throughout the second half of the year. Those IBC trends were broadly in line with the Pentagon's assessment of trends in the security situation. In the data collected by the Pentagon most casualties were Iraqis, even though 68% of the attacks targeted US-led coalition troops.

In terms of bombings, during the fourth year Iraq saw a particularly marked increase in mortar attacks, suicide car and roadside bombing attacks, and massive incidents each killing more than 50 people. In the last year there were 17 such large bombing incidents – 8 of them occurring in 2007, and the 2 most lethal ever (killing 137 and 120 civilians, respectively) which also occurred at the start of 2007.

Baghdad, the most populous region of the country, continued to be one of its most violent, experiencing about five times more deaths per capita than the rest of the country. By the end of year four, approximately 1 in 160 of its residents had been violently killed – an impact on the population that approached the effect on Fallujah after the two major US sieges of the city in 2004 (during which about 1 in 140 Fallujans were killed). Once again, by far the majority of casualties throughout the nation were among men. Young men in particular are both the most frequently targeted as well as the most exposed.

One of the most horrific aspects of the targeting of Iraqi males is the growing number of post-capture executions, which often include torture and mutilation. As these bodies are discovered, often piled together, or washed up at river barriers, they are sent to the morgues (Medico-Legal Institutes) for investigation and potential identification. The Baghdad MLI receives bodies found in the streets and outlying areas of Baghdad, as well as a number of unidentified bodies from bombings, which it photographs and tags to assist identification. Those that remain unidentified or unclaimed by relatives are sent for burial in mass graves in Najaf, Karbala and the outskirts of Baghdad.

About 10–20%, or roughly 200–250 per month, of the bodies received and autopsied at the Baghdad morgue were of people who died from non-violent but 'suspicious' causes requiring some degree of legal investigation. The morgue's total monthly autopsies were not solely of violent deaths. However, more intermittent figures collected by IBC revealed the number of deaths the MLI determined to have been deliberate killings, usually by gunfire, rather than non-violent sudden deaths (Table 2.2).

Though incomplete, these clearly exposed central Iraq's precipitous decline in civil security from almost immediately after the invasion.

Table 2.2: Deaths identified as murders at Baghdad Central Morgue

July 2002	21
Aug 2002	10
July 2003	498
Aug 2003	522
Aug 2004	386
Nov 2005	555
July 2006	1,417
Aug 2006	1,091

The bodies frequently showed signs of torture, a trend that accelerated since at least 2005 and continues to this day.

In the fourth year of the war, the daily violence remained Iraq's greatest civil concern. The data collected in the four years showed that there was never a sustained period of improvement on the security front, despite claims to the contrary by President Bush and Secretary of State Condoleezza Rice that there were 'encouraging signs' of progress in Iraq, and that 'things are going reasonably well'. Coalition forces, principally US as well as some UK forces, were identified to have killed at least 536 Iraqi civilians in year four. This compared with 370 in year three. With an average of three incidents a week in which a foreign army kills civilians, including the killing of a five-year-old girl and entire families with their children, could such an army ever be a stabilizing force?

Airstrikes, years of occupation and 'boots on the ground', as well as the instalment of a new 'democratic' government, all failed to quell the insurgency that erupted at the point of invasion. In the sixth year of the war, the response moved into the era of remote warfare, with President Obama relying on armed drones, special forces and private military companies. That counterinsurgency policy also failed and is failing still, as insurgency has persisted across the Middle East. In Iraq and in Afghanistan we see long-term damage, poverty, continuing terror and instability. Millions have been internally and externally displaced, hundreds of thousands of whom have sought refuge in Europe, legally and illegally.

At the root of the problem, argues Paul Rogers, is the failure of what might best be called 'the control paradigm centred on a military-industrial complex', which serves a political establishment that cares mostly about the short term and stems from elite power structures that own the narrative on national and international security (Rogers, 2019, p 147).

In the two decades since the 9/11 attacks that triggered the War on Terror, security solutions have centred on regaining and controlling through force. This approach disregards the causes of conflict, which it neither seeks to understand, nor seeks to respond to. As a result, 20 years on, the War on Terror continues. Rogers sees this as part of a wider security culture that only rarely recognizes that threats to elite security stem from what might be termed the 'majority margins'. The marginalization and exclusion of most people is the biggest threat to security, however, and this is where the paradigm has failed, these revolts from the margins have only been controlled by force (Rogers, 2019). The failed control paradigm has left a trail of weak and failing states, hundreds of thousands of people killed and millions displaced. It has also left a legacy of bitterness, resentment and anger, a long-standing policy and enduring legacy of the West in the Middle East.

3

The Beginning of the End of Sectarian Violence? Writing the War 2008–2009

By 2008, the UNHCR raised the estimate of refugees to a total of about 4.7 million, with 2 million displaced internally and 2.7 million displaced externally (UNHCR, 2008). But the death toll was to halve, then halve again the following year as Table 3.1 shows.

The numbers, despite being high, suggested a marked improvement, perhaps the beginning of the end of sectarian violence. The 'surge' appeared to have worked, but Iraqis were still far from secure.

2008: Iraq after the surge

Over 10,200 Iraqi civilians lost their lives in 2008, still a shockingly high number, although a substantial drop on the preceding two years: on a per-day rate, representing a reduction from 81 per day (2006) and 72 per day (2007) to 25 per day in 2008. The most notable reduction in violence was in Baghdad. For the first time since the US-led occupation of Iraq began, fewer deaths were reported in the capital than in the rest of the country (from 54% of all deaths in 2006–2007 to 32% in 2008).

While the US used a variety of means in its surge strategy, military force has remained central, with the predictable outcome of new civilian lives lost. Airstrikes – the most frequent mode of US military attack involving civilian victims – continued with regularity throughout the surge, killing close to 400 civilians in 2008. Roadside bombs killed 1,106 civilians. During 2008, 928 policemen were reported killed. Some three quarters of the reported civilian killings had no clearly distinguishable perpetrator.

Table 3.1: Civilian deaths by month 2008–2009

	Jan	Feb	Mar	Apr	May	Jun	Jul	Aug	Sep	Oct	Nov	Dec	Total
2008	861	1,093	1,669	1,317	915	755	640	704	612	594	540	586	**10,286**
2009	372	409	438	590	428	564	431	653	352	441	226	478	**5,382**

As well as extracting the daily data on civilian deaths, I followed the developments that revealed more human misery, its causes and its place in the larger context.

The vulnerable

3 Feb 2008

The rules of war are founded in 3 principles: discrimination, necessity and proportionality. They dictate that only combatants may be targeted (discrimination), that the tactics used should only be those necessary to achieve a certain military objective (necessity), and that the cost of the tactics used is not higher than the benefit of the objective itself (proportionality).

The basis and aim of all 3 principles can be summed up in a single phrase: the protection of the vulnerable. During any war civilians are the most vulnerable to attack, and it is the lives of civilians that any army, government, state or group has the responsibility to defend, protect or spare.

The failure to protect the most vulnerable members of society was evident again this week in Iraq, when nearly 250 civilians lost their lives. There were at least 13 children among them. In the recent Baghdad bombings, even the two suicide bombers were reportedly vulnerable people, Down's syndrome women, used by those for whom their own interests are paramount, for whom the lives of Iraqi civilians are expendable.

During the 'surge' year, February 2007–February 2008, the whole purpose of which was to effectively bring security to those who needed it the most, around 22,000 civilians lost their lives in violent attacks, as many as 1,300 of whom were killed by US forces. All sides failed to protect those civilians: the US army, the British, the insurgents, terrorists, even their 'legitimate' leaders; on the contrary, all parties contributed to their killings directly or indirectly. The latest example of this is last Sunday's air strikes that killed 9 Iraqi civilians (as many as 20, according to witnesses), for which the US army has apologised as usual. It seems that the principle of proportionality is lost on them, as the tactics they employ (air strikes on buildings, even whole neighbourhoods) show that the cost involved (the loss of civilian lives) is, to them, very low. Or at least low enough for them to be using these tactics repeatedly, for the past 5 years.

Already there have been 2 large-scale attacks this year, with 50 or more killed, despite the recent drop in violence. The first one, in Mosul, killed 57 civilians on January 23rd; the second killed 62 at a Baghdad pet market on February 1st. The pet market attack was one of two co-ordinated attacks that killed 99 people in two pet markets in Baghdad. Despite the optimism of the last few months, caused by the decrease in violence, 2008 has started badly. Violence aside, Iraq is still a politically and economically dysfunctional state. And, perhaps most tragically of all, it is still not sovereign, 5 years after our attempts to 'liberate' it and give it to its people to govern. There is still no one in charge, no one defending those ever-suffering Iraqis, no one to value their lives. No one to see beyond their own interest, be it power, wealth, control, or all of the above.

And the killings continue, every day. Literally. Not a day has gone by when Iraqi civilians have not lost their lives in shootings, bombings, air strikes... not one day since March 2003. This is perhaps the most shocking fact about this war. Its daily terror. Its daily promise of death.

Meanwhile, Brigadier Robert Aitken has criticised the conduct of some British soldiers serving in Iraq. They need to have a 'better understanding between right and wrong', he said. Indeed they do. Yet who has the moral authority to teach them such an understanding? Not their leaders, who declared a war with such a high civilian cost, a war that has unleashed a multitude of horrors, a war that has destroyed a whole society. Not their leaders, who still have not recognised or admitted the wrong they have done. Who still claim to be moral, pious even, driven by ideals such as altruism, self-sacrifice, and striving for liberty, democracy – a force of good against evil.

Who has the courage to teach them respect for a person's humanity, whatever their colour or nationality, whatever their 'otherness', the moral courage to stand up against injustice? Our armies may not lack the courage needed in battle, but they may lack the moral courage to stand up to what is wrong, to the victimisation of a country's civilian population, to the sacrifice of the vulnerable. Sadly, so do their leaders. Our leaders. (Hamourtziadou, 2008a)

According to an Iraqi MP who preferred to remain anonymous, during highly confidential negotiations representatives from American oil companies offered $5 million to each MP who voted in favour of the Oil and Gas law (*Mosul Observer*, 1 February 2008). During the week that followed, Suhaila, a 39-year-old Iraqi woman, the mother of a 4-month-old daughter called 'Zahra', decided to sell her because she could not feed her. She displayed her in a vegetable market in Baghdad. With a starting price of $500, she finally managed to sell her for $1,000.

Meanwhile, soldiers with the 1st Platoon, Company D, 1st Combined Arms Battalion, 68th Armor Regiment, 3rd Brigade Combat Team, 4th Infantry Division, Multi-National Division – Baghdad, made an impact by bringing presents to school children in Bayrk, a rural village in Fahama. Upon arriving at the school, the soldiers passed out backpacks, pencils and stuffed animals to the children. Making a positive impact on the lives of Iraqis, the army claimed, no matter how small, was a big part of current operations by coalition forces in the Fahama region. It was not the first time soldiers in the platoon had handed out treats to the children.

On 5 February US soldiers, acting on a tip, entered a tiny house in the village of Dour and opened fire on a sleeping family killing four of them: Ali Hamad, a farmer, his wife Naema Ali, their 19-year-old son and their 11-year-old daughter.

It was that February that a video was found, showing children being trained to kill and kidnap. The boys, estimated to be as young as nine, wore suicide vests and balaclava masks, as they held guns to the heads of mock kidnap victims. And the ugliness continued. The daily killings, the blood of innocents staining the streets of Baghdad, Mosul, Falluja, Baquba; the loss of all innocence as Iraqi children learnt to kill, to violate, to cope with a life without boundaries, without ideals, without security, without hope, in a state that had collapsed.

The consequences of state collapse

24 Feb 2008

Turkey invaded again this week. Thousands of Turkish troops marched into northern Iraq, bombing, shooting, attacking by land and by air. Over 100 Kurdish peshmerga have been reported killed so far; no civilian deaths yet, as most of the villages the troops attacked were devoid of people. They had already run for their lives. Where to? Who knows? Where do people run to when they flee their homes, as an army approaches? Where do they find food and shelter in an impoverished country, a country of terror?

The spokesman for the Iraqi government Ali Dabagh called on Turkey to respect the sovereignty and the unity of Iraq, and to stop the transgression of the Iraqi border. The 'sovereignty and unity' of Iraq. So this is what happens when a 'sovereign' state is attacked and its citizens are killed. Its government calls on the attackers to respect it. Its army does not even interfere. This is what happens in a state where there is 'unity'. The citizens have to defend it alone and fight the invading army themselves. As for the American 'protectors', they had been 'notified' of the attack, according to White House spokesman Scott Stenzel, by Turkey, their NATO ally, and they too chose not to interfere.

Because all that matters is alliances. Whose side one is on. Who cares about the citizens of Iraq? Who grieves over their deaths? Not the Iraqi government, that's for sure. As Iraq is rocked by bombings, as its citizens' blood is spilt, as yet another invasion is taking place, the PM, al-Maliki, leader of this 'sovereign state', flies to London for routine medical tests.

The consequences of state-collapse were evident in Iraq this week. The uncontrollable violence; the fleeing innocents; the population left defenceless; the lack of leadership; the vulnerability of the whole state as yet another country crosses its borders virtually unhindered.

Moqtada al-Sadr ordered his army to prolong its ceasefire for another six months. A good decision, no doubt. But he could have chosen not to. He could have decided to start fighting again, killing the innocent and the guilty alike. Who could have stopped him? Who is in charge in Iraq exactly? Whether there is peace or war, security or daily terror, depends on decisions made by various parties, at will, cruelly, recklessly, sometimes mercifully. One just never knows. This is what happens when a state collapses.

This week 235 civilians lost their lives to violence in Iraq. At least 11 of them were children. In the worst attack of the week, a suicide bomber killed 63 Shia pilgrims in Iskandariya; it was the third 'major' (with 50 or more killed) attack this year, and the second such attack in February. In fact, the death toll in February is already higher than that of January. For the first time since September, after the steady decline of the last few months, the death toll is up this month. (Hamourtziadou, 2008b)

'When you close your eyes and think of Iraq, what do you see in your mind's eye?' asked Jerry Schwartz, writing for the Associated Press.

> Is it a picture of charred bodies hanging from a bridge over the Euphrates River in Fallujah? Is it a picture of a Marine climbing a massive statue of Saddam Hussein to place an American flag on its face, hours after the fall of Baghdad? Or is it a picture of an Iraqi prisoner standing on a box, arms outstretched with wires attached, a fabric bag covering his head? (Oklahoman, 2008)

In my mind's eye, I saw the coffins, those cheap-looking boxes with the Arabic writing carried daily by Iraqi men, young and old, pain and anger visible on their faces. I saw the bodies, bullet-riddled, decomposed, unidentified, dumped or buried in mass graves. 'How many bodies will there be today?', I asked myself every morning. Because there were always bodies – without names, without identities. As if they had never been someone's sons, daughters, parents. Someone's beloved.

I saw the young assassins, the new generation of Iraq that should have been enjoying the joys of youth, the challenges and dreams of the future. Teenage boys learning how to make bombs, how to kill themselves and others, adding more cheap-looking coffins to the pile, to be carried in ever-increasing anger and despair. More than anything, I saw the grief: the screaming mothers, the fathers carrying their children's bodies in white shrouds. And I wondered, how could people bear so much grief?

The clear and biggest losers of this war are the Iraqis. The 2003 invasion and occupation of their country have brought them the following:

- terror
- poverty
- anarchy
- vulnerability
- collapse

Those that should have been the clear winners of this war are tragically by far the greatest losers. The other clear losers are the young men and women, over 4,000 of them, our soldiers, mainly American and British, who have so far lost their lives. Those young men and women who joined their country's armed forces intending to be brave, to protect, to save, to sacrifice their lives for the good of their nation and its civilians – their parents, children, friends, neighbours. Those men and women have instead died the death of the dishonourable, used and sacrificed by the winners of this war.

Who are those winners?

The clear winners at that time were those who had started this War on Terror, George W. Bush and Tony Blair, who had managed to get re-elected after invading and destroying another country, and after killing thousands of civilians, having cleverly redefined the war as an expression of Western values: freedom, democracy, equality. Their flattery worked: enough of us believed that we, noble, liberal, civilized and moral Westerners, were on a wonderful mission to save an oppressed population living in fear. Enough of us believed, because we wanted to believe, in our intrinsic goodness and in the good intentions of our leaders. Through us, their victory was assured, and through us they continued to be victorious.

The other winners were the extremists, who are still winning in Iraq, in Afghanistan and in Syria. Those who kill civilians daily. Those who torture and shoot women who wear make-up, who want to send their daughters to school. Those who blow up people in markets, who shoot innocents outside bakeries, inside schools, as they drive their cars. Those who abduct, torture and murder children, leaving their bodies in streets, fields, dumps, as though they were rubbish. The fanatics, the murderers, the terrorists, they have established a foothold in Iraq, they have now become what Iraq is famous for. What no country ever wants to be famous for.

Anyone who has become rich, even richer, or more powerful as a result of this war is also a winner. American and British firms and companies, 'the money men'. It was those winners that led to the destruction of Iraq.

A harsh neoliberal restructuring was introduced by the military invasion, in the most brutal and boldest way ever seen in the world, which turned Iraq into a neoliberal utopia. When Saddam Hussein's regime was defeated and replaced by the Coalition Provisional Authority (CPA), headed by Paul Bremer, a series of extensive neoliberal measures were quickly introduced in its first month without any waiting period, from privatization of 200 Iraqi state-owned companies to reducing corporate tax from 45% to 15%, and from allowing foreign firms to retain 100% of their Iraqi assets to a complete restructuring the Iraqi banking system. Iraq's oil revenues were put in a US-dominated development fund, the Development Fund for Iraq (DFI), held in an account at the Federal Reserve in New York and used for restructuring expenditure.

The Coalition Provisional Authority ran the occupation regime during its first 14 months and directed the most extreme version of neoliberal restructuring put in practice ever in the world, enforcing the market as the organizing and regulative principle of the state and society. In less than 14 months, Paul Bremer issued 26 orders, as a result of which the Iraqi state was deprived of economic sovereignty and control of its own affairs. More than half a million Iraqi citizens abruptly lost their jobs, after which over 50% of the workforce suddenly became unemployed. All these extensive neoliberal 'shock programme of economic reforms' were described by *The Economist* on 25 September 2003 as a 'Capitalist Dream' (*Economist*, 2003).

Following the invasion, the Coalition Provisional Authority paid large sums of compensation from Iraqi public sources to a number of international corporations, ostensibly as compensation for 'lost profits' or 'decline of business' due to Saddam Hussein's aggressive behaviour in the region since 1990. Sheraton received $11 million, Bechtel $7 million, Pepsi $3.8 million, Mobil $2.3 million, Kentucky Fried Chicken $321,000 and Toys R Us $190,000 – all US-based enterprises. Israeli farmers received $8 million, supposedly because they were not able to harvest fully due to the threat from Saddam's regime, and Israeli hoteliers and travel agencies received $15 million. A detailed account of these compensation payments were given in the book by

Eric Herring and Glen Rangwala, *Iraq in Fragments: The Occupation and its Legacy* (Herring and Rangwala, 2006).

The political and economic domination of Iraq started in the first year of the occupation, when about $50 billion of reconstruction contracts were commissioned to various US corporations, including Halliburton, Bechtel, SkylinkUSA, Stevedoring Services of America, and BearingPoint. During the same period, only 2% of the contracts were given to Iraqi firms. Research by the *Financial Times* showed in 2013 that the top 10 American and foreign contractors in Iraq have secured business worth at least $72 billion between them (*Financial Times*, 2013). A large amount of Iraqi money was paid to US contractors to implement local projects, many of them never finished, drowned in a sea of bureaucracy, corruption and open theft. No one knows quite how many such contractors were hired and how much money was paid to them for tasks never completed.

The Charge of the Knights

30 Mar 2008

Al Maliki's 'bold decision to go after the illegal groups in Basra shows his leadership and his commitment to enforce the law in an even-handed manner', George W. Bush declared last week. Nearly 30,000 Iraqi troops have been involved in the assault code named 'The Charge of the Knights', a series of attacks against militants in Basra, Baghdad and other cities in southern Iraq. An assault that lasted for most of last week, greatly contributing to the civilian death toll of nearly 400. Among last week's victims were 12 children, while 38 were killed by US and British forces, the allies of the Iraqi government, which, naturally, assisted in the killings.

'All explanations are possible for the current fighting in Basra', writes Fatih Abdulsalam ('Iraq's never-ending war' Azzaman, March 29), 'but the reality of the situation ... is the fact that war ... has been raging without interruption in Iraq for the past five years.' 'Iraq', he observes, 'has turned into a country of armies and militias, all with their own separate agendas and plans. All are bent on fighting each other over influence and privileges, whether material or political, and have nothing to do with the people and the country they are supposed to serve.' And all parties involved can provide a whole set of justifications for their presence, their fight and their use of force against any given target.

Two leading television stations broadcasting to Iraqi audiences have offered their own coverage of the clashes between government/US/British forces and those of the Mahdi Army.

Privately-owned Al-Sharqiya TV reported the government-led assault extensively, covered news of attacks against the Dawa Party (headed by Prime Minister Al-Maliki) in Baghdad and Kut, and of demonstrations against Iraq's 'new dictator'.

The Iraqi government's TV station Al-Iraqiya, in contrast, showed not one news bulletin. According to BBC sources, 'the channel aired a repeat of an interview with the interior minister, discussing various political and security issues. This was followed by patriotic songs, urging unity, and patriotic poetry. The only "urgent" caption screened was on a Sunni-mounted attack against civilians in Baghdad. The caption read: "Terrorist takfiris from Al-Qa'idah terrorist organization attack residents in Al-Shurtah area in Baghdad, forcing them out of their houses"'.

As for Falah Shanshal, Sadrist bloc MP, he described this assault as 'mass punishment' (National Iraqi News Agency, March 28). The government measures, he said, were as good as imposing martial law, 'leaving the people in Iraq's provinces in tragic situations'. The former Iraqi army, he observed, was disbanded for being 'a tool to oppress Iraqi people'. But, he wondered, 'will this army be disbanded for following in the footsteps of its predecessor?'

All explanations are possible, as are all justifications, reasons, myths and narratives. But above and beyond all those narratives and justifications, as March 2008 comes to an end, at least another 1,378 Iraqi civilians (52 of them children) are added to the list of the fallen 'for freedom and democracy', both of which are yet to be seen in this war-torn country. (Hamourtziadou, 2008c)

As al-Maliki's 'Knights' charged, a suicide bomber was preparing to kill mourners at a funeral, one of the easiest and most common targets of suicide bombers. A report of the bombing in McClatchy included an image of blanket-covered corpses. The blankets had cheerful floral patterns. Freshly killed, the corpses lay on the desert-like terrain, wrapped in flowery blankets of red and pink, blue and white, their bloody, burnt bodies hidden from the view of those who, numb with grief, sat by their side or stood by as if unsure of what to do (photo in McClatchy (2008a), 'Suicide bomber attacks funeral in tiny Iraqi village, killing 60', 18 April 2008). As many as 60 people were reported killed in this suicide attack on a funeral procession on 17 April, in a small village in Diyala.

They were only some of the 505 civilians killed that week. US forces killed 19 of them as they assisted al-Maliki in his efforts to rid Iraq of 'criminals' and his own government of any opposition. Among the dead were 23 children.

A month into the 'Charge of the Knights', Dr Maha al-Douri, Iraqi MP representing the al-Sadr Trend, declared a huge humanitarian disaster in Basra and Baghdad's Sadr City. 'There is a huge media blackout', she said. 'There are hundreds of martyrs and thousands of injured. Hospital morgues are stacked with martyrs and hospitals cannot accept wounded people anymore. Any convoy that carries humanitarian aid is being turned back or fired upon by the occupation forces. The entire city is being annihilated' and members of the Trend are being 'liquidated for the sole reason that we choose to resist'. She added, 'We have not raised our weapons in the face of the government; our weapons and resistance are directed against the occupation only; we want to drive the occupation out of our land' (interviewed on Al-Jazeera, 19 April 2008).

For Ali, Sajad, Ayat and all the other children

4 May 2008

Ali Hussein was buried in the clothes he died in: a white-and-blue t-shirt and a pair of little orange shorts. It was what he wore the day his dust-covered body was pulled out of the rubble of his house, after it had been flattened by an American bomb. Ali was 2 years old.

At least 30 people died in that bombing in Baghdad's Sadr City, on the 29th of April, 12 of whom were children.

'Ya'mma, Ya'ba' ('Oh mother, oh father'), cried Amira Zaydan, a 45-year-old spinster, slapping her face and chest as she grieved for her parents Jaleel, 65, and Hanounah, 60, whose house had exploded after apparently being hit by an American rocket.

'Where are you, my brothers?' she sobbed, lamenting Samir, 32, and Amir, 29, who had also perished along with their wives, one of whom was nine months pregnant.

'What wrong have you done, my children?' she howled to the spirits of four nephews and nieces who completed a toll of 10 family members in the disaster that struck last Tuesday (The Times, *4 May*).

As neighbours were trying to dig out her family's bodies out of the rubble, another rocket landed, killing 6 rescuers.

Um Aseel Ali lost her husband and 3 sons, aged 6, 4 and 2, when a rocket hit their house, while another woman, Um Marwa Muntasser, kept under sedation, lay unaware that her *husband Samir and her children, 4-year-old Sajad and 2-year-old Ayat, had been killed when their home was hit. All three women may qualify for condolence payments (made for death, injury or battle damage resulting from US military operations) usually around $2,000–$3,000, which should ease their pain of having had their families exterminated inside their own homes.*

Overall, 218 civilians were killed in Iraq last week, 25 of them children. 20 of those children were killed by US forces, as they tried to kill Iraqi 'criminals' through bombing house after house, neighbourhood after neighbourhood, in a city of 2.5m people.

As April 2008 came to an end, the Iraqis mourned another 1,400 civilians... perhaps as many as 1,900. At least 66 children were reported killed in April, while US forces killed a minimum of 136 civilians (and possibly as many as 600), with the blessing of the democratically elected Iraqi government.

How can we do this? How can we 'enlightened', 'liberal' and 'moral' citizens of a culture that has allegedly reached the 'end of history', a culture that stands for freedom, human rights and equality... how can we commit such crimes? We think we can fight humanitarian wars inhumanely, we find it acceptable to meet 'evil with evil'. We, who think our morality and our ethics to be superior to those of others, less civilised, how can we bear to be so cruel?

When did we lose our faith in our principles, those principles that were true for us, that defined our western civilisation? When did we abandon those principles that made our lives a little more meaningful than the simple struggle for survival in a jungle, a little more meaningful than the basic survival of the fittest – or, in this case, the mightiest? (Hamourtziadou, 2008d)

The language of having 'liberated' and 'democratized' Iraq absolves Western forces of any complicity in the suffering of Iraqis. It deliberately fails to acknowledge the legacy of pain the West has left to the civilian population, pain that goes beyond the physical, pain that is trauma.

Psychological trauma arose from a bodily metaphor. Before the nineteenth century, the word (Greek in origin) referred to a physical wound. In the nineteenth century, however, with the development of a science of mind and memory that wrested the human soul from religion and drew new boundaries around the human memory, the word was 'psychologized' (Hacking, 1998). Trauma, like mental illness, rests on a concept of individual mind. 'The symptoms of trauma, as codified in PTSD [post-traumatic stress disorder], include hypervigilance, the intrusion of the past in memory, and emotional numbing' (Fierke, 2007, p 125). These constitute the individual as fundamentally isolated and correspond with the collapse of community (Summerfield, 1998). They also lead to a loss of feeling of being protected (Edkins, 2003). Trauma results from an environment conducive to extreme shock, an environment such as war. It is not merely the actual initial shock, however, that produces trauma, but rather the wider experience of human encounters of hatred, humiliation or betrayal. We see this in cases of child abuse or genocide, where one's family or the state, that is, bodies that would normally be the source of protection, become a sources of danger (Edkins, 2003, p 4).

Within a social context of war and through interactions of hatred, humiliation, defeat, or a denial of humanity, we can move from individual trauma to an understanding of trauma as 'the social and political experience of a population' (Fierke, 2007, p 132). The traumatic experience of a community, an experience of widespread social suffering, the trauma of military defeat and foreign occupation, a community's loss of identity and agency, are all conditions present and prevalent in 'democratic' Iraq. Collecting the data and looking at the figures concerning loss of life in Iraq only goes so far in understanding the traumatic legacy of the invasion: 'trauma in war has a political component that arises from a loss of control or powerlessness over an environment, which is related to an experience of defeat, humiliation or conflict over who will control in a situation of instability' (Fierke, 2007, p 136). Fierke writes:

> the brutalization of Iraqi civilians and the humiliation of Iraqi prisoners by American soldiers at Abu Ghraib is conducive to a redefinition of the liberation as a 'trauma'. American soldiers, including female soldiers, engaged in face-to-face acts of sexual and other humiliation with Iraqi prisoners. These acts, which violated many taboos of Islam, were then widely publicized. In addition to the obvious element of humiliation, these events magnified an implicit betrayal: the 'liberator' appeared increasingly to be a brutal occupier. (Fierke, 2007, p 136)

Adding to the sense of powerlessness and betrayal, the Iraqi government – any Iraqi government after 2006 – has failed to protect the population from any attacks (internal or external), instead launching campaigns that result in more loss of civilian life, moving from the role of protector to that of – yet another – attacker. An attacker that, just like the foreign invaders, has never been held accountable, either nationally or internationally. An attacker that remains above the law.

On 8 September 2008, in what was already becoming ordinary violence in Iraq, bodyguards of the minister of displacement and migration, who had been telling Iraqis it was safe to come home after five years of war, were involved in a rush-hour shooting that police said killed a woman and injured six other people. Circumstances surrounding the incident were unclear. The ministry said traffic police fired towards the minister's convoy and that the bodyguards only fired into the air. Police said the bodyguards were trying to clear traffic by shooting into the air and that one of them accidentally aimed his gun into nearby cars. Witnesses said the shooting was the result of a dispute between the ministry bodyguards and traffic police. The head of the ministry's planning directorate, Ali Shaalan, called the incident 'totally unacceptable' but said the ministry guards had done nothing wrong. However, Shaalan added that the guards had surrendered and that their detention proved 'no one is above the law' (Susman and Ahmed, 2008).

So no one was above the law in Iraq. Those foreign soldiers who bombed a whole neighbourhood in Sadr City on 29 April, killing 30 civilians, 12 of them children, were not above the law. The killers of two-year-old Ali Hussein, and two-year-old Moqtada Raed, four-year-old Sajad and two-year-old Ayat were not above the law. That same army that had killed some 500 Iraqi civilians that year alone was not above the law. Or so we were told, by their allies, the government that existed – and still exists – on the strength of the army that occupied their country and regularly killed its civilians. An army that arrested and detained whoever they decided, for months, even years, without charge. An army that remains unpunished. And still welcome.

And the minister of displacement and migration had just been saying how 'safe' the country was. As if a country that was occupied, ruled by a government supported by the occupying forces, could possibly be safe. As if a country as lawless, in effect, as Iraq, where the strong do just as they please and are clearly above the law, a country where bombs and guns kill civilians every day, could be safe for anybody.

To make Iraq even safer, Britain and America, its allies and occupiers, revealed plans to sell Iraq sophisticated weapons, including F-16 fighter jets. To a government that, much like Saddam Hussain's, had already used weapons against its own civilians. A government that had repeatedly stood by as foreign soldiers had killed Iraqis.

Every time an American soldier shoots an Iraqi, The Iraqi government uses weapons against its people; every time an American plane bombs an Iraqi home, every time a man, woman or child is thrown into a filthy jail indefinitely, the government acts against its people. Every time a bomb explodes, every time a family looks for its loved ones in a morgue, and every time bodies are unearthed from mass graves, the Iraqi government fails its people.

The true weapons of this war, more than IEDs, guns, bombers and fighter jets, greatly resemble its causes. They are gain, doctrine and fear. They constitute both the reasons behind the War on Terror and the weapons used in the course of the wars fought within it.

Gain is the most obvious cause of any war. 'Territorial expansion and conquest initiated the Second World War, the Napoleonic War and contemporary wars such as the Gulf War', writes Hough (2008, p 58). 'A war which enhanced the power of the state initiating the conflict, without upsetting the balance of power to a dangerous extent, would better fit the bill as a Realist war of gain ... The wars of European imperial expansion also clearly come into this category' (Hough, 2008, p 58). In the invasion of Iraq, according to the hegemonic/political explanation, gain perhaps played the biggest role, as the invaders expected to gain after the regime change, and have indeed gained the most since. American and British plans for Iraq's future economy went beyond 'reconstruction'. The emerging state was going to be treated 'as a blank slate on which the most ideological Washington neoliberals can design their dream economy: fully privatized, foreign-owned and open for business' (Klein, 2003). Those whose homeland it was, the Iraqi public, were absent from these decisions. Without any democratic process, the 'charity', the 'gift' of liberal and democratic Western states was barely disguised exploitation. In the name of that 'democratic' dream of a privatized, foreign-owned and 'reconstructed' Iraq, hundreds of thousands of Iraqi civilians have lost their lives. Political and economic domination, the neoliberal transformation, have left Iraq impoverished and with an annual death toll from the violence in the thousands since the invasion.

Doctrine. The Cold War was an example of this, as were the religiously inspired Crusades, as is the war/clash of civilizations thesis. This last explains the War on Terror in terms of an idealistic conflict of clashing values and cultures. Like gain, doctrine has been both a reason/cause of the wars in the Middle East in the 21st century, according to the ideological explanation, and a weapon used to sustain those wars and triumph (either materially or morally) over opponents. Doctrine as weapon has also been used by the insurgency and the terrorist groups, as well as anti-government forces in Iraq, both Shia and Sunni, justifying and explaining their violence in terms of a higher set of religious values or an ongoing anti-Western/anti-imperialist struggle.

Fear. Wight considers fear to be a distinct cause of war. This is not necessarily the fear of imminent invasion, but the fear of longer-term consequences for the power of the state in *not* resorting to armed conflict. An example of this was Japan's attack of Pearl Harbor in 1941, designed to provoke the US to enter World War II, fearing being marginalized and economically dominated by the US if it remained outside the war (Bull and Holbraad, 1978). Similarly, the invasion of Iraq in 2003 was motivated by 'a rational apprehension of future evil', though not the evil (the alleged imminent WMD attacks) presented at the time. Rather, the regime had to be removed so as to avert future evil in the form of political and economic loss. Fear as a weapon has been used in Iraq every day since the 'Shock and Awe' campaign, as airstrikes and terrorist attacks have become commonplace and irregular warfare dominates every sphere of life.

Fear and doctrine as weapons were used by the American military in Iraq as part of a nation-building process; as a project of building nations the military way.

'Army issues new manual for nation-building', read the headline on 6 October 2008. It continued:

> The U.S. Army on Monday released a new field manual that for the first time gives nation-building the same top priority as major combat operations in conflicts involving fragile states. The Stability Operations Field Manual, derived from the Army's experiences in Iraq and Afghanistan, provides commanders and other Army personnel with a guide for supporting broader U.S. government efforts to deliver development, reconstruction and humanitarian aid in war-torn nations. Army officials described the document as a roadmap from conflict to peace. 'Our objective, when we go into a foreign country, is to leave but to leave with that country safe and secure,' said Lt. Gen. William Caldwell, commander of the U.S. Army Combined Arms Center. The 'coercive and constructive capabilities' of military force, it says, can establish security; facilitate reconciliation between adversaries; establish political, legal, social and economic institutions; and ultimately transition responsibility to a civil authority. (Reuters, 2008)

Never mind ideology, ancestry and glorious past as the building blocks of national consciousness and identity. Never mind shared values and goals, trust, brotherhood and loyalty to the motherland. Forget unity when faced with threats. Nation-building the new, military way involves, instead, 'going into a foreign country' and, using 'coercive and constructive capabilities' to build a nation. When 'going into a foreign country' actually means attacking, bombing, killing. This is no way to build a nation.

Building nations – it is hard to see this as the role of a military. The intervention of a military, even domestic, is always regarded as something bad, something that violates civil rights and liberties. When the army is foreign, it is called 'war' and 'occupation'. Moreover, armies can reconstruct buildings they have destroyed, but they cannot resurrect those they have killed, or those whose deaths they have caused during their 'nation-building' efforts. This is beyond the 'constructive capabilities' of even the most powerful army in the world.

Death of a child

2 Nov 2008

Khudaer Muhammad Abdullah, 49, and his wife had already lost 2 sons; 19-year-old Muazzaz was kidnapped and killed last year, while 21-year-old Saad was killed by a suicide bomber last month, at the police academy in Kirkuk.

'On Sunday he lost his last son, and his 4-year-old daughter is now hospitalized with serious wounds. His last son, Muhammad Khudaer Muhammad, 7, was killed when part of a rocket-propelled grenade exploded on a vacant lot where he was playing soccer with three other children, according to police reports.

Muhammad was killed instantly in the blast. His friend Ahmed Hamid Jelu, 9, lost both legs and died at a hospital shortly afterward. Two other children – Hassan Dhaya, 7, and Muhammad's sister, Ahlan Khudaer Muhammad – were seriously wounded.

Mr. Abdullah, a shepherd, said that he had just returned from leading his sheep to pasture when Muhammad asked permission to play soccer with some friends in the lot across the road from the family's home.

About 15 minutes later, around 3 p.m., Mr. Abdullah heard an explosion.

' "Their bodies were completely torn apart by the blast," Mr. Abdullah said. His son, he surmised, must have been sitting on the ground waiting for the ball to be passed to him, because he found Muhammad seated. An official at Kirkuk's morgue later said that Muhammad's head had been blown off' (New York Times, 2 November 2008).

Meanwhile, the US is warning of terrible consequences if the Iraqis don't sign the security agreement that gives immunity to US soldiers in Iraq. Should the agreement not be signed, Iraq 'would lose $6.3 billion in aid for construction, security forces and economic activity and another $10 billion a year in foreign military sales' (McClatchy, 2008b). The US army will no longer 'protect' Iraq, 200,000 Iraqis will lose their jobs, and NGOs that provide essential services and support for displaced people will cease their operations.

So no protection, no money, no jobs and no food. Unless they agree to let a foreign army kill their civilians unpunished. A great threat indeed. Makes the years of economic sanctions look like Iraq's Golden Era.

The threats are not empty but real, grave and to be taken very seriously. Yet those they are threatening have already lost so much. When a family has lost its child, its father or mother, how much more can anyone threaten to take from them? When people have lost members of their family to violence, hunger, disease, how much more can you hurt them? People like Khudaer Muhammad Abdullah and his wife... how much can the threat of unemployment, or the cessation of US protection, affect or frighten them, after having lost 3 children?

Asked who he would like to see winning the US election, Abu Karrar al-Sa'aidi, a real estate broker in Baghdad, replied 'I hope the winner will be the person who can return what Americans have taken from Iraq' (Reuters, 2 November).

The most important things cannot be returned. Such as a life taken too soon. A child lost for ever.

This week 109 civilians lost their lives in Iraq. 10 of them were children. (Hamourtziadou, 2008e)

Iraq in 2009

As 2009 came to an end, the year's trends and losses were marked. This IBC analysis of 2009 trends began with a cautionary note:

> *a distinction must be drawn between abstractions represented by varying rates of violence and the reality of that violence for those experiencing it. Every statistic on this page can be traced to a human life violently ended, none of whom are any less a victim for having been killed during a downward trend in violence.*

There were many improvements in levels of armed and non-state terrorist violence in Iraq. However, the violence continued to affect Iraqi civilian life on a daily basis.

The annual civilian death toll from violence in 2009 was the lowest since the 2003 invasion, at 5,382 and had the lowest recorded monthly toll (226 in November).

The most violent city was Mosul, with 799 recorded deaths out of a population of 1.8 million. On a per capita basis, Mosul became significantly more deadly than Baghdad (1,725 deaths out of a population of 6.5 million), despite none of the year's largest-scale bombings occurring in Mosul. Additionally, Mosul's absolute number of violent *incidents* deadly to civilians in 2009 (592) far exceeded Baghdad's (459).

Civilian deaths caused by coalition forces were much lower than in the preceding year, at 87 reported. Deaths involving Iraqi forces were to 122 in 2009. Of these deaths caused by US coalition and Iraqi state forces, the number killed in joint actions fell from 120 in 2008 to 16 in 2009; the overall number of civilians killed by state forces (US coalition, Iraqi, or both) was 1,122 in 2008 and 193 in 2009.

The weapon of choice increasingly became the magnetic bomb, or adhesive explosive device (AED). Magnetic bombs secretly attached to cars changed from a relatively rare to a common form of assassination (61 killed in 2008, 200 killed in 2009). Individuals continued to be the targets of summary executions, often involving torture, although numbers fell from 2,380 in 2008 to 288 in 2009. Large-scale bombings killing more than 50 civilians per attack increased in their severity of impact, claiming 758 lives in 8 attacks during 2009, compared to 534 in 9 attacks during 2008. With roughly two explosions deadly to civilians every day in 2009 (769 explosions causing 3,126 deaths), Iraq continued to be the non-state terrorism capital of the world, suffering more deaths from such attacks than any other country.

The long-term impact of the War on Terror was becoming clearer, as those with power and claims to global leadership were failing to gain support and to provide the most basic security to the ailing population of Iraq.

Arche and hegemony: leadership, power and a story of cooperation

Raw power is 'ineffective when applied in a politically unsophisticated way and at odds with prevailing norms and practices' (Lebow and Reich, 2014, p 6). In Iraq and Afghanistan it eroded rather than enhanced

American influence; a material basis was not enough – a social one was needed. 'The power of the mighty hath no foundation but in the opinion and belief of the people', as Hobbes wrote in *Behemoth*.

Power requires influence, which rests on understanding and on persuasion, rather than coercion. The invasion (whatever the narrative that attempted to justify it) and the occupation that followed were clear manifestations of coercive tactics by the US and Britain. The continued use of force resulted in death, destruction and chaos, rather than cooperation, peace and any sense of loyalty. What the Americans needed was a way to influence, convince and persuade the Iraqis that they had common goals, interests and objectives. A common vision for Iraq.

> Persuasion depends on shared values and acceptable practices, and when it works, helps to build common identities that can make cooperation and persuasion more likely in the future. Influence of this kind also benefits from material capabilities but is not a function of them. It is restricted to common goals and requires considerable political skills ... By influence we mean the ability to persuade others to do what one wants, or refrain from doing what one does not want. (Lebow and Reich, 2014, p 6)

The first responsibility of hegemony is *normative,* according to Reich and Lebow. Leadership involves the capacity to shape the policy agenda, knowledge and manipulation of discourses, insight into how others define their interests and their problems, and what responses they consider appropriate. The Greeks used the term *arche* to describe rule based on force, or the threat of force. It is rule by a despot, a tyrant or a dictator. It is rule that is ephemeral and largely lacking legitimacy. Hegemony, on the other hand, requires acceptance by those ruled, creates loyalty and can endure longer than power. '*Hegemonia* requires material capabilities, but those capabilities must be used to advance the common interests of the community' (Lebow and Reich, 2014, p 47).

It was the need to combine force with influence, *arche* with hegemony, destruction with reconstruction, that led to the 'surge', but also to the Human Terrain System, both of which were launched in 2007 and whose impact we observed in the years that followed. As Iraq continued to be 'the non-state terrorism capital of the world', as civilians continued to die in their hundreds each week, the force of weapons and the cognitive forces of political and specialist minds, in the form of Operationally Relevant Social Science Research in Iraq and

Afghanistan, began to work in unison, reaping temporary rewards: a reduction in violence, the mobilization of Iraq's tribal 'Sahwa' and the illusion of power sharing.

By the end 0f 2009, British forces had left Iraq, while US forces, under the leadership of the new president, were also preparing to leave. The newly transformed Iraqi state they were leaving behind was blighted by economic, political and societal threats to its security, with outcomes and impact felt both inside and outside the country.

Security and vulnerability; threats to the vulnerable state

In *People, States and Fear*, Buzan wrote of 'a duality of state security and societal security, the former having sovereignty as its ultimate criterion, and the latter being held together by concerns about identity' (Buzan, 1983, p 105). Society is about identity, about the self-conception of communities and of individuals identifying themselves as members of a community. A state lacking community identity (that is, society security), puts its own security (in terms of sovereignty and legitimacy) at stake. Such states and such societies are weak and vulnerable to a variety of threats.

Weak states lacking sociopolitical cohesion – like post-invasion Iraq – are vulnerable to most threats, internal and external, military and political. The state created after the 2003 invasion, the 'new, democratic Iraq', already displayed clear signs of weakness in terms of power and in terms of societal cohesion. Iraq, under Saddam Hussein, never enjoyed sociopolitical cohesion; Iraqi society was fragmented and divided both before and after 2003. With a strong leadership, however, though still not a strong, powerful state, Iraq's vulnerability lay mainly in the great likelihood and occurrence of political threats to its leadership – Saddam's regime. The new Iraq, from its first democratic election to its last, as a state and as a society, showed political vulnerability: weakness and inadequacy of the political powers, their policies, their legitimacy, their planning and control. The new Iraq was characterized by socioeconomic vulnerability: socio-spatial segregation, large inequalities of wealth and social disorganization. It has also suffered from psychological and cultural vulnerability: inadequate security or risk perceptions; cultural weakness; risky behaviour and incapacity to protect oneself and others. The growing sectarian identities and insurgencies, among a population increasingly poor, miserable, displaced and dying in horrific daily violence, started to become the biggest threats to security, understood both as state security and as societal security. Already poor under Saddam Hussein, Iraq after the invasion and by 2009 was weak and vulnerable in all its contexts, the political, the social and the economic, being exploited, lacking internal support and any capacity to cope with the total breakdown of security. Moreover, its citizens suffered the daily attacks of neighbouring states, mainly Turkey, and those of the occupying forces.

Post-invasion Iraq continued to suffer the effects of human insecurity. Its lack of development, services and resources, its food scarcity, poverty and unemployment, meant that there was still no 'freedom from want'. The human rights violations, as well as the daily terrorist attacks, meant there was no 'freedom from fear'. While the lack of good governance, in a state supported and maintained largely by occupying forces, meant there was no 'freedom to live in dignity'.

The new state faced threats to human rights, human dignity and human life. Even as the occupation was officially nearing its end, the damage done to Iraq went beyond the personal safety of its citizens; it extended to the identity and values of its communities, their sense of belonging and of being protected, their sense of living in a 'homeland'. This damage has proven long-lasting, if not permanent. The outcomes are multiple: a country filled with criminals and warlords, and run by a corrupt regime, an alienated and marginalized population, an economy in crisis and, tragically, an annual death toll from armed conflict and terrorist attacks still in the thousands. The greatest victims have been the most vulnerable segments of an already vulnerable society: the children, the women, the elderly, the poor and the minorities.

Energy security

An aspect of security that needs to be addressed in the context of Iraq, and which is inextricably connected to all other aspects of its security, is energy security.

The rising global demand for energy, combined with fears of dwindling supplies and increased instability in energy-rich regions, ensures that the sources, locations and stability of world energy supplies remain a core concern of security, at national and international levels, military, political, economic and human. Energy security is a growing problem that intersects with a range of wider security concerns (Raphael and Stokes, 2016).

> Energy security exists when there are energy sources large enough to meet the needs of the political community (the energy demands), which include all military, economic

and societal activity. Those sources must be able to deliver such quantities of energy in a reliable and stable manner, and for the foreseeable future. As soon as these conditions are not met, there exists a problem of energy (in)security. (Raphael and Stokes, 2016, p 344)

For industrialized states and their citizens, the existence of robust infrastructure usually means that the existence of a stable energy supply at state level is sufficient to ensure enough energy for the population. Insecurity arises when the state fails to secure the resources from another, energy-rich state. That is not the case for communities that live in conditions of energy insecurity in states like Iraq, where shortages of energy supply are a fact of life, even though abundant local sources of energy exist (there are still daily power cuts in Baghdad and other Iraqi cities). Iraq, an energy-rich state, suffers from energy insecurity and such insecurity has effects on the quality of life for many, with health, education and transport services affected.

The existence of reliable supplies of energy underpins economic activity, Raphael and Stokes argue, and can be seen as a prerequisite for any significant degree of economic security. In attempting to ensure the stability of supplies, core powers are increasingly militarizing their approach to energy security, as we see in the Middle East through the War on Terror. This 'may have significant consequences for *international security*, as inter-state cooperation threatens to break down into a struggle over the control of key energy reserves. Likewise, this militarization often has a profound impact upon the human security of those living in oil-rich regions in the South, as the use of armed force is used to "stabilize" energy-rich areas' (Raphael and Stokes, 2016, p 344). In energy-rich states, oil wealth has another impact. In states in the Middle East, states like Iraq, oil wealth is directly linked to regime security, when it becomes bound up with the collection of oil 'rents', a method of income generation that allows governments to become politically insulated from their citizens, increases corruption and causes deterioration of political and civil rights. This process negatively impacts on development and security, as oil wealth fails to filter down to the wider population.

The global reliance on fossil fuels as a source of energy impacts on all of us. We collectively face the growing problem of energy insecurity. While demand is growing, it is not clear that reliable and stable sources of supply will continue to match that demand and this leads to a demand/supply 'energy gap'. Fossil fuels supply over 80% of global energy (Nunez, 2019). Energy supply, however, has peaked in many parts of the world and is declining, particularly oil production. Moreover, the geographical distribution of world energy stocks and the location of the largest energy consumers creates an 'energy–security nexus', whereby energy security becomes entwined with the foreign and security policies of the great powers. For this reason, the stability and friendly orientation of key oil-producing states and regions is a central concern for strategists. Foreign and security policies reflect this, as the 'consuming states', the large economies, have made it a priority to secure regimes friendly and responsive to their energy needs. In regions like the Middle East where instability is endemic, and where there exists a range of forces seeking to challenge existing geopolitical configurations, great powers have deliberately bolstered 'friendly' governmental and non-governmental actors. Billions of dollars of economic and military assistance have been granted to oil-rich regimes to ensure that enough oil keeps flowing. In the context of global capitalism, 'oil remains the lifeblood of the current order – an order that is based upon an unequal distribution of wealth and power in favour of global economic elites. In this regard, those who benefit most from the prevailing order are driven to ensure that the flow of energy under favourable conditions continues to underpin their position in the global system' (Raphael and Stokes, 2016, p 347).

The 'blood for oil' thesis gives credence to the 'Imperialism by a Hegemon' explanation of the War on Terror. The war is understood as another intervention by capitalist powers in an oil-rich region, designed to serve specific corporate interests, especially those of 'Big Oil'. In this understanding, the capitalist state is an instrument for ruling economic elites, with foreign policy subsumed under a logic of profit maximization. US foreign policy of oil capitalism is conducive to business opportunities and profit maximization for huge energy multinationals.

The installation of friendly regimes to serve those interests leads to corrupt governments, as it has done in Iraq, to the reduction of legitimate political space for most of the population and to vast inequalities in wealth distribution. All of these factors are causes of domestic unrest and insurgency. All of them also impact on national and regional security, especially when the states involved are weak and, therefore, vulnerable to most threats.

Iraq has held several parliamentary elections since the invasion, the first one in 2005 and the latest in 2018. Since 2003, at least 27 prime ministers, presidents, vice-presidents and governing councillors came to power, either democratically elected or through a provisional government, representing different political parties/coalitions, none of whom managed to satisfy the serious and rightful demands of the Iraqi people: to end corruption, to increase living standards, to create jobs and opportunities for the increasing number of young people, to provide security and adequate funding for services. What contributed to this failure were the constant violence, the longstanding divisions of the country along ethnic and religious lines, the desperate state of the economy and corruption as a result of a contracting system put in place by the US pro-consul Paul Bremer. Successive Iraqi governments pursued the project of neoliberal transformation of Iraq, sometimes willingly, but mostly reluctantly and as a result of already tightly established links with the International Monetary Fund (IMF) and global financial institutions through loans and debt rescheduling. Iraq's debt was restructured on terms that made the country subject to fully applying IMF austerity policies, even after the occupation officially ended in 2011. An example of this was the 2006 fuel liberalization programme, which the Al-Maliki government accepted, following the IMF recommendations, which cut off all subsidies of fuel and gas products, resulting in a sudden explosion of prices of fuel and gas-related items.

The neoliberal measures taken by the Coalition Provisional Authority, following the 2003 invasion, reinforced macroeconomic stabilization, cut government expenditures and ended state subsidies. They opened up the Iraqi economy to foreign investment by selling state-owned enterprises. All these bold neoliberal measures have produced a dystopian economy and a failed state, incapable of controlling its own affairs.

The overwhelming motivations of the people who took to the streets in Iraq in the autumn of 2019 were the low standards of living, high unemployment among the young, an inefficient welfare state, food shortages and the continuing conflict and disorder. All these Iraq shares with those countries that witnessed serious protest movements in the early 2010s, the so-called 'Arab Spring' countries – Tunisia, Egypt, Libya, Syria and others. What these states in the Middle East and in North Africa (MENA) also have in common is that they have all experienced an intense economic transformation, imposed by the IMF and the World Bank, during the previous couple of decades, away from the state-command economy model of 'Arab Socialism' of the 1960s and 1970s, and towards market-dominated neoliberal capitalism in the 1980s and 1990s. Through the guidance and assistance of the IMF and the World Bank, the MENA region pursued neoliberal economic policies (entrepreneurial freedom, strong property rights, free markets and free trade) which led to great income inequalities and a concentration of wealth among the small political elite. The 'Arab Spring' uprisings took place within these conditions of sharply increased poverty, very high youth unemployment and lack of opportunities for young people. Neoliberal restructuring was directed by the IMF and was put into practice by the regimes, with similar devastating results.

The continuing protests in Iraq and the killing of protesters in their hundreds by government forces, combined with a persisting insurgency, demonstrate the lack of identification of the population with 'the state'. What we see contributing to this weakness is the new colonialism masked as political and economic development, through the principle and the process of globalization. The preoccupation in globalization discourse with the benefits of interdependence is a distraction from confronting new forms of colonialism 'through policies and systems designed to distance its perpetrators from unseemly motivation' (Poku and Therkelsen, 2016, p 265). Neoliberal ideology has been promoted to the developing world by the chief advocates of globalization, the IMF and the World Bank, through their liberalization programme.

As predicted, neoliberalism has fostered inequality; a growing unemployment that has gone hand in hand with poverty and mass migration. Globalization makes security interdependent; terrorism, gun crime and illegal migration are spillover effects of structural, political and economic insecurity in the developing world. Iraq today shows how globalization incites rebellion and radicalization. The advancement of the neoliberal agenda by industrialized states through globalization has failed to deliver the economic stability and growth it promised. Instead, globalization continues to increase the gap between rich and poor, between and within states. 'Globalisation services the interest of its advocates, the elites of the core capitalist economies, at the expense and immiseration of the majority of people in developing economies – arguably a form of neo-colonialism – and the weaker segments of their own societies' (Poku and Therkelsen, 2016, p 271).

Ultimately, inequality is the biggest threat to global security.

4

Iraq 2010–2013

'It is time for us to transition to the Iraqis. They need to take
responsibility for their country and for their sovereignty.'
Obama on his single visit to Iraq, 7 April 2009

By 2010 British forces had left Iraq and US forces were preparing to do
the same. President Obama promised a new direction in domestic and
foreign policy, dropping the phrase 'War on Terror' entirely, defining
the struggle as a battle against terrorist organizations. His rejection of
neoconservatism was a rejection of Bush's policies in the Middle East,
which included the occupation of Iraq.

US combat troops left Iraq in 2010, although over 50,000 military
support troops remained until the end of 2011 (Gabbatt, 2010). Though
the daily killing of civilians continued, the years following Obama's
election saw the violence claiming fewer lives than ever before, since
Iraq was invaded (Table 4.1).

Iraq's human security would be affected by three factors during this
period: the Human Terrain System, the Awakening Councils and the
Arab Uprisings, all of which demonstrated America's tactics, power
and influence; all of which caused further violence, the escalation and
spillover of wars fought in the Middle East and North Africa, and
ultimately the deaths of thousands of Iraqis.

Iraq 2010

While 2010's civilian death toll in Iraq was the lowest since the war
began, for those who have lost loved ones in 2010, there was no sense
in which the year could represent an 'improvement' on 2009. Iraq
Body Count recorded 4,167 civilian deaths from violence in 2010
(compared to 5,369 in 2009). Evidence of these deaths was extracted

Table 4.1: Civilian deaths by month 2010–2013

	Jan	Feb	Mar	Apr	May	Jun	Jul	Aug	Sep	Oct	Nov	Dec	Total
2010	267	305	336	385	387	385	488	520	254	315	307	218	4,167
2011	389	254	311	289	381	386	308	401	397	366	288	392	4,162
2012	531	356	377	392	304	529	469	422	400	290	253	299	4,622
2013	357	360	403	545	888	659	1,145	1,013	1,306	1,180	870	1,126	9,852

from some 8,250 distinct reports collected from 143 sources, covering 1,685 incidents.

The data collected in 2010 showed the smallest year-on-year reduction (proportionally as well as in absolute terms) since violence levels began to reduce from late 2007 onwards: 2008 reduced deaths by 63% on 2007, 2009 by 50% on 2008, but 2010 only improved by 15% on 2009.

The 2010 data suggested a persistent low-level conflict in Iraq that would continue to kill civilians at a similar rate for years to come. The within-year trend for 2010 was somewhat more hopeful: the US 'end of combat mission' on 31 August 2010 was followed by an immediate halving in the number of civilian deaths between August and September, and lowered levels continued into the winter months, with December showing the lowest toll of the year.

The geographic spread of violence showed the continuity typical of that year's casualty data. Mosul remained extraordinarily violent relative to its size, with more events recorded there than in Baghdad for the early part of the year. However, roughly from the declared 'end of combat mission' Baghdad again became the city in which violence was most prevalent in absolute terms (but given its much greater size, proportionally less so than Mosul).

Civilian deaths resulting directly from actions involving US-led coalition forces were half as many as in 2009, with a total of 32 reported, while Iraqi forces caused 98 civilian deaths in 2010. Of these deaths caused by US coalition and Iraqi state forces, the number killed in joint actions was also almost the same in 2009 (16) as in 2010 (15); the overall number of civilians killed by state forces (US coalition, Iraqi or both) was 189 in 2009 and 115 in 2010.

Many of the perpetrator groups behind civilian deaths in Iraq's post-invasion armed conflict are difficult to identify, which means that most of the deaths recorded by IBC are assigned to the 'Unknown' agent category. However, even from the minority of incidents where perpetrators could be positively identified, it was apparent that 2010's violence profile remained one where 'anti-occupation' activity continued to play a central part in the deaths of Iraqi civilians. This was most obvious when the targets were policemen or government-allied individuals (police forces members accounting for 1,083 – 26.0% – of the deaths recorded in 2010).

'Unknown agents' are those who appear to attack civilian targets lacking a clear or unambiguous link to the foreign military presence in Iraq. This may include some overlap with other groups as well as with criminal murders. 'Anti-occupation forces' are those whose targets are either US-led coalition personnel or Iraqis working for, or in collaboration with, the coalition forces.

Once again in 2010, as in previous years, what was striking was the 'everyday terrorism' that had become the pattern of life in Iraq. After nearly eight years of occupation, insurgency and terrorism, the security crisis in Iraq was still notable for its sheer relentlessness: 2010 averaged nearly two explosions a day by non-state forces that caused civilian deaths: 691 explosions killed 2,677 people. Those lethal explosions occurred in 13 of Iraq's 18 governorates and were responsible for 64% of all Iraqi civilian deaths in 2010.

Yet it was in 2010 that the world started to be optimistic about Iraq. People were still being killed every day, but in 2010, 2011 and 2012 the annual death toll fell to between 4,000 and 5,000 civilians, a far cry from the shocking 29,451 of 2006. As the American troops left Iraq and security passed to the Iraqi government, it appeared as though the violence could be handled and contained. The following years, however, were to show little change, except in one area: the addition of the Iraq War Logs, 391,832 US army field reports disclosed to WikiLeaks. The existence of those logs that covered the 2004–2009 period revealed knowledge of the escalating violence in the country, contrary to what American and British politicians had claimed. As it turned out, they *did* do body counts.

The data in the Iraq War Logs revealed hundreds of previously unreported civilian deaths and incidents caused by coalition forces, as well as torture and human rights abuses in detention facilities. The documents, recorded by soldiers operating on the ground, bore witness to the sectarian violence and civil war sparked by the occupation. Together, they make up a database known as 'SIGACTS'.

At the time each report was classified as 'Secret' but the information contained is no longer militarily sensitive. The files were made available to a select group of media outlets, including the Bureau of Investigative Journalism, *The Guardian*, *The New York Times*, the German weekly *Der Spiegel* and French newspaper *Le Monde*. Iraq Body Count was also given access to the data.

The revelation that came towards the end of 2010 sparked a controversy that continues to this day, but it also added a new source of casualty data. When IBC civilian data, official Iraqi and US combatant death figures and data from the Iraq War Logs released by WikiLeaks were combined, it was estimated that since the invasion 162,000 people had lost their lives in Iraq, of whom 79% were civilians. Of the civilian dead, 64,702 were reported killed by small arms gunfire, 39,283 by explosive weapons (such as IEDs, suicide attacks and aerial bombardment) and 5,820 by airstrikes (including cannon-fire, bombs and missiles).

Of the 45,779 victims for whom IBC was able to obtain age data, 3,911 (8.54%) were children under the age of 18, while the most targeted group were police officers.

Of all documented civilian deaths up to 2011, 15,142 (13%) were reported as being directly caused by the US-led coalition. US forces killed far more Iraqi civilians than any other members of the US-led coalition, including Iraqi military forces. Of the 4,040 civilian victims of US-led coalition forces for whom age data was available, 1,201 (29%) were children. On average, US-led coalition forces killed Iraqi civilians in one or two incidents per day, and over three civilians per day, for three straight years, 2005–2007 (1,512 incidents, 3,617 deaths averaging 3.3 deaths per day; with 1.4 incidents per day, or almost 10 per week, averaging 2.4 deaths per incident).

Over half of the civilian deaths caused by US-led coalition forces occurred during the 2003 invasion and the sieges of Fallujah in 2004. The highest intensity of civilian killings over a sustained period occurred during the first three 'shock and awe' weeks of the 2003 invasion, when civilian deaths averaged 319 per day and totalled over 6,716 by 9 April, nearly all attributable to US-led coalition forces.

Iraq and casualty recording in 2011

During 2011 4,162 civilian deaths were recorded, a level of violence almost identical to that of the previous year, when 4,167 civilians deaths were recorded. Evidence of these deaths was extracted from some 6,828 distinct reports collected from over 90 sources, covering 1,911 incidents.

There was a noticeable increase in civilian deaths attributable to anti-government/occupation attacks (1,214 in 2011, up from 911 in 2010). There was a decline in deaths caused by the coalition, while the rate of civilian deaths caused by Iraqi state forces increased, with deaths resulting directly from actions involving US-led coalition forces falling to their smallest number ever, at a total of 19 reported by year end (down from 32 in 2010), and deaths involving Iraqi forces rising from 98 in 2010 to 147 in 2011.

There was a gradual decrease in violence by US forces, as they prepared to withdraw from Iraq, following Obama's election in 2009, or at least from being those responsible for Iraq's domestic security. The handing over of power to the Iraqi authorities was, as the figures show, done with knowledge of the government killings, mostly in the form of daily shelling of areas and cities with high levels of insurgency. The killings and human rights violations of the democratically elected government of Iraq had started long before the American withdrawal of 2011; more importantly, they were being carried out with the full knowledge and endorsement of the coalition. The new regime was no less brutal than the old Baath regime of Saddam Hussein, yet it had the full backing of those Western states that had allegedly fought for 'Iraqi freedom' from an evil dictator. Now the brutal regime was an ally of the West and could kill with licence, as long as it served the interests of those who still controlled Iraq, even by proxy.

The release of the Iraq War Logs by WikiLeaks enabled IBC to carry out some preliminary research into the number of casualties the Logs might contain that have not been reported elsewhere. The Logs would reveal another 15,000 civilian deaths beyond the previously known death toll, including 3,000 deaths of policemen. Many of the previously unreported deaths caused by US-led forces found in the Iraq War Logs were of small-scale but frequent 'Escalation of Force' (EOF) cases where ordinary civilians were shot in their cars at checkpoints or similar circumstances due to a variety of tragic, and often shocking, failures in communication.

The Logs also allowed IBC to provide for the first time an estimate for (mainly Iraqi) combatant deaths since 2003. Updating these figures with deaths that occurred throughout 2010 and 2011, and combining them with IBC's documented deaths, provided the totals shown in Table 4.2.

In 2011 it was estimated that the Iraq War Logs would add unreported details of 23,000 violent incidents in which Iraqi civilians were killed or their bodies were found.

The number of violent deaths in a conflict is an important, and generally difficult and painstaking, fact to establish. The task requires access not just to raw numbers, but to the victim- and incident-level data which produced them: details describing who was killed, where, when and how. The unprecedented level of detail in the Iraq War Logs made this task possible in a way which previous, aggregate, releases of data by the US Department of Defense did not allow. Despite the death counts in the logs apparently being *lower* than the numerical totals provided in existing sources, detailed, incident-level analysis indicated that the logs were likely to *add* some 15,000 civilian deaths.

The fact that the Iraq War Logs contained this many previously undocumented deaths would have been impossible to discover if they were only presented as a set of death totals, as is all too often the case with official announcements or publications. Without sight

Table 4.2: Iraq Body Count 2003–2011

Iraq Body Count 2003–2011	114,212
Iraq War Logs new 'Civilian' and comparable 'Host Nation' remaining – central estimate	13,750
Iraq War Logs 'Host Nation' combatant – central estimate	5,575
Iraq War Logs 'Enemy' (minus IBC overlaps) – central estimate	20,499
Insurgents killed June–December 2003	597
Insurgents killed May 2004	652
Insurgents and Iraqi soldiers killed March 2009	59
Insurgents and Iraqi soldiers killed 2010–2011	2,187
TOTAL IRAQI	**157,531**
US and coalition military killed 2003–2011	4,802
TOTAL	**162,333**

of the incident- and victim-level details contained in the Logs, there would be no way to know how these data in fact compared or might contribute to other sources.

Comprehension and humanization of the data in the Iraq War Logs

As well as allowing more complete numbers to be reliably derived from them, incident and victim details such as those found throughout the Iraq War Logs provided important insights in their own right, in terms of the actual violence and in the human casualty factor. The Iraq War Logs provided far more detail for many of the deaths that had been documented and listed only in aggregated form by IBC. These details allowed those deaths in the IBC database to be disaggregated into newly defined and much more clear-cut 'incidents', which included accompanying details regarding their time, location and the identity of victims.

One case vividly illustrates how the logs would add a dramatic increase to detailed knowledge of the war, even when not necessarily adding new numbers to the deaths total.

IBC entry k4435 simply recorded 35 bodies of persons found, typically killed execution style, across Baghdad over the course of 1 November 2006. These few data points – the number, city, date and general cause of death – were the highest level of detail that existed

Table 4.3: Entry of incident before Iraq War Logs

Time	Number killed	City	Sub-city	Weapons	Victim details
	35	Baghdad		Gunfire, executed	

in the public domain about these deaths. The Iraq War Logs also contained 35 bodies found on the same date in Baghdad, but spread across 27 logs specifying a wide range of details, including the precise neighbourhood and time of day where particular bodies were found and, in many cases, the demographics and identities of those killed.

Details in IBC entry k4435 in its original form are shown in Table 4.3.

Table 4.4 shows 27 incidents in the logs recording bodies found in Baghdad on 1 November 2006, that eventually replaced the single IBC entry in Table 4.3. The columns in the table show the wealth of incident and victim details that would be added to the public record when the Logs were fully integrated into the IBC database.

Once fully analysed and coded by IBC, this one day's account of deaths in Baghdad, rather than being presented as a single database entry of '35 bodies found', with little accompanying details about the specific incidents or victims involved, would be split into over 20 more detailed incidents whose usefulness extended not just to a properly detailed historical account of the conflict, but possibly also to anyone whose loved ones went missing on or near that day.

The Iraq War Logs contain an unprecedented level of detail regarding individual Iraqi victims. This first became obvious when matching an entry in the logs to another previously reported case where bodies were found, this time in a mass grave containing 28 dead, recorded in the IBC database entry k4724. While the logs list the same event, they also note that the families of the dead were able to identify the victims involved, and then list all 28 names.

Based on preliminary analysis of 860 logs, matching these to IBC entries for incidents in the same locations and timeframes, it was estimated that the Iraq War Logs would add around 25,000 newly specified incidents to the IBC database, of which 23,000 would define events involving civilian deaths and around 2,000 would relate to the deaths of police and Iraqi security forces killed after capture. As noted in the previous section, some of these new incidents would also add new deaths (estimated at roughly 15,000), while others would provide new event and victim details for deaths already recorded in a more aggregated, less detailed form.

Table 4.4: Entry of incident following release of Iraq War Logs

Time	#	City	Sub-city	Weapons	Victim details
1:22	1	Baghdad	Route Al Amin, Al Sadr district	Gunfire, executed	
8:13	2	Baghdad	Karkh district	Gunfire, executed	Names, occupation, sects
10:35	1	Baghdad	Route Kamaliyah, Al Sadr district	Tortured, strangled	
10:45	1	Baghdad	Washshash village, Karkh district	Gunfire, executed	Age, gender, sect
12:00	1	Baghdad	Haifa Street, Karkh district	Gunfire, executed	
12:30	1	Baghdad	Al Mammon, Karkh district	Gunfire, executed	Gender
13:00	1	Baghdad	Diyala Bridge area, Al Resafa district	Gunfire, executed	Gender
13:00	4	Baghdad	Bab Al Muadam area, Al Resafa district	Gunfire, executed	Gender
13:45	1	Baghdad	Kadhimiya area, Kadhimiya district	Gunfire, executed	Name, age, gender
14:00	2	Baghdad	Al Mammon, Karkh district	Gunfire, executed	Names, ages, genders, sects
14:18	1	Baghdad	Al Mammon, Karkh district	Gunfire, executed	Age, gender
14:30	1	Baghdad	Route Al Rasheed, Hay Al Amil, Karkh district	Gunfire, executed	Gender
14:40	1	Baghdad	Karkh district	Gunfire, executed	
14:50	1	Baghdad	Al Mammon, Karkh district	Gunfire, executed	Name, age, gender, sect
15:00	1	Baghdad	Route Al Ghazaliya, Karkh district	Gunfire, executed	Age, gender, occupation
15:15	1	Baghdad	Route Al Shames Market, Hay Al Adel, Karkh district	Gunfire	Name, gender
15:30	1	Baghdad	Route Al Mansour, Al Ghazaliya, Karkh district	Gunfire, executed	Gender
16:00	3	Baghdad	Route Al Ghazaliya, Karkh district	Gunfire, executed	
16:20	1	Baghdad	Route New Baghdad, Al Amin, Al Sadr district	Gunfire, executed, tortured	Gender

(continued)

Table 4.4: Entry of incident following release of Iraq War Logs (continued)

Time	#	City	Sub–city	Weapons	Victim details
16:25	1	Baghdad	Karada, Al Resafa district	Gunfire, executed	Gender
16:30	1	Baghdad	Route Al Thawra, Sadr City, Al Sadr district	Gunfire, executed	Gender
17:00	1	Baghdad	Mada'in district	Gunfire, executed	Gender
17:00	1	Baghdad	Route Kamaliyah, Al Sadr district	Gunfire, executed	Gender
17:10	1	Baghdad	Al Sadr district	Gunfire, executed	Gender
17:30	1	Baghdad	Route Al Rashid, Al Saydiya, Karkh district	Gunfire, executed	Gender
18:35	2	Baghdad	Route Al Mansour, Karkh district	Assassinated	Names, genders
18:40	1	Baghdad	Al Mansour area, Karkh district	Assassinated	Name, age, gender, occupation

While it is important for incidents to be as clearly defined and distinguishable from each other as possible, the same holds even more true for victims. A full list of every victim of the conflict, individual by individual, name by name, remains the ultimate long–term goal of the IBC project.

It is almost impossible to convey the pain contained in the experiences behind the numbers. Although we may speak of dozens killed in a particular incident or thousands over a span of time, it is human beings who die and are mourned human beings who deserve the final dignity of recognition not as a mass, but as individuals. It is not enough to establish only how many, but also who was killed as a result of the US/UK's 2003 invasion of Iraq and the country's subsequent collapse in civil security. Like all the other casualty details, names too belong in the public domain – as a memorial to the dead and public recognition of the loss suffered by their families, and, indeed, as another means of understanding the full impact of the war.

Iraq 2012

During 2012 Iraq Body Count recorded 4,622 civilian deaths from violence. Evidence of these deaths was extracted from some 7,000

Table 4.5: Civilian deaths by province in 2012

Province	Deaths in 2012	Per 100,000	Population	Province capital
Diyala	574	39.77	1,443,173	Baqubah
Salah al-Din	522	37.07	1,408,174	Tikrit
Anbar	511	32.73	1,561,407	Ramadi
Ninewa	861	26.33	3,270,422	Mosul
Tameem	295	21.14	1,395,614	Kirkuk
Babylon	341	18.73	1,820,673	Hillah
Baghdad	1,116	15.82	7,055,196	Baghdad
Wassit	63	5.20	1,210,591	Kut
Qadissiya	53	4.67	1,134,313	Diwaniyah
Basra	103	4.07	2,531,997	Basra
Thi-Qar	65	3.54	1,836,181	Nasiriyah
Kerbala	33	3.09	1,066,567	Kerbala
Missan	22	2.26	971,448	Amarah
Sulaymaniyah	37	1.97	1,878,764	Sulaymaniyah
Erbil	11	0.68	1,612,692	Erbil
Najaf	7	0.54	1,285,484	Najaf
Dahuk	6	0.53	1,128,745	Dahuk
Muthanna	1	0.14	719,069	Samawah

distinct reports collected from more than 80 sources covering 2,101 incidents. The 2012 figures brought the number of civilian deaths recorded by IBC since March 2003 to between 113,805 and 124,513.

2012 marked the first year since 2009 where the death toll for the year increased, even though slightly. Overall, 2012 was more consistent with an entrenched conflict than with any transformation in the security situation for Iraqis in the first year since the formal withdrawal of US troops, a low-level war little changed since early 2009, with a 'background' level of everyday armed violence punctuated by occasional larger-scale attacks designed to kill many people at once. The majority of incidents and civilian deaths occurred in provinces in the central regions of the country. In 2012 43% of deaths occurred in just two provinces: Baghdad and Ninewa. As some provinces had much larger populations, however, Table 4.5 indicates the risk which residents of other provinces continued to face.

Moreover, while police forces were always targeted in post-invasion Iraq, 2012 saw both an increase in the absolute number of police killed in comparison to 2011 (724 versus 946 in 2012), and an increase in their proportion of all deaths (17.4% of deaths in 2011 versus 20.5% in 2012).

During the height of sectarian violence in the years from 2006/7, most deaths were from small arms fire, often in targeted killings. Such killings continued: in 2012 there were 989 reported incidents involving deadly shootings, or cases of bodies found shot dead, with a death toll of 1,644. Of these deaths, 690 were of a single individual.

As 2013 commenced, Sunni discontent grew and erupted, doubling the civilian death toll and introducing a new enemy: the Islamic State.

The trenching of faults

Fault lines

There were fault lines in Iraq before 2003. The state was weak economically; it was weak politically, with an unpopular dictator, at home and abroad; it was weak societally, clearly divided into Sunnis, Shias and Kurds.

The fault lines were to widen so much that they reached the size of trenches. Many factors contributed to that. The initial unprovoked attack of 2003 by one of the world's most powerful states was the first one. It was followed by years of occupation, insurgency, terrorism and increasingly competing interests. Internally, the interests of the Sunnis, the Shias, the Kurds, the religious fanatics, the secular, the non-Muslim; externally, the interests of the US and the UK, Iran and Syria, all of which want to expand their political and ideological sphere of influence at any cost. Those competing interests led to the internal collapse of Iraqi society and remain the sad legacy of the invasion.

The struggle for power

National power is composed of quantitative and qualitative factors: geography, resources, industrial capacity and military capabilities; national character, national morale, quality of government. In all of these, Iraq has been stripped of any power it may have had. The resources it was lucky to have, due to its geographical location, are being exploited by others, while a third of the population live below the poverty line. Its army was dismantled by its occupiers and is still struggling to regroup and manage the daily violence. Whatever national character and morale it had before, it lost in a sea of betrayals, collaborations, mutual attacks and accusations, while its government, elected twice under occupation, only inspires mistrust and revolt among its people.

Iraq is now a fragmented state, where each party struggles to gain power, at the expense of the others, as they have incompatible security requirements, which means that the security of each cannot be assured at the same time as the security of its rivals or enemies. Thus they seek relative gains, where their own gain is a loss to another, rather than absolute gains, which require cooperation. In a state as weak and fragmented as Iraq, all sides see the struggle for power and its acquisition as a means to their survival.

Iraq 2013

The year started with protests and rising discontent. The Sunnis demanded reforms, while the government of Nouri al-Maliki abandoned any efforts to be cross sectarian, targeting Sunni politicians, arresting and interrogating and forcing some into exile. After the April 23 protest turned violent and the Iraqi Security Forces attacked protesters, killing 49 of them, the retaliation resulted in the number of civilian deaths tripling in the next 6 months. While 1,900 civilians were killed between October 2012 and March 2013, 6,300 were killed between April and October 2013.

Overall, nearly 9,500 civilians died in violence in Iraq this year, which is almost equal to the 2008 figure, when 10,000 were killed. Back in 2008, however, that figure represented a decline in violent deaths (down from 25,800), whereas now it represents an increase; it has more than doubled since last year, when the recorded civilian deaths were 4,500.

Al Qaeda in Iraq has found fertile ground in all this discontent and has attacked the Iraqi government, as the Syrian government is being attacked this year, by killing members of its army, its police force, its politicians and journalists, as well as its Shia population. Indeed, the last six months have seen the massacres of entire families, as they sleep, or travel to a holy place, sometimes 5, sometimes 12 family members at a time... The faults are now as wide and as deep as trenches.

As the Sunnis protest and feel their government has failed them, so the Shia protest and they too feel their government has failed them, by failing to protect them. Civilians have continued to die every day this year. Daily they are still blown up, shot, stabbed, abducted and beheaded. Yet among all the death and savagery, a glimmer of hope and humanity, as Ayyub Khalaf, a 34-year-old policeman and father of two, throws his arms around a suicide bomber, sacrificing himself to protect the Shia pilgrims, on December 18. Let him serve as a symbol, a hope that not all is lost. (Hamourtziadou, 2013a)

On the 10th anniversary of the invasion, on 20 March 2013, the impact of war, regime change and 'liberation' was evident. My own thoughts were as follows:

10 years in Iraq: contains flashing images

There was no reason why Saddam Hussein should not be defeated swiftly and easily; Iraq was a country deeply divided by religion and ethnicity, broken by war and impoverished by years of economic sanctions. It was a vulnerable state. A weak state, one easily threatened militarily, politically and economically, one that could be controlled with little effort and few casualties. And so operation 'Shock and Awe' began on March 19 2003. And the bombing of Baghdad commenced.

Millions of us sat transfixed before our TV screens, watching in shock and awe as bombs and missiles exploded. The reports came with the warning they contained flashing images, and true enough the sky over Baghdad flashed orange and golden, the sounds of war filling our ears. On the ground, it must have been deafening. Terrifying. The narrative of terror that began on March 19 2003 was to last for years: terror from the sky, terror on the ground, terror from the foreign soldier, terror from one's neighbour... It would become, in turns, a narrative of justifications, of explanations, of accusations. 10 years later, it continues.

The bombing emerged from and was justified, in the minds of many, by the 20th century belief in the goodness of empire. For the imperialists, writes Beau Grosscup, 'those outside the core of Western culture were deemed undeserving of or unprepared for self-determination ... The European and North American collective and individual selves found their identity and place in the world in terms of privilege, dominance and hegemony' (Grosscup 2006: 29). Who but we the good, we the powerful, we the privileged, was best placed to intervene?

It is a violence we have been powerless to stop – those of us who opposed the invasion, who opposed the 9-year occupation of Iraq, who oppose terrorism. As civilians started to get killed daily in their hundreds, we watched, we documented. Over 122,000 civilians recorded killed so far, 4,180 of them children, 14,900 known to have been killed by our coalition forces. Civilians such as those 17 members of one family, killed in an air strike on April 4 2003 (IBC incident page x093; the 2 children machine-gunned at a checkpoint on May 28 2003 (x083); 7-year-old Afrah Moneem, shot dead at a Baghdad market on September 10 2003 (IBC individual page d4224-sa1478); the 2 killed in a helicopter strike on June 25 2007 (d3702); the 2 elderly people killed in a raid as they slept on a rooftop in Sadr City on May 30 2007 (k6583); the 17 killed in another raid in Sadr City on October 21 2007 (k7815), 2-year-old Ali Hamed among them (k7815-su932). Civilians like little Ali Hussein, the boy in the orange shorts, who died in a Sadr City air strike on April 29 2008 (k10366), where 30 people lost their lives; or 8-year-old Sa'adiya Saddam, shot dead in Diwaniya on February 7 2009 (k12175)... Collateral damage.

The killings were committed by many different perpetrators and by a variety of methods; coalition forces, insurgents, terrorists, American soldiers, British soldiers, Sunnis, Shia have brought about the death of innocents through air strikes, suicide bombings, car bombs, shootings, IEDs... The victims, people from all walks of life: shepherds, street cleaners, construction workers, policemen, doctors, clerics, teachers, journalists, politicians, school children... Killed as they walked, shopped, worked, drove, slept, changed a tyre...

Dr Haidar al-Baaj was shot dead in Basra on October 15 2003 (x194-hs132), one of 145 doctors and medics to be killed since the invasion. Other victims include:

• Hana Abdul Qader, politician, shot in Mosul on March 6 2005
• Widad al-Shaml, teacher, shot in Baquba on May 11 2006
• Mohammed Shihab al-Dulaimi, politician, shot in Baghdad on September 16 2006
• Asmaeel Taher, teacher, shot in Mosul on May 2 2007
• Abdul-Amir Ezz Al-Din, labourer, shot in Kirkuk on August 10 2007
• Maron Awanis, taxi driver, shot in Baghdad on October 9 2007
• Salih Saif Aldin, journalist, shot in Baghdad on October 14 2007
• Paulos Faraj Rahho, priest, abducted and killed in Mosul on March 13 2008
• Ahmed Salim, cameraman, shot in Mosul on September 13 2008
• Mohammed Akeel, schoolboy, blown up in Baghdad on July 9 2009
• Nazhan Isam Aziz, labourer, shot in Dubiz on April 21 2012

Images of the last 10 years include the wooden coffins, the bodies in white shrouds, the names – foreign to our ears – the faces – some smiling in old photographs – the blood, the blown-out cars... The suspects – blindfolded and handcuffed... the heroes, like 18-year-old vendor Ahmed Draiwel, who picked up a bomb and ran with it, away from the busy market, in Sadr City, in March of 2007 (k5752-xc826), the only one who died when it exploded.

Thousands of civilians have been killed each year, since the night of the flashing images. At its peak, the terror claimed 29,027 in 2006; at its calmest, 4,073 in 2010.

Meanwhile Iraq was 'liberated' and 'democratised', with elections taking place during the years of occupation. As the killing continued. Every day as I turned the page in my notepad and wrote the new date on top, I feared the daily count, the names and ages of the newly dead... Baghdad: 5 by car bomb... Mahmudiya: 4 children by IED... Karbala: 45 by suicide bomber... Mahmoud Modher... Junaid Mohammed Khairallah... Nora Sabah Gadan... family of Saler Hamzeh Ali Moussawi...

The narrative of terror is the narrative of justifications, the narrative of explanations, the narrative of accusations. It is the narrative of the names and faces of the innocent. It is the narrative of the helpless and the poor, the millions of refugees, the bodies found and picked up from the streets of Baghdad, buried in mass graves, unidentified, unclaimed. We are the lucky ones, who witness the horror from afar, our TV screens, our newspapers, our computer monitors. We can watch in shock and awe, as it all unfolds, less and less frequently now, safe *from the missiles, safe from the car bombs, the only danger those flashing images hurting our eyes. That's why those reports come with a warning.* (Hamourtziadou, 2013b)

The Human Terrain System (2007–2014): managing the 'far enemy'

> 'Agricola first laid waste the land. Then he displayed to the natives his moderation.' (Tacitus)

'Are there interdependencies between insurgencies, societies, and economies? Does the language of war require a sociological grammar in order to be understood?' (Sims, 2015, p 1).

The three functions of hegemony, as described by Lebow and Reich, all require influence rather than the blunt exercise of power. Leadership requires the capacity to shape policy agendas and appeal to shared norms; economic management to stabilize and undergird the functions of the economic system; sponsorship requires the capacity to enforce initiatives through dialogue, negotiation and the use of regional or global institutions as venues. 'Sponsorship requires the implementation of consensual goals that are consistent with self interest' (Lebow and Reich, 2014, p 8).

The self-interest, in other words, needs to be served through dialogue, cooperation, negotiation and, above all, through, at the very least, the semblance of shared goals. All of which require 'a sociological grammar', a language based on an understanding of the society in question. The focus then becomes not only the securing of land and resources, as provided by the armed forces, by also the creation of an ideological hegemony grounded on the development of 'shared' values and goals. It is through the creation of the latter that the former is better served. In order to secure those shared goals, at the height of insurgency and terrorist attacks on Iraqis and American soldiers alike, the US army developed the Human Terrain System (HTS).

This support programme employed social scientists from the areas of sociology, anthropology, political science and linguistics to provide the military with an understanding of the population, the *human terrain*, in Afghanistan and Iraq. The concept of HTS was first developed by Montgomery McFate and Andrea Jackson in 2005, and proposed a pilot version of the project as a response to 'identified gaps in [US military] commanders' and staffs' understanding of the local population and culture' (McFate and Jackson, 2005). The programme was run by the United States Army Training and Doctrine Command

(TRADOC) with five HTS teams deployed to Iraq and Afghanistan. This was to grow to 31 teams and a $150 million annual budget, the HTS becoming a permanent US army programme in 2010 (McFate and Fondacaro, 2011).

On 7 February 2007, a five-person military–civilian Human Terrain Team (HTT) embedded with the US army 4th Brigade Combat Team in Khost province, Afghanistan.

> Designated AF1, this experiment in hybridized civil–military relations was the first embedded team in the Human Terrain System (HTS), an ambitious proof-of-concept program managed by the U.S. Army Training and Doctrine Command (TRADOC). The team's mission was to provide BCT – approximately 3,000 personnel – commanders: with operationally relevant, sociocultural data, information, knowledge and understanding, and the embedded expertise to integrate that understanding into the commander's planning and decisionmaking process. (Sims, 2015, p 2)

This 'embedded expertise' was an attempt to combine and apply social science scholarship to military instruments so as to 'wage more effective population-centered counterinsurgency (COIN) campaigns in and among the population'. Teams were to be geographically located, to develop understanding of a particular area in order to 'preserve and share sociocultural knowledge' across unit rotations (Sims, 2015, p 2).

> The teams would conduct granular social science research among the civilian population and report directly to the brigade staff. Thus they were plugged in to the highest levels of planning on the ground with the ability to influence all aspects of the brigade based on their findings. As a former HTT member observed, while other brigade elements 'directly engage the people on a continual basis' focusing on development projects and influencing the local population, the HTT's unique contribution was in 'understanding the people'. (Sims, 2015, p 3)

In Iraq and Afghanistan, 'understanding the people' required fluent language skills, robust knowledge of research methods, and field experience. Such skills required social science expertise identified as only available in the US civilian reservoir. According to Clifton Green,

HTS was developed as a response to concerns about mismanagement of US military operations in Iraq and Afghanistan, in particular the lack of cultural understanding of these countries demonstrated by the US military. Soldiers were being asked to navigate a complex foreign environment with little or no training, and they were failing. Cultural research and analysis had only a small place in the army thought process. HTS was designed to provide a better understanding of indigenous populations in these countries, to help US and allied forces dampen the insurgencies. The army, facing progressively worsening situations, needed new ideas and thus backed a $20 million, five-team HTS proof of concept. Within a year, the requirement for Human Terrain Teams mushroomed to 26 teams as the price tag surpassed $100 million annually (Green, 2015, p 62).

The HTS then can be described as a counterinsurgency tool providing sociocultural knowledge. The American Anthropological Association argued that the programme was performing a 'tactical function in counterinsurgency warfare' (American Anthropological Association, 2008, p 3). Lamb argued that the population-centric approach to counterinsurgency required 'protecting and eliciting cooperation from the population' and that 'the principal instruments for delivering this understanding to [General David] Petraeus' military forces in the field were Human Terrain Teams' (Lamb, 2013, p 1). Retired US army officer Ralph Peters noted that it was part of 'a growing sense that the reality on the ground in Iraq and elsewhere contradicts the theories we were fed' (Peters, 2007).

Seen as part of a 'trend for cultural awareness', HTS was thus part of a cultural turn in the War on Terror. Paul Joseph, Professor of Sociology at Tufts University, in his 2014 book, asserted that the very existence of the programme reflected a trend in the Department of Defence for deeper understanding of operations 'among people whose reactions to those operations will significantly influence, if not ultimately determine, success or failure' (Joseph, 2014, pp 2–3). It was necessary to understand the adversary, so as to be able to attack the network behind the IEDs. The need to understand the terrain on a cultural level stood in marked contrast to the hubristic beginnings of Operation IRAQI FREEDOM, in which there was 'a relative lack of concern by the President and the top military leadership' regarding Iraqi culture and consultation with academic experts (Emberling, 2008, p 449). As Sims writes, in the HTS there was a requirement to 'understand the cloak in which the insurgent wrapped himself in: the population'. 'Focusing on the insurgent would lead to collateral damage and popular support for the insurgency', but 'if the population's needs were met, the insurgents can be exposed and isolated' (Sims, 2015, p 147).

The HTS became the subject of much controversy. In 'Human Terrain System is Dead, Long Live … What? Building and Sustaining Military Cultural Competence in the Aftermath of the Human Terrain System', Major Ben Connable, US Marine Corps (retired), writes that many of them thought organic capability was the right approach.

> We made three arguments: (1) outsourcing cultural competence would ensure its inevitable disappearance and the equally inevitable path to grievous tactical errors in the next war, (2) training and educating everyone to a reasonable level was the only way to ensure the even and widespread cultural competence needed in a massive distributed counterinsurgency operation such as Iraq or Afghanistan, and (3) cultural information could be classified or unclassified, but it had to be integrated into a holistic intelligence understanding of the battlespace. (Connable, 2018, pp 25–26)

The idea was to build a 'cultural information clearinghouse' to meet the needs of commanders to understand culture, tribes and other complex issues (Connable, 2018, p 28). Connable continues:

> In a mostly earnest and sometimes aggressive effort to improve cultural intelligence capabilities, some intelligence staffs worked to enhance cultural intelligence collection and analysis, to integrate culture into analytic products, and to build cultural databases. For at least the first decade after the invasion of Iraq, the undersecretary of defense for intelligence did its best to coordinate defense intelligence cultural activities, but full integration of cultural information into the all-source analysis process – in which all types and sources of information are supposed to be fused to generate holistic understanding – never really took hold. (Connable, 2018, p 29)

Cultural intelligence cells emerged in the community, some of which, like the Human Terrain Analysis Branch at US Central Command, were highly successful, but short-lived, while it remained unclear how they contributed to a holistic understanding of the environment. Culture was at the core of all operations, from humanitarian assistance missions to counterinsurgency to conventional warfare. Culture was 'inaccurately and perhaps indelibly branded as an irregular warfare thing'. That despite the fact that culture rarely appears in the literature or doctrine on conventional warfare, and it is excluded from tactical and operational narratives.

> Proponency only emerges when culture becomes a problem, and this usually occurs in irregular conflicts such as Vietnam, Afghanistan, and Iraq. Cultural competence training and cultural intelligence do not appear to offer any assistance in direct tactical combat, which happens to be the primary conventional war purpose of the military's combat arms. ... if culture does not matter in conventional war then it can and should be shelved so the military can dedicate more time to combined arms training. (Connable, 2018, p 30)

Or should it? This thinking, argues Connable, is short-sighted, first of all, because rapidly developing cultural competence is impossible; generating real, service-wide cultural competence takes time. 'Abandoning culture because it is perceived to be an irregular war consideration makes another deadly culture crisis inevitable', he warns. It is like repeating the Vietnam War cycle: start by entering an irregular war, then make terrible cultural errors, scramble to create cultural training, education, and intelligence, and finally dump everything. Connable sees remarkable parallels between the late 1970s and today (Connable, 2018, p 30).

Culture, he writes, must not be separated either from irregular or from conventional war, as the US military views warfare as a fundamentally human endeavour. Joint Publication 1, *Doctrine for the Armed Forces of the United States*, the capstone doctrine for the US armed forces, describes war as a complex human undertaking and a Clausewitzean contest of opposing, independent wills. Both army and Marine Corps doctrinal publications agree. If this is true, argues Connable, 'then even tactical and operational combat require understanding human behavior, and human behavior is rooted in culture' (Connable, 2018, p 30). According to him, culture lies at the heart of warfare. For a military to be able to identify and break the enemy's will to fight, it needs to understand what motivates or weakens them. For a military to be able to secure and count on allies, it needs to understand what will keep them in the fight.

'Understanding the enemy' also formed the basis for the mission to turn that enemy into an ally – into turning the 'bad' into 'good'. The civilizational and moral changes that were required, as the first and second narratives made clear. If the clash of civilizations was behind the War on Terror, then civilizational adjustments had to be made; if the War on Terror was the battle between good and evil forces, then the evil ones had to become good and join all the other good ones in their fight, to secure victory over evil. The first 'evil-turned-good' during that period were the Sons of Iraq that formed the Awakening Councils, or *Sahwa*. As they joined the coalition in their fight against al-Qaeda in Iraq, they became the next target: 1,732 Awakening Council members were killed in Iraq by 2017 (IBC database).

The Awakening Councils

Sheikh Abdul Sattar Abu Risha, who led the Anbar Awakening (*Sahawat al-Anbar*), was the grandson of a tribal leader in the Iraqi revolt against the British occupying forces in 1920 and the son of a commander in the Anglo-Iraqi War in 1941. After becoming an ally of US forces and the Iraqi government, he united Sunni tribes in opposing al-Qaeda in Ramadi in 2007. *The Washington Post* reported that he was 'a warlord and a highway bandit, an oil smuggler and an opportunist' (Partlow, Scott Tyson and Wright, 2007). In the summer of 2006 he began enlisting his fellow sheikhs in *Sahawat al-Anbar* and encouraging members of his tribe to join the local police force, to secure their own neighbourhoods. Tribal meetings took place under security provided by US forces at Sattar's compound in western Ramadi and by March 2007 the council counted 41 clans from Anbar province (Pitman, 2007). However, many of the Awakening leaders, despite the councils being US-sponsored and funded, are believed to have supported the Iraqi insurgency.

> U.S. Marines worked with local tribal leaders to expel al-Qaeda in Iraq (AQI) from the governorate. In September 2006, the process was expanded and formalized when Sheikh Abd al-Sattar al-Rishawi (known as Sattar Abu Risha,) convened the first Sahwa meeting, drawing together 45 tribal leaders from around Ramadi to successfully convince 4,500 Sunni Arabs, including many former insurgents, to join the Anbar police. (Knights, 2009)

'The Awakening Councils were seen as an Iraqi solution to an Iraqi problem' (Watani, nd). Sunni tribesmen and former resistance fighters were paid by the US to man security checkpoints; however, coalition forces did not coordinate Sahwa/Sons of Iraq (SOI) activities across provinces beyond funding and general direction. The Awakening Councils were also known as Sons of Iraq (*Abnā' al-'Irāq*), National Council for the Salvation of Iraq (*al-Majlis al-Waṭanī li-Inqādh al-'Irāq*), Sunni Salvation movement (*Ḥarakat al-Inqādh al-Sunnī*), National Council for the Awakening of Iraq (*al-Majlis al-Waṭanī li-Ṣaḥwat al-'Irāq*), Sunni Awakening movement (*Ḥarakat al-Ṣaḥwah al-Sunnīyah*). The US military referred to them as 'Concerned Local Citizens Groups' (US Department of Defense, 2007).

Abu Risha was killed in September 2007, days after meeting and publicly shaking hands with President Bush. Reuters reported:

> Sunni Arab Iraqis and U.S. forces in Anbar province vowed on Friday to keep fighting al Qaeda after the assassination of a tribal leader who worked with Americans to create one of Iraq's few security success stories. Abdul Sattar Abu Risha was killed in a bomb attack on Thursday near his home in Ramadi, provincial capital of what was once one of Iraq's most dangerous areas. 'All the tribes agreed to fight al Qaeda until the last child in Anbar', his brother, Ahmed Abu Risha, told Reuters. An al Qaeda-led group said on Friday it was responsible for the killing of Abu Risha, according to an Internet posting. The self-styled Islamic State in Iraq called the killing of Abu Risha a 'heroic operation' and vowed to assassinate more tribal leaders who cooperate with U.S. and government forces. (Reuters, 2007)

The statement was posted on a main Islamist website. The Islamic State in Iraq (ISI) called the assassination of Abu Risha 'a new setback for the crusaders' plans and Bush's new strategy'. His brother, Ahmed Abu Risha, was named as the council's new head, 'hours after the death of his charismatic, chain-smoking brother, who wore flowing white and gold robes as he shook hands with Bush'. Iraq's national security adviser Mowaffaq al-Rubaie, Interior Minister Jawad al-Bolani, Defense Minister General Abdel Qader Jassim and Lieutenant-General Raymond Odierno, second in command of US forces in Iraq, joined about 1,500 mourners at Abu Risha's funeral amid tight security. President Bush 'praised Abu Risha's bravery and pointed to the improved security in Anbar as evidence that US strategy was making headway'. 'He was a significant figure, there's no doubt about it. I'm sure this is a loss', added Major Jeff Poole, a US military spokesman in Anbar (Reuters, 2007).

'Understanding the enemy' resulted in turning some of the 'bad' into 'good', which involved, if not civilizational, certainly moral changes. If more 'bad' ones could be turned 'good', then victory would be secured for the West. Looking at the functions of hegemony again, we see that they require influence: leadership requires the capacity to shape policy agendas and appeal to shared norms; sponsorship requires the capacity to enforce initiatives through dialogue, negotiation, and the use of regional or global institutions as venues. The interest of the leader will be served, but through dialogue, cooperation, negotiation and the establishment of shared goals and of shared enemies.

The creation of the Awakening Councils was not free of controversy or a guarantor of the West's triumph over Iraq's insurgency. In 2011 Myriam Benraad, in 'Iraq's Tribal "Sahwa": Its Rise and Fall', wrote

> From 2007 to 2008, Iraq's tribal 'Sahwa' (Arabic for 'Awakening') was a key component of the U.S. 'surge' strategy and largely credited for its role in the dramatic reduction of violence across the country. In the last two years, though, members of the movement have increasingly become the target of a retaliation campaign led by al-Qaeda's 'Islamic State of Iraq' and other insurgent groups still active on the battlefield, with almost daily assassinations and attacks in which hundreds have died. In the present context of resurgent violence, persistent political tensions triggered by the 2010 stalemate and the U.S. military's scheduled withdrawal of its remaining troops by the end of 2011, the Sahwa's future looms as one of the most crucial tests of Iraq's stabilization and successful 'democratic' transition. (Benraad, 2011)

The dramatic reduction of violence during that period can be seen in the IBC 2007–2009 monthly and annual figures (Table 4.6). The reduction continued and stabilized through to 2013, as we saw at the start of this chapter (Table 4.7).

As Benraad observes, when several sheikhs from the Albu Mahal tribe around the city of Qaim began to cooperate with US troops, they did so in order to drive al-Qaeda out of their territory, but at the time, 'this shift had much to do with the tribes' growing awareness of the benefits that such a rapprochement could mean for them in the longer

Table 4.6: Civilian deaths by month 2007–2009

	Jan	Feb	Mar	Apr	May	Jun	Jul	Aug	Sep	Oct	Nov	Dec	Total
2007	3,035	2,680	2,728	2,573	2,854	2,219	2,702	2,483	1,391	1,326	1,124	997	**26,112**
2008	861	1,093	1,669	1,317	915	755	640	704	612	594	540	586	**10,286**
2009	372	409	438	590	428	564	431	653	352	441	226	478	**5,382**

Table 4.7: Civilian deaths by month 2010–2012

	Jan	Feb	Mar	Apr	May	Jun	Jul	Aug	Sep	Oct	Nov	Dec	Total
2010	267	305	336	385	387	385	488	520	254	315	307	218	**4,167**
2011	389	254	311	289	381	386	308	401	397	366	288	392	**4,162**
2012	531	356	377	392	304	529	469	422	400	290	253	299	**4,622**

run, especially in terms of political participation and power' (Benraad, 2011). Indeed, this may not have been about anyone becoming 'good', or about any party embracing democracy and freedom, or even accepting the authority of a benevolent hegemon. Power, the struggle for it, always seems to rear its head, whatever name we try to give to it.

The rise of Awakening Councils, coupled with the American 'surge' in 2007, resulted in a reduction in civilian deaths and in the Sahwa becoming a major actor in Iraq. Sahwa councils spread throughout Sunni Arab communities as

> a forum where US military and tribal leaders could talk and coordinate security actions. Sahwa councils also participated in US-brokered reconciliation talks between Sunni and Shia community leaders. Sahwa councils increasingly became a place where local reconstruction needs were discussed, drawing in Iraqi local municipal and military officials. In essence, the Sahwa operated in parallel to official provincial, district and sub-district councils where they did not include local Sunni Arab leaders. (Knights, 2009)

Tribes were given arms and financial resources to fight al-Qaeda and delegated important authority prerogatives in their areas to establish order. From the start, the Sahwa were driven by economic motives and opportunism,

> a clear warning sign of the serious possibility of the movement's falling apart in time and the tribes' turning back to violence if their alliance of convenience with the United States ceased to bring sufficient benefits or to be satisfyingly rewarded. This risk seemed all the higher, as the U.S. coalition had pledged to devote funds in support of the movement and provide Sahwa fighters with long-term employment by their progressive incorporation into Iraq's new security forces. (Benraab, 2011)

The promise made by the coalition was not kept by the Iraqi government. From the start, 'Baghdad opposed the Sahwa, looking at its alliance with the United States with suspicion and resentment, concerned that its successes on the ground might translate into actual legitimacy and political power' (Benraab, 2011). In addition, 'this attempt and others quickly lost steam through al Qaeda's murder and intimidation campaign against tribal leaders and anyone, regardless of sect, associated with receiving US help' (Watani, nd).

The relationship between the Awakening Councils and the Maliki government deteriorated after the US withdrawal from Iraq. Ahmed al-Rishawi (Abu Risha) became the leader of the Awakening Movement in Anbar. In the 2010 election, they were part of the Coalition of Iraq's Unity (CIU), also known as the Iraq Unity Alliance (IUA). Led by Interior Minister Jawad al-Bolani, members shared a secular-nationalist vision for Iraq and favoured a US-style government, a constitutionally based political system that would transcend sectarian or ethnic affiliations, with 'three equal branches of government, a free press as a "fourth" power, equal rights for women and an emphasis on stopping domestic violence against them, care for the handicapped, partnership with international institutions, and a move towards a free market economy' (Watani, nd). Coalition candidates promised security, jobs, a place to live, healthcare and education.

In 2012 Ahmed Abu Richa joined anti-government camps in Anbar and made the same demands as the protesters, such as releasing detainees, more Sunni representation in government institutions, and more integration of Sunnis into the political process. In March 2013 he was arrested on terrorism charges.

In *Al-Anbar Awakening Volume II Iraqi Perspectives: From Insurgency to Counterinsurgency in Iraq, 2004–2009* we read, through a series of interviews, revealing perspectives (religious, tribal and political) on insurgency and counterinsurgency in Iraq.

> The 17 paramount-dignified sheikhs of the major Anbari tribes and tribal federation turned away from al-Qaeda for survival purposes and toward U.S. forces for the same reason. They will tell you that Iraqis were being hunted down and killed by both the terrorists and the Coalition forces in Anbar. They knew the unbending terrorists would never meet them halfway, but they were confident that the Americans would – and they were right. Many of these men were once as much a part of the insurgency as Zarqawi was, albeit for different reasons. (Montgomery and McWilliams, 2009, p viii)

Where Iraqis once avoided them, Montgomery and McWilliams write, so as not to jeopardize their lives and those of their families at the hands of al-Qaeda terrorists or nationalist insurgents, they now sought them aggressively in order to engage with them, in the spirit of friendship and cooperation. Montgomery and McWilliams see this as the result of a successful campaign plan, where Iraqis began to see marines as a force that was 'sharing in their agony' (Montgomery and McWilliams, 2009, pp ix–x). During an interview with Colonel Montgomery, in answer to the question 'What role did Coalition forces play in the Awakening?', Anbar Governor Mamoun Sami Rashid al-Alwani replies as follows:

> Mamoun:
> They were supporting first the local government, whether it was the governor or provincial council. In addition, they were supporting us and starting dialogue with the tribes. So they will start the dialogue with the tribes in order to work together to stop the insurgency, together with the local government. Because the military force was in the hands of the Americans, that reinforced the position of the governor, helped the legislation and execution of the laws or orders issued from the provincial council. They were recruiting and establishing the police. They trained those people. They equipped them with weapons, vehicles, and fuel. Sometimes, the military relied on the Coalition forces to feed them. They played the main role. I always called them the main referee, who refereed the whole game. (Montgomery and McWilliams, 2009, p 157)

Staff Brigadier General Haqi Isma'eel Ali Hameed, Commander 2nd Region Directorate of Border Enforcement, recalls the initial stages of the mobilization, at Sheikh Abdul Sattar Abu Risha's house, on 14 September 2006. At that first meeting it was decided who would provide financial support and who would provide weapons and ammunition. The Iraqi government approved the establishment of the police in al-Anbar Province, to which it was going to provide support with weapons and salaries. Thousands of tribal sons were inducted immediately into the police forces. Training support was provided by the Americans and by the Iraqi army (Montgomery and McWilliams, 2009, p 227).

Building on those collective goals, dialogue and cooperation, which make clear the influence and leadership of the hegemon, Staff Brigadier General Haqi Isma'eel Ali Hameed continues,

> The most important thing was that the goal was the same for the Marine Corps, for the Iraqi government, and for the Awakening – to destroy the terrorists, to keep the security situation in good condition, to stop these groups from targeting honest people, and to stop these groups from targeting the Coalition forces. ... It became normal to have meetings with the Marine officers and with people who provided us with information attending these meetings. So at that time, the Marine officers were visiting the tribal sheikhs' houses, and they were eating lunch with them, and it was something normal to be together as friends. (Montgomery and McWilliams, 2009, p 232)

In addition to exercising brute force through an invasion, occupation, air raids and shootings, we see America attempting to play the role of the hegemon by providing leadership, appealing to shared norms and persuading as well as coercing; and sponsorship through dialogue and negotiation, creating and implementing consensual goals consistent with self-interest. Power was a combination of coercive tactics, resulting in death and destruction, and cooperation, resulting in the creation of shared interests and objectives. The Awakening Councils were persuaded to do what the coalition wanted and to refrain from doing what the coalition did not want. The US-led coalition provided an *arche* but also a *hegemonia*, for a while at least; it was rule based on force, rule that lacked legitimacy, but it also became rule accepted by some of the ruled, seemingly loyal members of the local community, on the illusion of power-sharing. The impact of American rule on Iraq, the lesson learnt by the Iraqis, was summed up by Lieutenant General Ra'ad al-Hamdani: 'Now we have a saying that "it's stupid to trust the American administration policies". Another is that "it is ignorant to object to the American political decisions"' (Montgomery and McWilliams, 2009, p 297).

The combination of force and influence, destruction and reconstruction, the 'surge', but also the Human Terrain System and the Awakening, impacted on the later years of the invasion, politically and in terms of security, in the ways chapters 3–4 have discussed. As the overall civilian death toll in Iraq declined and stabilized to between 4,000 and 5,000 a year during 2009–2012, a new development in Syria and other Arab states led to the doubling of casualties and to the opening of new fronts in the War on Terror. It was a development that combined insurgency, terrorism, popular uprisings and Western support: the Arab Spring. As the West was fighting armed groups in Iraq, with the cooperation of the Iraqi government, it was simultaneously supporting such armed groups in Syria, against the Syrian regime. Before we look at the impact of this new development on Iraq's security, we need to ask how this Arab Spring fits into our War on Terror.

The Arab Spring

> The Arab Uprising was a reaction to the authoritarian, West-centric and in-egalitarian rule of the post-populist era, a revolt manifest in the overthrow of presidential monarchies and initial empowerment of the outsider Islamic movements. It was encouraged by diffusion from the West of Internet technology and the parallel spread of Western discourses of democratisation and human rights that de-legitimised local political practices. (Hinnebusch, 2015, p 103)

In this uprising we again see the following, by now familiar pattern, in the West's security policy in the Middle East: Western support for armed anti-regime groups, as part of an attempt to remove regimes no longer friendly, and attempts to spread Western values (moral and political).

At the same time, we observe the anti-West nature of many of those groups taking part in the uprising, a challenge to authority and a strengthening of Islamic ideology, all arguably morbid symptoms alongside America's attempts to enforce the power and influence it had been losing. A time of crisis, a time of change, a time of transformation, but also a time of great human loss. Arguably a clash of civilizations, a clash of values, a power struggle and a structural shift, where identity became the referent object in the process of securitization. The uprisings opened contests over identity, between sub-state, state and supra-state loyalties. The demands and grievances of the anti-regime youth movements that led the uprisings were state-centric, marginalizing traditional pan-Arab agendas and discourses, whether anti-imperialist, anti-Zionist or pan/unionist (Rahim, 2011). Post-revolutionary empowerment of Islamic movements (variants of the Muslim Brotherhood in Tunisia, Egypt, Morocco, Yemen and Syria) gave a new impetus to transnational Islam; while those movements sought to Islamize states, they were linked by trans-state networks that strengthened a pan-Islamic identity (Hinnebusch, 2015).

The hope and expectation for a democratized, pacific Middle East, where revolutions would bring regional autonomy, were unrealized, as the region became afflicted with sectarian violence, civil wars, regional struggle for power and failed states. In addition, Western intervention in the form of financial and material support, as well as airstrikes, not only escalated the violence, but, at least in Iraq and Syria, added to the civilian death toll. Syria was no longer the state Iraqi refugees fled to for security and protection; instead, Syrian refugees began to flood Iraq, which itself was starting to see new levels of conflict reminiscent of the 2006–2007 period, with renewed government mortar attacks, ISIS executions and American drone strikes. In the words of Hinnebusch, Iraq and Syria became 'battleground states', states where 'unconsolidated regimes and fragmented societies were highly vulnerable to spillover of the conflicts unleashed by uprisings in their neighbours' (Hinnebusch, 2015, p 277).

As the War on Terror expanded its military and ideological battlefronts, Iraq and Syria became the two states characterized by deconstruction and trans-state sectarianism. In Iraq the alienated Sunnis that had already formed the backbone of the insurgency became part of the new terror: the Islamic State. The deconstructed and debilitated Iraqi state lacked control over its territory, and could not provide security or deliver services. A decade after the invasion, 'the country was increasingly balkanised' (Hinnebusch, 2015, p 288). The Syrian uprising also led to the deconstruction of the Syrian state. 'The mostly Sunni protesters felt empowered by the rising influence of Sunni movements across the region and particularly that of the Muslim Brotherhood, whose Syrian branch was the historical alternative to the Ba'th regime' (Hinnebusch, 2015, p 288). The discourse of Islamist terror, as in Iraq, led to government violence, further radicalization and armed resistance. Like Iraq, Syria became a failed state made up of government-controlled areas, areas under the control of various insurgent groups and tribes, Kurdish-controlled areas and, finally, areas under the control of Islamist jihadists.

The start of 2014 saw the abandonment of HTS, the entrance of ISIS and the dominance of armed unmanned combat aerial vehicles. Over 3,000 Iraqi civilians would be killed in the next three years by coalition airstrikes and at least 22,500 by ISIS forces.

> For America, Britain, and the Western powers, the rise of ISIS and the caliphate is the ultimate disaster. Whatever they intended by their invasion of Iraq in 2003 and their efforts to unseat Assad in Syria since 2011, it was not to see the creation of a jihadi state spanning northern Iraq and Syria, run by a movement a hundred times bigger and

much better organized than the al-Qaeda of Osama bin Laden. (Cockburn, 2014, p 38)

There was short-sightedness or 'failure to see that, by supporting the armed uprising in Syria, they would inevitably destabilize Iraq and provoke a new round of its sectarian civil war' (Cockburn, 2014, p 73).

5

Iraq 2014–2017: Obama and the Banality of Killing

During Obama's presidency foreign policy aimed to maximize the protection of military personnel through the use of drones (Chamayou, 2015). Rather than maintain a costly military presence in the Middle East, the Obama administration used surrogate warfare as a means of preserving national interests (Krieg, 2016). The drone-killing programme was stepped up and targeted killing was normalized in no-boots battlefields. During his presidency over 3,000 Iraqi civilians were killed in airstrikes. The death toll doubled in 2014, going from nearly 10,000 in 2013 to over 20,000, remaining high in 2015 and 2016, as Table 5.1 shows, finally dropping to just over 13,000 in 2017, when 'the battle for Mosul' ended and ISIS in Iraq was declared defeated. As the War on Terror and the Arab Spring continued to claim victims, in Iraq through the brutality of ISIS and the coalition airstrikes, which resumed at the start of summer 2014, we were celebrating the triumph of our technology. 'Advancements in technology, improved capabilities for target discrimination, and limited risk of collateral damage made RPAs the weapon of choice for targeting High Value Individuals (HVI)' (Fowler, 2014, p 109).

Limited risk of collateral damage? As the British Parliament began to debate further intervention in Syria in September 2014, to 'dismantle and ultimately destroy what President Obama has rightly called "this network of death"' (House of Commons, 2014), the question of precision bombing could not be ignored. While the House did not yet endorse air strikes in Syria (that would come the following year), it did endorse the resuming of air strikes in Iraq:

> [The House] acknowledges the request of the Government
> of Iraq for international support to defend itself against the

Table 5.1: Civilian deaths by month 2014–2017

	Jan	Feb	Mar	Apr	May	Jun	Jul	Aug	Sep	Oct	Nov	Dec	Total
2014	1,097	972	1,029	1,037	1,100	4,088	1,580	3,340	1,474	1,738	1,436	1,327	**20,218**
2015	1,490	1,625	1,105	2,013	1,295	1,355	1,845	1,991	1,445	1,297	1,021	1,096	**17,578**
2016	1,374	1,258	1,459	1,192	1,276	1,405	1,280	1,375	935	1,970	1,738	1,131	**16,393**
2017	1,119	982	1,918	1,816	1,871	1,858	1,498	597	490	397	346	291	**13,183**

threat ISIL poses to Iraq and its citizens and the clear legal basis that this provides for action in Iraq; notes that this motion does not endorse UK air strikes in Syria as part of this campaign and any proposal to do so would be subject to a separate vote in Parliament; accordingly supports Her Majesty's Government, working with allies, in supporting the Government of Iraq in protecting civilians and restoring its territorial integrity, including the use of UK air strikes to support Iraqi, including Kurdish, security forces' efforts against ISIL in Iraq; notes that Her Majesty's Government will not deploy UK troops in ground combat operations; and offers its wholehearted support to the men and women of Her Majesty's armed forces. (House of Commons, 2014)

The precision of air strikes was already in question. By September 2014 over 15,000 Iraqi civilians had already been killed in coalition air strikes since the invasion, according to IBC records. Another thousand Iraqi civilians would be killed through air strikes by December 2015, when the House of Commons finally endorsed further air strikes, this time in Syria. The need to address the security of vulnerable persons in the continuing (though a little altered, in terms of strategy and tactics) War on Terror was urgent.

The words 'precision bombing' or 'precision-guided missiles' are used to make us think that British warplanes can go there and help the good guys, the so-called moderate rebels, without much, if any, collateral damage. To emphasize, this point is considered important not just because many people think it is morally wrong to cause civilian casualties, but also because the killing of civilians can be used as a recruitment tool for the terrorist groups (Gokay and Hamourtziadou, 2015).

How precise are these precision bombs? The word precision bombing (or smart bombing) refers to the aerial bombing of a target with some degree of accuracy, with the aim of limiting unintended, collateral damage. Such bombing allows fast high-flying aircraft to engage targets in urban environments with very little collateral damage. We have seen such weapons used by all major powers for the last 20 years, in Operation Desert Storm, Afghanistan, Kosovo, Libya, Iraq and currently Syria. Modern 'smart weapons', laser-guided munitions can be and are more effective in hitting the clearly identified targets. Yet the level of precision is still no more than 60%. During Operation Desert Storm, less than 60% of bombs hit their targets. In the US/NATO war on Kosovo, only 58 strikes were successful out of a total of 750.

During the 2003 invasion of Iraq, several US 'precision-guided' bombs managed to miss Iraq entirely, falling into Turkey and Iran (Gokay and Hamourtziadou, 2015).

'In Iraq for a year and three months there have been no reports of civilian casualties related to the strikes that Britain has taken. Our starting point is to avoid civilian casualties altogether', said Prime Minister David Cameron during the debate relating to 'ISIL in Syria' in the House of Commons, on 2 December 2015 (House of Commons, 2015). The sad truth was that in the past 'year and three months', that is, since August 2014, over 1,400 civilians had been killed as a result of those air strikes, according to the Iraq Body Count database.

Had the coalition air strikes at least reduced the overall killings of civilians? Since August 2014, according to IBC, more than 22,000 civilians were killed in Iraq, in mass executions, bombings, shootings, mortar attacks. 'The result of our intervention has not been the creation of a peaceful state, it has not defeated ISIS, it has not stopped the violent deaths of innocents, it has not abated sectarian conflicts, and it has not alleviated suffering. All violence has continued unabated, violence to which we added more than a thousand deaths in 15 months' (Gokay and Hamourtziadou, 2015).

After the coalition renewed its air strikes in Iraq, the country witnessed its largest bombing in years: 120 civilians were blown up by a suicide bomber on 17 July 2015, in Khan Bani Saad. The violent regime change brought anarchy, death and devastation, from which Iraq has been unable to recover. Overthrowing dictators in the name of freedom, and bombing in the name of peace has been our country's foreign policy for over a decade. The consequences of this policy have been plaguing not only the Middle East, but Europe as well: terrorist attacks, migrant crisis, anarchy, rising global insecurity. If our 'precision bombs' are supposed to free and secure, they are failing.

Airwars has been monitoring international airstrikes against the so-called Islamic State and others in Iraq and Syria. As a result of a total of 8,657 precision air strikes an estimated 23,000 ISIS members have been killed, and up to 2,104 civilians. Civilians like Mohannad Rezzo, a university professor, and his 17-year-old son, Najeeb; his sister-in-law Miyada and her 21-year-old daughter, Tuka. The four family members were killed when a coalition air strike flattened their home as they slept, on 21 September 2015 (Airwars, 2015). What if Najeeb was your son? Tuka your daughter? Miyada your wife? What if you were Mohannad Rezzo? Would you sacrifice your own life, or your family's lives to help defeat ISIS? It is easy for us who are far from the daily killings to justify the bombings, to dismiss or downplay fears of civilian casualties. It is easy also to downplay our role in the deaths of thousands. But what if the lives of those we love were at stake? What if it was our own country that was collapsing, together with our livelihoods? What might our perspective be then? Which would we consider the greater evil?

With the approach of the 11th anniversary of the invasion in March 2014, there were so many reasons to question just what had been achieved in Iraq. Peace? Democracy? Liberation?

The blurring of war and peace, tyranny and democracy, captivity and liberation

Eleven years after the invasion there were still questions about the decision to intervene in Iraq based on humanitarian claims. After the WMD fears were shown to have been unfounded, those that still justified the invasion increasingly stressed the humanitarian concerns, Saddam Hussein's cruel regime, internal insecurity, lack of freedom and violation of human rights, all of which not only justified the intervention, but also demanded it. Officially Iraq was 'at peace', officially a democracy and it had officially been 'liberated'. Yet the lines between peace and war, democracy and oppression, freedom and entrapment were blurred.

On 26 February 2003, four weeks before the invasion, George W. Bush stated: 'The nation of Iraq, with its proud heritage, abundant resources and skilled and educated people, is fully capable of moving toward democracy and living in freedom.' After the invasion, and after the war was officially over, in November 2003, he spoke of the American mission to spread democracy and freedom. 'Freedom can be the future of every nation', he said to the National Endowment for Democracy. 'The advance of freedom leads to peace' (The Baltimore Sun, 2003). In the UK, Prime Minister Tony Blair was also talking of a 'roadmap for peace', 'a larger global agenda – on poverty and sustainable development, on democracy and human rights, on the good governance of nations'. He spoke of his 'detestation of Saddam'. Before him, he said, Iraq was wealthy, but

> today it is impoverished, 60% of its population dependent on food aid. Thousands of children die needlessly every year from lack of food and medicine. Four million people out of a population of just over 20 million are in exile. The brutality of the repression – the death and torture camps, the barbaric prisons for political opponents, the

routine beatings for anyone or their families suspected of disloyalty are well documented. I recall a few weeks ago talking to an Iraqi exile and saying to her that I understood how grim it must be under the lash of Saddam. 'But you don't', she replied. 'You cannot. You do not know what it is like to live in perpetual fear.' And she is right. We take our freedom for granted. But imagine not to be able to speak or discuss or debate or even question the society you live in. To see friends and family taken away and never daring to complain. To suffer the humility of failing courage in face of pitiless terror. That is how the Iraqi people live. Leave Saddam in place and that is how they will continue to live. (*The Guardian*, 2003)

Years later, Blair had 'no regrets' over his decision, as he stated at the Chilcot Inquiry in January 2010. By then, over 110,000 civilians had been killed in Iraq. How peaceful was that? What sort of peace were the Iraqis living in? The daily conflict led to millions of Iraqis living as refugees, in poverty and disease, both internally and externally, in need, in fear, in uncertainty. The war-like conditions of their lives make a mockery of any claim to have brought them peace, security or a sense of safety and protection from violent death. War is not over for them. It has not been over since 20 March 2003, but has been allowed to continue and flourish, adding more corpses of men, women, children, poor, wealthy, young, old, professionals, unemployed, educated, illiterate, hopeful and hopeless alike. The bombers and the shooters, American, British, Iraqi or any other nationality, have killed people of all ages, social class and religion – almost indiscriminately.

Iraq is now as dangerous as it was in 2003, when our coalition planes dropped bombs every night, and no city, town or village is safe. No street, or building. No home, or school, or office. No mosque, no church and no market. It is what happens in war. To say that a war is being fought on Iraqi soil would be too simple. Since 2003 Iraq has, in fact, witnessed not one, but many types of war: pre-emptive, aggressive, civil, guerrilla, religious, proxy, as well as war of liberation.

The first was the 'pre-emptive' attack on Iraq by American and British coalition forces, to, it was claimed, gain a strategic advantage in an impending war before that attack (by Saddam Hussein) materialized. This military offensive was a war of aggression, an invasion, which was illegitimate and unauthorized by the UN Security Council and which gave the coalition forces control of and authority over Iraqi territory.

It was followed by eight years of occupation and resulted in thousands of Iraqis losing their lives.

Civil war followed the 2003 invasion, as the fragmented Iraqi society started to further divide and as the cracks deepened. Alliances started to form against perceived enemies, on the basis of religion, political affiliation and ideology. Organized groups struggled to gain power over others to achieve independence and, later, to change government policies or to overthrow it, as the grievances increased. It was in 2006 and 2007 that Iraq experienced its highest levels of sectarian violence, when the fighting between Sunni and Shia peaked. The insurgency was to last to the present day.

Iraqi insurgency has taken several forms. It has been a fight against the occupying forces, a fight against the Iraqi government, as well as a fight against another faction, or even against former members of the same faction, as in the case of Sunnis who sided with US forces in 2008, during the 'Sunni Awakening'. In short, those seen as terrorists, or collaborators, or both. Following the American withdrawal in December 2011, a renewed wave of sectarian and anti-government insurgency swept Iraq, raising fears of another civil war.

This asymmetric warfare has had several actors. There are perhaps as many as 40 different groups, but the major groups of armed insurgency have been:

- Baathists, supporters of Saddam Hussein's administration, including army or intelligence officers, whose ideology is a variant of pan-Arabism. Their goal was the restoration of the former Baathist government to power, and later joined forces with guerrilla organizations that opposed the US-led invasion. They are increasingly under Syrian influence.
- Iraqi nationalists, Iraqis who believe in Iraqi self-determination and advocate the country's territorial integrity. They also rejected the presence of the coalition forces and took up arms against them.
- Sunni Islamists, Salafi/Wahhabi 'jihadists'. Salafis advocate a return to a strict understanding of Islam and oppose any non-Muslim groups and influences, and regularly attack the Christian, Mandean and Yazidi communities of Iraq. They also attack Shia Muslims, whom they consider apostates.
- Shia militias, including the Iran-linked Badr Organization and the Mahdi Army. Shia Islamists are thought to be Iranian-run groups, influenced ideologically and armed by Iran. The Badr Organization was formed by the Iranian government to fight the Saddam Hussein-controlled Iraq during the Iraq–Iran War 1980–1988. Following

the 2003 invasion, they moved back to Iraq, from Iran, to fight alongside the US-led forces against other insurgents. They now support the al-Maliki government. The Mahdi Army was made up of supporters of Muqtada al-Sadr. They were the first serious opposition to the US-led coalition from the Shia community and fought against the occupying forces for the next five years. At his most popular, Al-Sadr had the support of 68% of Iraqis, according to a poll by the Iraqi Centre for Research and Strategic Studies, as he fought to liberate Iraq. The Mahdi Army was also thought to have been trained by Iran: 'There seems to have been a strategic decision taken sometime over late winter or early spring (of 2006) by Tehran, along with their partners in Lebanese Hezbollah, to provide more support to Sadr to increase pressure on the U.S.', according to a senior American intelligence official (*New York Times*, 2006).

• Foreign Islamist volunteers, including those often linked to al-Qaeda and largely driven by the Salafi/Wahhabi doctrine. They are mostly Arabs from neighbouring countries, primarily Syria and Saudi Arabia, Wahhabi fundamentalists who wish to assist the insurgency against Western forces and their allies in Iraq. They are fighting a jihad under the ideological umbrella of al-Qaeda and Ansar al-Islam.

The warring parties, including the US-led coalition forces and the current Iraqi government forces, have acted to and claimed to: liberate, occupy, subjugate, control, defeat, avenge and defend – territories (the Iraqi state, or parts of it), people (the Iraqis, or various religious and ethnic groups within Iraq) and values (Western, Muslim, democratic, national).

Tyranny and democracy

Iraq has had a democratically elected government since 2006. Nuri al-Maliki and his party were again elected in 2010 in yet another election taking place under occupation. Officially, Iraq is now a democracy, a far cry from the cruel dictatorship of Saddam Hussein, as echoed in the speeches of George W. Bush and Tony Blair, with its repression and brutality, torture, perpetual fear and terror. Or is it?

A tyranny is a cruel and oppressive government or rule, with unrestrained exercise of power and undue severity or harshness. Iraqi democracy has all the characteristics of a tyranny. Since 2006 thousands have been arrested, imprisoned and tortured by the regime. Protesters have been shot at and killed; any insurgency is met with shelling that kills insurgents as well as civilians; while political opponents have been persecuted. After the US army left Iraq, the nightly shelling and mortar attacks by the Iraqi army commenced, killing civilians in addition to the terrorist acts, which never ceased. In Ramadi and Fallujah, residents accused government forces of illegally detaining citizens, torturing and raping them, while doctors and NGO workers have accused the government of war crimes. The Iraqi army is reported to have prevented medical supplies from entering the cities.

On 14 February 2014, Nikolay Mladenov, UN Secretary-General Ban Ki-Moon's Special Representative for Iraq and Head of the United Nations Assistance Mission for Iraq, expressed great concern about the deteriorating security situation in Fallujah. 'More than 60,000 families have been displaced since the fighting broke out in the Anbar province', he said, and 'the displaced families are running out of food and drinking water and suffer from poor sanitation and limited access to health care' (Jamail, 2014). Angry protesters demanded 'an end to checkpoints', 'an end to unlawful home raids and detentions', and 'an end to gangsters and secret prisons'. It sounds like something out of the Saddam Hussein era and not like a democracy where the power lies with the people and the laws made to protect their rights, where there is equality and equal representation, where there is respect and where citizens are not subjected to torture and killing by the state.

It was this 'democracy' that Gilbert Achcar described in 2007:

> What Washington wants, and what it means by democracy, is the installation of governments under US control with democratic facades, and nothing more … The Bush administration used to say that a post invasion Iraq would serve as an attractive model in the region. Now, Iraq has definitely not become an appealing model in the Middle East; on the contrary, it has become an appalling model, because people now associate this democracy with deep insecurity and civil war. (Chomsky and Achcar, 2007, p 51)

Captivity and liberation

As has already been established, there is no peace in Iraq, but is there freedom?

An essential feature of liberty is the freedom from external restraint. 'The free man is the man who is not in irons, nor imprisoned in a gaol, nor terrorized like a slave by the fear of punishment', according to Helvetius (Berlin, 1958, p 122). The free citizen has freedom of movement, of religion, of speech; they are free from constraints put on their right to protest, to participate in government, to have their voices heard and their concerns recognized; finally free citizens are able to fulfil their potential.

In war-torn Iraq, where children are blown up on their way to school, where daily hunger torments nearly a third of the population, where fear rules in every town and every village, how free can people be? How free can people be when they fear for their lives, when they fear their neighbours, their rulers? How free can people be when they fear roadside bombs when driving, car bombs when shopping, gunfire and suicide bombers when stopping at checkpoints or attending a funeral? How free can people be when they fear mortar fire and shelling as they go to sleep? And how can people, children, fulfil their potential in such a state?

The Iraqis are captives of their own leaders, they are captives of their fragmented society and they are captives of the legacy left by American and British forces. Moreover, they are trapped in this captivity and are not allowed, by those in power and by those with the power of weapons – in Iraq, in the wider Middle East and in the West – to escape it. Ultimately, it is the interests that are being fought on Iraqi soil that hold the population captive.

'The core of security, the protection from harm, assumes a field of relationships, including a threatener, the threatened, the protector or means of protection, and the protected' (Fierke, 2007, p 46). In today's Iraq the blurring of the lines between war and peace, tyranny and democracy, freedom and oppression has resulted in confusion as to who is threatened, who is the threat, who is the protector and what the means of protection are. The relationships between protector and protected, threatener and threatened, are in disorder.

During 2014, control of Falluja would rest with two groups: ISIS (Islamic State of Iraq and Syria) and the Military Council for Tribal Revolutionaries, a mixture of tribal representatives and militants drawn from the Saddam-era army. They both tried to assume the role of protectors, yet both were feared by most residents, largely due to their brutality, which matched that of the government that arrested and tortured them routinely.

In Buhriz, in the province of Diyala, militants burnt homes and shops, targeting the families of security forces and those rejecting extremist organizations and cooperating with security forces. At the same time, those security forces continued the shelling of Falluja and Ramadi and the killing of civilians, under the direction of the government. The line between the saviours and the aggressors was again blurred, as it was in 2003, when our coalition forces came to Iraq as invaders and as liberators. As deep as the internal divisions have become since 2003, as much as the existing fault lines have been turned into trenches, Iraq remains unclear, undefined and deeply insecure, caught up in a perpetual war.

As ISIS entered Iraq and the Caliphate started to become a reality, Western efforts redoubled to help and protect the people of Iraq, this time invited to do so by the Iraqi government. As the body count rose and national, regional and global security in this War on Terror once again took top position on our security agenda, how was the *human* security of Iraqis assured by this support?

Support and its casualties

'We will have to re-think our strategy towards Syria; support the Iraqi Government', wrote Tony Blair (2014). Support: the shouldering of someone else's burden; the sharing of responsibility; the assistance and provision of what is needed to do better, to recover, to flourish. The casualties of the support provided by the coalition had reached nearly 141,000 dead civilians by 2014. They were the victims of our support. Direct victims, killed by our military, or indirect, killed by the insurgency and the terrorism that followed the invasion and occupation of Iraq, as well as the 'democratic elections' also held with our support. And, increasingly, direct victims of Iraqi government forces.

The US was to offer further support, by selling to the Iraqi government nearly $1 billion worth of warplanes, armoured vehicles and surveillance aerostats. The deal included 24 AT-6C Texan II light-attack aircraft, a turboprop plane manufactured by Beechcraft that has .50 calibre machine guns, advanced avionics and can carry precision-guided bombs. At the same time the US was offering support to Syrian insurgents, arranging their training in Qatar in the use of sophisticated weapons and fighting techniques. Support for the rebels in Syria, support for the government in neighbouring Iraq. Support that has resulted in thousands of innocents perishing every year, in both countries. 'There is no sensible policy for the West based on indifference', insisted Tony Blair, 'whether we like it or not'. So we must intervene and we must support, to be sensible. Why we should support the Iraqi government, yet not support the Syrian government, which is fighting the same insurgency, remains unexplained.

Blair was to continue to have no regrets over the decision to attack and occupy Iraq, claiming there were a few fairly 'good years' in Iraq, following the carnage of 2003–2007. Yet it never ceased in Iraq. The cracks never filled. The wounds never healed. Our continued support has been catastrophic, costing thousands of innocent lives and delivering the final blow to a divided society.

Iraq 2014: civilian deaths almost doubling

On 1 January 2015, IBC's annual report was published, having recorded the deaths of over 17,000 Iraq civilians in one year.

A total of 17,049 civilians were recorded killed in Iraq during 2014, roughly double the number recorded in 2013 (9,742), which in turn was roughly double the number of civilian deaths recorded in 2012 (4,622). During this period, not a single day passed without Iraqi civilians being killed. The year 2014, however, reflected an increase in violence to levels not seen since the worst years of 2006 and 2007. The rise of ISIS as a major force in the conflict, as well as the military responses by the Iraqi government and the re-entry of US and coalition air forces into the conflict, all contributed to the elevated civilian death tolls (Table 5.2).

While post-invasion Iraq has never been conflict-free, the years 2010–2012 had seen a relative reduction in levels of violence, with annual civilian death tolls ranging from 4,116 to 4,622, and the monthly rate ranging from a low of 218 to a high of 529. Still, even during those relatively stable three years, an average of two deadly bombings a day

Table 5.2: Civilian deaths by month 2012–2014

	2012	2013	2014
January	531	357	1,097
February	356	360	972
March	377	403	1,029
April	392	545	1,037
May	304	888	1,100
June	529	659	4,088
July	469	1,145	1,580
August	422	1,013	3,340
September	400	1,306	1,474
October	290	1,180	1,738
November	253	870	1,436
December	299	1,126	1,327
Totals	4,622	9,852	20,218

took place. 2013 almost paved the way for the explosion of violence witnessed in 2014, starting with June, when 4,088 civilians lost their lives, mainly as a result of summary executions by ISIS. A violent August (3,340) and October (1,738) followed, with figures higher than any monthly toll since 2007. At the end of 2014, the monthly average for the second half of the year stood at over 2,000. The June peak marked the beginning of the ISIS offensive, worsening an existing trend in rising civilian casualties.

Most civilians were killed in Baghdad, Ninewa, Salahuddin and Anbar provinces, which between them accounted for close to 80% of civilian deaths.

Baghdad	4,078 civilians killed
Anbar	3,797 civilians killed (half by Iraqi airstrikes)
Salahuddin	4,274 civilians killed (mostly by ISIS)
Ninewa	4,474 civilians killed (mostly by ISIS)

Among the 20,218 civilians recorded killed, many deaths were attributable to the actions of specific armed groups, while the perpetrators of many killings remain unknown.

Iraqi military airstrikes	1,821 civilians killed
ISIS attacks	6,667 civilians killed
Coalition airstrikes	338 civilians killed
Unidentified actors	11,392 civilians killed

Total cumulative reported deaths for the entire period 2003–2014 passed 200,000 during 2014. Over 154,000 (around 75%) of these were civilian.

By the end of 2014 ISIS had become a major player in Iraq. Public executions and decapitations, the massacre of the Yazidi community in Sinjar, the rape and selling of women as slaves in Mosul markets, all pointed to a new brutality on the ground, while renewed attacks from the air added to the human catastrophe. ISIS and the Iraqi army caused thousands of civilian deaths, while the international coalition, for the first time since US withdrawal three years previously, resumed killing Iraqi civilians. In 2014, largely in connection with the rise of ISIS and the military response to it, the death toll nearly doubled again, making 2014 the third most lethal for civilians (after 2006 and

2007) since the 2003 invasion. Since the invasion, the violent deaths of civilians have risen at times, fallen at times, but have never ceased.

Iraq in 2015: the moral chaos of war

Philosophers, historians and political theorists have tried to provide a set of ethical principles with which to assess war. From the time of Thucydides writing about the Peloponnesian war in the 5th century BC, to Augustine in the 5th century AD, to Thomas Aquinas in the 13th, to Kant's Just War Theory, to the 20th century UN Charter defining human rights and establishing international courts to try war criminals, to Michael Walzer's *Just and Unjust Wars*, war has not ceased and nor have attempts to justify military action, or to declare it immoral. Death and destruction are often justified, if a 'Just Cause' is offered. Most wars begin with moral clarity and a conviction of the right course of action, yet before long the ethics become 'situational', dependent upon a particular context and evaluated in its light.

The Iraq war back in 2003 started with moral clarity: terrorism must be fought; the people of Iraq must be liberated; democracy must prevail; human rights must be protected; the WMDs Saddam purportedly possessed had to be found and destroyed. After it became clear that none of those moral and political goals had been achieved, and with Iraqis continuing to live in daily terror, including new terrors hardly imaginable 12 years ago, the international community once again took action to try to achieve those desirable ends. A US-led coalition resumed aerial bombardment of Iraq in 2014, and during 2015 17,578 civilian deaths were recorded by IBC, 1,363 killed by the coalition. The lowest number of killings by the coalition was in March (32 civilians) and the highest in September (290 civilians).

Back in 2006–2007 we thought the situation could not get any worse, as thousands of civilians were being killed every month. What could be worse than the daily loss of life through bombings, air raids and execution-type killings? What could be worse than millions of people living as refugees in camps, hungry and in unsanitary conditions? What could be worse than fearing arrest and torture by your own military? What could be worse than foreign armies conducting air strikes over your cities?

During 2015 Iraq continued to experience old and new horrors, as people were sold, as they perished in refugee camps, as they died in hideous ways at the hand of ISIS (beheadings, crucifixions, electrocutions, immolations, drownings, shootings, stonings, hangings and bombings), at the hands of extremists, Sunni and Shia, at the hands of their own government and the international coalition.

The reasons given for their killing? Watching football, practising witchcraft/sorcery, objecting to a religious ruling, being gay, trying to flee, not swearing allegiance, collaborating with security forces and simply being in the wrong place. Those killed were people of all ages, from children to a 70-year-old woman who was burnt alive for refusing to pay ISIS members the money they demanded. A year after the international coalition started air strikes in Iraq, not only were civilians still killed at the same rate, but many areas in Anbar, Ninewa and Salahuddin were under ISIS control.

All parties involved in the violence declare some kind of moral justification:

- the people must be liberated;
- the terrorists must be killed;
- moral order must be restored;
- those 'against Islam' must die;
- the government must be in charge;
- peace and stability must be enforced;
- the threat must be removed.

What that threat is varies according to the ends of each party: the threat to liberty, the threat to democracy, the threat to Islamic values, the threat to humanity, the threat of terrorism, the threat of Western imperialism, the threat of human traffickers, the threat of fundamentalism. With all the reasons and justifications given, all of which continue to this day, Iraq has been witnessing a moral as well as a physical chaos.

Although 2015's death toll (17,578) was lower than 2014's (20,218), it was far from reverting to the earlier relatively low levels of 2010–2012, and belonged much more to the later, more catastrophic conditions which began in 2013. The level of deaths in 2015 was very similar to that in 2014. More Iraqi civilians were killed in 2015 than in the three years 2010, 2011 and 2012 combined. IBC's original figure for 2014 was 17,049, but that was later revised to 20,218. The increase of about 3,000 was partly due to newly emerging eyewitness accounts and discoveries of mass graves in areas where control was retaken from ISIS.

The provinces of Ninewa, Baghdad, Anbar, Salahuddin and Diyala accounted for 90% of all civilians killed in Iraq during 2015. These trends largely tracked the activities of ISIS, with large numbers of executions, and killings by coalition and Iraqi forces engaged in combat with them, including through air strikes and artillery. Baghdad's violence was not far behind Ninewa's or Anbar's, having remained at a consistently elevated level throughout the year. Diyala experienced the year's worst car bombing, which killed some 120 people on 17 July in Khan Bani Saad. Of the 17,578 civilians recorded killed, 1,532 were killed by Iraqi forces. The lowest death toll was in October (10 civilians), the highest was in May (358 civilians).

Since the new phase of the conflict began in June 2014, clashes between Iraqi military and allied militias on the one part and insurgent groups such as ISIS on the other continued to be common, including throughout 2015, causing thousands of deaths among these groups. Daily reporting on combatant casualties continued to be sketchy and sometimes questionable, however Iraqi and Kurdish officials began to release information on losses among their forces, reporting that over 4,000 Iraqi soldiers and allied militia were killed. Over 1,500 Peshmerga and Kurdish security force members were killed fighting ISIS in the north, mainly in Ninewa. Some 13,000 ISIS fighters were killed between June 2014 and December 2015.

Total reported deaths for the entire period 2003–2015 passed 240,000 during 2015. Over 170,000 (roughly 71%) of these were civilian.

On the 13th anniversary of the invasion, any assessment of the West's – and by now Iraq's – War on Terror could not ignore the casualties of the wars that have been fought on Iraqi ground as a result. My anniversary report stressed the impact of the wars that had, since the invasion, been fought in Iraq and acknowledged some of the casualties of those wars.

Iraq 2016: wars and casualties

Roman philosopher Cicero wrote that in times of arms, the laws fall silent. Men and women, soldiers and civilians, must do what they can to save themselves and others; what happens in war lies beyond moral judgement, beyond the law, according to some. Political realists argue that war is outside the sphere of morality, that the relations between self-seeking political entities are necessarily amoral. Yet men and women, historians, philosophers and politicians have talked and written about war in terms of right and wrong. Wars are called 'just', 'unjust', 'aggressive' or 'defensive'; there are 'wars of independence', 'freedom wars', 'civil wars', 'world wars', 'humanitarian wars', 'wars of resistance' and others, each with its own justification or condemnation explicit or implicit in its name or description. What receives less in-depth discussion are the casualties of war. Human casualties, war's first, principal and defining outcome; and also other casualties, including the conditions that make life good, safe and worth living.

Since March 2003 a number of wars have been fought in Iraq: aggressive, humanitarian, pre-emptive, civil; they have taken the form of air raids, shootings, executions, mortar attacks, IED explosions and car bombs; they have been fought by several parties, some Iraqi, others non-Iraqi, some occupying, others state-controlled, some insurgent, others terrorist. As many as 40 different groups have been active in Iraq, groups that have fought hard wars, with bombs, mortar shells, guns and knives. Though featured ever less frequently in Western media, hard wars are still fought every day on Iraqi soil. Although less prominently reported, they are still evident, for they are material and can be seen and photographed: the burnt-out car that concealed the bomb, the blackened building where the explosion happened, the blood staining the pavement, the wreckage of the market stall where the IED was planted, the bullet holes and shrapnel through concrete, through metal and through flesh. Incidents include the suicide bombing in Hilla, on 6 March 2016, when 60 civilians were killed; the execution of 10 children by ISIS members in Fallujah, on 23 January 2016; the killing of 29 civilians by air strikes over Mosul on 29 September 2015.

But there are other, non-material wars being fought: wars of words, wars of ideas, discourse wars. They are wars that speak of enemies, of threats, of hegemony and of counter-hegemony, of freedom and of enslavement; less obvious and not as photographable. Every hard, material war has its ideational counterpart, but discourse wars can take place without any shots being fired, or bombs dropped. The effects of such wars are felt much longer, even for generations after the gunfire has ceased. We still see them now, as the people of Iraq fill the streets in daily protests; as the government of Iraq allies itself with Trump's America and Khamenei's Iran; as militia continue to 'protect' and contain; as a global capitalist system facilitates the transition of transnational capital for the benefit of its liberal core, through the silencing of those that threaten it.

Old wars have continued to rage, while new wars have been declared and justified – wars of arms and wars of words. Old enemies remain, as new enemies are created.

The casualties of war are first and foremost measured in the loss of human life. In the period 20 March 2015–20 March 2016 almost 16,000 civilians lost their lives in Iraq. That brought the total civilian death toll to more than 174,000, with the total violent deaths (including combatants) up to 242,000. The dead were civilians,

Table 5.3: Iraq Body Count database entries

IBC page	Name or personal identifier	Age	Sex
a1912-kb3258	Khalid Jabar Ali	Adult	Male
a1912-xm3313	Hilal Berar	Adult	Male
a1912-ka3332	Hassan Ali Hassan	Adult	Male

Table 5.4: Iraq Body Count database entries

IBC page	Name or personal identifier	Age	Sex
a1916-hn3336	Miyada (Bassim's wife, Tuka's mother	Adult	Female
a1916-fe3379	Tuka Bassim Rezzo	21	Female
a1916-fs3321	Najeeb Mohannad Rezzo	17	Male
a1916-nx3340	Mohannad Rezzo	Adult	Male

Table 5.5: Iraq Body Count database entry

IBC page	Date	Name or identifier	Age	Sex	Location
a4007b-xz3192	11 Mar 2016	Fatima Samir	3	Female	Taza, southwest of Kirkuk

soldiers, insurgents, terrorists; they are Iraqi, American, British, Italian, Sunni, Shia, Yazidi, Kurdish; killed while fighting, shopping, walking, sleeping.

While it is not possible to name them all, as there are at least a dozen incidents a day where civilians lose their lives, victims of 2015 include Hasan Ali Hasan, Hilar Berar and Khalid Jabar Ali, Iraqi army officers, executed in Badush prison by ISIS members on 23 September 2015 (Table 5.3). They also include Mohannad Rezzo, Najeeb Mohannad Rezzo, Tuka Bassim Rezzo and Miyada, family members, killed in an airstrike on 23 September 2015 (Table 5.4). Another casualty was three-year-old Fatima Samir, who died in a chemical attack in Taza on 11 March 2016 (Table 5.5).

Moderation has been another casualty in this struggle for power. The wars have resulted in increased Muslim hostility, jihadism and radicalization. Hard-liners have prevailed, while moderates are marginalized and silenced. The prevalent narratives are now the hegemonic and the counter-hegemonic.

As the wars reached their 13th year and a generation was coming of age, childhood was another casualty. Millions of children have grown up in daily violence, bombings and shootings, lack of education, poverty and fear, witnessing violent death as part of a 'normal' life. Some have even been recruited as child soldiers, featured in propaganda videos as they carry out executions. What adults are those children growing up to be? How will the trauma of war affect their lives?

As the wars continue, more casualties become apparent. One of them is the Iraqi state, a failed state unable to control its territory and incapable of maintaining security. A state so internally divided and externally penetrated that any sovereignty it struggled to possess after 2003 now seems a delusion. It is a state that (even now in 2020) is characterized by sectarian conflict, economic debilitation and violence, a state reliant on external intervention and support.

A tragic casualty has been hope. The most frequently asked question on Iraq, for years, was 'How can the war end?' So many are still looking for the answer, the solution, the path to peace, yet even now no answer can be given. The continuing struggle for hegemony, the battle of interests and the battle of rival identities are slowly killing hope, along with thousands of innocents. As we reach more sad anniversaries, the question becomes 'How many more people, dreams and ideals will be sacrificed at the altar of this power struggle?' Whether moral, immoral or amoral, these wars have resulted in an endless cycle of violence, recriminations, enmity, suffering and death. The hard and discourse wars have reinforced each other, co-constituting a political reality that has prevented, rather than facilitated the search for solutions.

In 2016 the world's attention was once again on Fallujah, a city that had been at the heart of Iraq's insurgency since 2003. A new offensive against ISIS began in May, an assault that highlighted life and death in this city in fear of insurgents, of the state and of the occupying forces. Tahsin Ali Abbas al-Saadi died on the second day of the offensive. He was a war correspondent covering the latest battle of Fallujah, to liberate the city from Islamic State control. In the photo made public he was smiling, looking away from the camera, a scarf around his neck, his young face like those of thousands of other young Iraqis who have met violent death in battles, shelling, air strikes, explosions. He died on 23 May 2016, the day after Iraqi PM Haider Al-Abadi announced the start of the latest assault on Fallujah.

The Iraqi army's assault on Falluja began one of the biggest battles ever fought against the Islamic State, with the government backed by world powers, including the United States and Iran, determined to win back the first major Iraqi city that fell to the group in 2014. Fifty thousand people were thought to be trapped inside the city, with limited access to food, or healthcare. Those trying to flee were killed. Those who disobeyed the Islamic State were summarily executed, as were those suspected of collaborating with security forces. Others fell victim to their own state army. Entire families committed suicide, after suffering from starvation and disease:

> Other citizens confirmed that they are eating fodder for lunch. As for water, they receive it once per week on Monday and only for one hour. The citizens told Asharq Al-Awsat that suicide in their city is happening on a daily basis. They noted that starving Fallujah was preplanned as the government and coalition forces have been practicing mass punishment against the city, which resisted them during their invasion. (Asharq Al-Awsat, 2016)

Fallujah, a bastion of the Sunni insurgency that fought both the US occupation and the Shiite-led Baghdad government that took over after the fall of Saddam Hussein in 2003, is a city where US troops fought some of their biggest battles in 2003–2011, a city that has been subjected to almost daily shelling by Iraqi forces since 2012. Between 2012 and June 2016, 1,627 civilians were killed by Iraqi forces. While under the control of the Islamic State, 2014–2016, 1,200 were killed by Islamic State fighters. During the same period, 78 Iraqi civilians were killed by coalition air strikes in Fallujah. And this year 18 (5 of them children) were reported to have starved to death. Overall, since the start of the 'War on Terror' more than 7,000 civilians have been killed in Fallujah.

Tahsin Ali Abbas al-Saadi was covering the latest 'human catastrophe' in Fallujah, but he would have been a young boy back in 2003, when his country was first attacked and occupied, starting an insurgency that continues 13 years on. He would have been just a boy when the first battles of Fallujah were fought in 2004.

Local resentment was evident from the day US forces arrived on 23 April 2003. Five days later, on 28 April, a demonstration calling for the soldiers to leave, including from a school building they were occupying, turned violent. According to protesters, US soldiers fired on them without provocation, killing 17 people and wounding more than 70 (Human Rights Watch, 2003).

Participants in the demonstration stated that the protest was peaceful. They chanted slogans like 'God is great! Muhammad is his prophet!' and 'No to Saddam! No to the US!' A total of 17 persons were killed in the school shooting and 75 were wounded. Thirteen people were killed at the scene, according to a local doctor, and their corpses were brought to the hospital for collection. An additional four persons died in the hospital over the following days.

At a protest in town two days later, 30 April 2003, a US military convoy opened fire, killing three. According to Dr Ahmad Ghanim al-'Ali, two people were killed right away and a third died during transfer to the hospital in al-Ramadi. Sixteen people were wounded. (IBC's pages for these two incidents and the people killed in them, with name, age and other details where known: x066 and x069.)

Two battles of Fallujah in 2004

April 2004: 572–616 killed in siege of Fallujah

The First Battle of Fallujah, Operation Vigilant Resolve, was an operation to root out extremist elements of Fallujah and an act of retaliation for the killing of four US contractors in April 2004.

On 31 March 2004, Iraqi insurgents in Fallujah ambushed a convoy containing four American private military contractors from Blackwater USA. The four armed contractors were killed by machine gun fire and a grenade thrown through a window of their SUVs. A mob then set their bodies ablaze, and their corpses were dragged through the streets and hung.

On the night of 4 April 2004, American forces launched a major assault. Of the approximately 800 reported deaths, 616 were of civilians, with over 300 of these being women and children. As reporters were barred from entering the city during the siege, IBC's number of 572–616 civilians killed (IBC Entry x360) is based on reported cumulative totals, rather than a series of individual reports, providing only glimpses of the totality of events that took place inside Fallujah. One set of cumulative numbers was derived from growing hospital and NGO figures which had reached 600 by the 12th and ultimately passed 800, swelled by deaths during a series of nominal 'ceasefires' as well as by the gradual recovery of bodies buried in the rubble of destroyed buildings or in makeshift graves in private gardens. The first 600 deaths included a breakdown showing that 160 women and 141 children under the age of 12 were among the dead.

November 2004: 581–670 killed in nine neighbourhoods

The Second Battle of Fallujah, Operation *Al-Fajr* and Operation Phantom Fury, was a joint American, Iraqi and British offensive in November and December 2004.

In April, Fallujah had been defended by an estimated 1,500 insurgents. By November, it was estimated that the numbers had doubled. The assault began on 8 November 2004 and the fighting continued until 23 December 2004. In this battle, 581–670 civilians were killed in nine neighbourhoods of Fallujah.

The only well-sourced number to have appeared in mainstream outlets regarding these deaths comes from a report by Integrated Regional Information Networks (IRIN), a UN agency. The IRIN report is limited to bodies recovered 'from rubble where houses and shops stood', doesn't include earlier recoveries of bodies from open areas and streets, and is confined to 9 of 27 neighbourhoods (IRIN News, 2005). The IRIN figures were: 'more than 700' bodies recovered, of which over 550 'were women and children'; 'a very small number of men were found in these places and most were elderly'.

Following the withdrawal of US forces from Iraq, Anbar was under daily and nightly attacks by Iraqi forces, as the Shia PM tried to suppress the Sunni insurgency. The shelling of Fallujah and Ramadi caused thousands of civilian deaths, while the arrival of ISIS forces added a few more thousands.

Living in Fallujah in 2016 was living with insurgency, living with terrorism, living with air strikes and mortar attacks. It meant living with hunger and disease, in fear and despair. Living in Fallujah meant death in explosions, death by fire, by bullet and by water, by lack of care and lack of food. Death came to Tahsin Ali Abbas al-Saadi as he tried to report yet another battle; it came to 18-year-old Hussein Merhij al-'Ubaidi as he protested, in April 2003; it was death by fire for 15 men burnt to death for trying to escape Islamic State in April of this year, their bodies hanging hog-tied over the flames.

Irregular warfare: insurgency and terrorism

Who were those insurgents who made their base in Fallujah, and who were these terrorists? Were they 'Saddam's men'? Were they 'evil forces'? Were they 'anti-Western'? And what were they fighting for?

Certainly, their methods fall into the category of irregular warfare, as they used violence to achieve power, control and legitimacy, through unorthodox or unconventional approaches to warfare. The recent history of Fallujah has been one of resistance through insurgency and terrorism, resistance to the foreign occupier and to its subsequent allied Iraqi state. Groups looking to challenge the US and its allies know their ability to dominate militarily almost every operational environment: land, sea, air, even near-Earth space. One response to superior conventional military power is to challenge the established militaries using irregular forces, such as insurgents, terrorists and other paramilitary forces that can disperse, choose when, where and how to attack, then blend into the population.

After the fall of Baghdad in 2003, the US secretary of defense forbade the use of the term 'insurgency' to describe the violence, but spoke instead of 'pockets of resistance' in order to minimize the gravity of the threat and to create the impression of Western victory, in military and political terms, but also in terms of 'hearts and minds'. It was important to show the gratitude and collaboration of the Iraqis with the occupying forces; it was equally important to draw attention away from the insurgency and its causes: At its core, irregular warfare is based on and caused by grievances, such as ethnic or religious persecution, foreign occupation or domination, or other perceived injustice.

In Fallujah, and in Iraq more generally, the types of insurgency we have seen are anarchist, aiming to weaken and destroy the existing order, apocalyptic-utopian, looking to mete out religious rewards or punishments, and traditionalist, trying to change the existing order to serve traditional norms. Most groups adopt irregular warfare because other forms of political violence are unavailable to them. They favour indirect and asymmetrical approaches to erode an adversary's power, influence and will, but also to proselytize, coerce and intimidate. They try to gain supporters, both local and international, at the same time causing enough instability and spreading enough fear to prevent the local population from assisting their enemies. Any such attempts regularly result in public summary executions.

Guerrilla tactics are conducted to achieve operational and strategic goals, short- and long-term: to weaken the resolve of their political adversaries and cause the withdrawal of competing occupying or government forces. The subsequent vacuum is then filled by the insurgent political structure. The groups have targeted the civilian population and symbols associated with the state (police, military, government employees and buildings and so on) to spread fear and to demonstrate their power and reach.

Living and dying in Fallujah have changed little since 2003. The 'city of mosques' has been home to over 300,000, or roughly 1% of Iraq's population: civilians and militia, al-Qaeda and IS fighters, living, fighting, starving and perishing in violence, under siege or under sentence of death. As the latest offensive raged in 2016, it was feared that yet another human catastrophe would visit the city. Indeed 2016 would turn out to be yet another year of relentless violence in Iraq.

2016: another year of relentless violence

As another year came to an end, a year during which IBC recorded the violent deaths of 16,393 Iraqi civilians, IBC released its annual report detailing the violence and analyzing the latest security developments. The report revealed that 2016 had seen deadly violence continue to impact Iraqi civilians on a daily basis. This was most significant in Mosul and surrounding areas in Ninewa, which were under the control of ISIS. At the same time, the region was under constant bombardment by US coalition and Iraqi government forces seeking to oust ISIS. As for Baghdad, it continued to witness daily attacks by roadside bombs, shootings and executions, as well as occasional mass casualty bombings. During 2016 civilians in Iraq continued to lose their lives at levels similar to those that have characterized Iraq since mid-2013. Out of 16,393 civilians killed, 6,539 could be identified as men, women or children, based on information extracted from reports. Of this number,

- 5,008 (77%) were men;
- 729 (11%) were women;
- 802 (12%) were children.

The demographic was typical of the conflict, as shown in Tables 5.6–5.8. Death by execution (by ISIS) continued to account for the largest number of civilians killed. Executions accounted for the greatest number of men killed. Women were also killed most often by execution (Table 5.7). Deaths from air attacks and shelling also remained at high levels, killing 2,732 men, women and children (Table 5.8). Air attacks and shelling accounted for the highest number of deaths among children. The second highest cause of death among children was execution.

Large-scale attacks

2016 also witnessed a large-scale attack by ISIS, when bombs placed in a crowded Baghdad market on 3 July killed 324 civilians. The market in Karrada was full of shoppers, including entire families, preparing for Eid al-Fitr.

Table 5.6: Victim demographics

Year	Victim records	Identified as men, women, children	Of whom men	Of whom women	Of whom children
2014	20,218	9,797 (48%)	7,977 (81%)	1,003 (10%)	817 (8%)
2015	17,578	7,740 (44%)	6,062 (78%)	934 (12%)	744 (10%)
2016	16,393	6,539 (40%)	5,008 (77%)	729 (11%)	802 (12%)

Table 5.7: Executions 2016

January	666
February	607
March	700
April	465
May	413
June	626
July	354
August	757
September	314
October	1,336
November	731
December	269
Totals	**7,238**

Another large attack, this time a suicide bombing involving a fuel tanker, claimed 100 lives. It took place in Shomali village, southeast of Hilla, on 24 November, when a suicide bomber driving a tanker targeted buses carrying Muslim pilgrims returning from the religious rituals of Imam Hussein Arba'een in Karbala. The explosion took the lives of Iraqi civilians, but also Iranians, Afghan and Pakistani civilians.

Perhaps the most shocking attack this year, though not as large scale as the other two, was the suicide bombing that killed 17 children. On

Table 5.8: Airstrikes and shelling 2016

January	161
February	133
March	282
April	293
May	176
June	192
July	118
August	209
September	73
October	158
November	485
December	452
Totals	**2,732**

25 March an ISIS child recruit detonated his suicide belt at a trophy award ceremony in Alexandria, north of Hilla, taking the lives of children as young as 10.

The last attack highlighted a practice not previously seen in Iraq: the recruitment and indoctrination of children in institutionalized military training camps and the exploitation of child soldiers in combat and in suicide operations. During its Caliphate project, 2014–2017, the Islamic State recruited and indoctrinated thousands of young boys under the age of 14. The 'cubs' were 'recruited' locally, mostly in Mosul, Sinjar and surrounding towns and villages in Ninewa province, through a variety of coercive and cooperative methods, which included kidnapping and forced conscription.

The 'cubs' and the Islamic State

As an aspiring state, ISIS needed compliant and committed civilians, as well as soldiers. 'The group's ambitions, reflected in its battle cry *baqiya wa tatamadad* ("lasting and expanding"), go beyond territorial control and political power and extend to the notion of engineering a new society with distinct social and cultural mores' (Berti and Osete, 2015, p 49). ISIS does not only see children as expendable soldiers and suicide bomber, but also as an investment in its future society and crucial to the stability of the 'State' (Anderson, 2016). For this reason, the 'cubs' received military training, but also religious education, to ensure life-long commitment to the group's ideology. This terrorist indoctrination set them apart from the traditional enlistment of minors in purely military roles as 'child soldiers' (Vale, 2018). The punishment for disobedience or 'desertion' was death, the first instance of which we see on 28 February 2015, in Sinjar, when five boys were executed for 'deserting the fight against the Peshmerga' (IBC a1178). The greatest mass execution of child recruits took place in Mosul on 21 August 2015, when 15 boys were executed on accusations of collaborating with the Iraqi security forces and for fleeing battlefields in the Baaj area (IBC a2076).

Primarily through abductions and forced conscriptions from family homes, orphanages and schools, ISIS recruited thousands of boys under the age of 14 in Iraq. 'It is estimated that children under 14 account for over a third of the 6,800 Yazidis abducted in Sinjar in 2014, with a further 800–900 reported to have been kidnapped from Mosul' (Vale, 2018, p 3).

> The United Nations and Kurdish officials have estimated that a total of 400,000 Yazidis were living in Sinjar at the time of the attack. An extensive retrospective survey of those killed and kidnapped has calculated an approximate 9,900 deceased and 6,800 abducted, with children under 14 constituting 33.7% of those kidnapped. (Vale 2018, p 13)

The children were exposed to and expected to participate in acts of brutality, including the execution of men disloyal to the Islamic State, thus 'normalizing' violence and death. The boys would watch stonings, beheadings and amputations as a means to serve the Caliphate. 'Such emotional "reprogramming" culminates in children's acceptance of violence as a "natural" way of life, and facilitates the progression for children to conduct violence themselves as combatants, torturers and executioners' (Vale, 2018, p 3). Eventually, they would be expected to carry out those acts themselves, when ordered to do so. If they disobeyed, they faced the same punishment.

Through 'positive governance', ISIS were able to exploit the poverty, deprivation, unemployment and illiteracy of the Iraqi population, which had still not recovered from the wars resulting from the invasion and occupation of the country, to start education programmes based on its particular curriculum and populating classrooms that had been empty for years. Their ideology was to become 'knowledge' for more than 100,000 Iraqi children in over 1,300 recruitment centres masquerading as schools. Similar to the sexual grooming of children:

> Symbols of group membership – including uniforms, weapons and gifts – played on local children's financial motivations for enlistment and fuelled peer pressure to conform to and join the privileged 'in-group'. Combining rewards of status and camaraderie, the group exploited children's desire for a sense of purpose and belonging. Through social bonding, physical adventure and ideological purification, with roles for even the youngest recruits, IS sent a clear message that it valued Syria and Iraq's children. (Vale, 2018, p 4)

Trusted figures in the form of 'hypermasculine' fighters emerged, becoming role models for the boys. Given the mounting death toll and the living conditions, ISIS was also able to use the boys' anger and desire for aggression and revenge, to punish those responsible and to build a new world free of the enemies of Islam. The radicalization of children ensured in-group security, if successful. By fulfilling the children's emotional needs and by constructing a convincing moral narrative (in the good-versus-evil manner we saw in Chapter 1), ISIS hoped to create loyal and committed warriors. It also integrated violence into everyday life in the areas it controlled.

The group professed radical ideological and moral opposition to anything 'Western', building a narrative that not only expressed grievances of disenfranchised Muslims, but also provided moral and ideological explanations of the War on Terror similar to those of the West: the moral Muslims were fighting against an immoral Western culture and against a corrupt (by Western values) Muslim state/region. This explanation combined the clash of civilizations argument and the good-versus-evil narrative, much in the way securitizing actors in the West have done. It was with this narrative that ISIS hoped to educate its children. Isn't that what states do?

When the Islamic State first appeared on the global arena, much was said about its right (or lack of right) to call itself a state and our refusal to use the term when referring to the terrorist group, choosing the word 'Daesh' instead, so as to not give them any legitimacy, credibility or status. It was the latest 'new' actor to enter the conflict, although the violence it brought was not new, as the violence against the civilian population had not ceased, even for one day, since 'Shock and Awe'.

When the Islamic State joined the battleground in Iraq, it was closely followed by the returning US and UK air forces.

The new group called itself a state. It was, at least, aspiring to be a state. It certainly believed itself to be as entitled as the Iraqi state, as entitled as the American state, as entitled as the UK and also France, Jordan, Canada, the Gulf states and others, entitled and justified to be there, to seek power, to pursue its own interests and to kill for them.

How entitled were they, any of them, to be there, to seek power, to pursue their own interests and to kill?

International boundaries are a distinctive social relation between human beings organized as sovereign states. And just like the states themselves, the boundaries between them are social constructions: they can be instituted, they can be defended, they can be disregarded, they can be violated, they can be dismantled, they can be moved, and their significance and uses can be changed. The map of Europe of 1400 was different from that of 1700, which was again different from the map of the present time (Jackson, 1998, p 157).

If boundaries are violated, moved, defended and created all the time, why wouldn't the Islamic State believe it had the right to be there, challenging those boundaries and trying to create new ones, by drawing a line around themselves and constituting a sovereign state? Why wouldn't they believe they had the right to pursue their lives in accordance with their own ideas, free from external intervention, in the territory they demarcate as their own? Much like Western states have done for centuries, in Europe, in the Americas, and in much of the colonized world – always with heavy civilian casualties. The fact that the Islamic State is currently a non-state, a terrorist group, is used to contrast it with those who kill legitimately – the states. In international law state violence can be legal, whereas non-state violence cannot.

In other words, 'state' is good, 'state' is legal, while 'non-state' is bad and illegal. History, however, indicates that the bloodiest wars with the highest death toll, in terms of soldiers and civilians, in the last 100 years, have been fought by states. World War II, in the space of six years, led to the deaths of an estimated 20,000,000 people. A state used nuclear power not only to kill, but also to maim and make future generations suffer the effects of the atom bomb; another state executed millions of civilians in concentration camps; yet another state committed atrocities using chemical and biological weapons, used women as sex slaves, tortured and buried people alive.

Words are not neutral. Language helps make the world; it affects our cognition and our emotions. It makes us perceive a 'hero' or a 'terrorist'; it helps us describe an act as 'legal', another as 'illegal', to express our approval or disapproval of it, to declare it 'right' or 'wrong'. Language is used to create a sense of outrage, fear, pride, compassion. Worlds and realities are constantly being constructed, where state violence appears reasonable and non-state violence does not, where good battles evil, where a 'war on terror' appears rational and imperative.

The Islamic State uses similar tactics when it attacks and destroys places of religious and cultural significance in Iraq that do not conform to its 'takfiri' doctrine, when it brands others as apostates and kills those who are 'bad' and enemies of its interests. It justifies its violence using religious language and divine entitlement. Its killings are done according to 'God's will', the public beheadings of Westerners are the fault of the West.

The question of legitimacy and illegitimacy, when it comes to the use of force, is not one that has an easy answer. Everyone claims to be justified in using their forces and weapons and all sides kill civilians – states and non-states; Iraq, the US, the UK, the IS, al-Qaeda, the Mahdi Army and many others over the years. The principle of universality is never entertained, as each side believes it and only it is justified in its actions; it and only it has been provoked to act in this way; it and only it has the right to strike, to kill, to defend, or to change the status quo. To apply the same logic to the other side is inconceivable.

In the midst of all the legitimations, the justifications and divine references, the innocents are blown up and gunned down – young, old, infant, male and female. When looking for those barbarians, we may want to remember that we are all capable of barbarism, the legal and the civilized included.

Every day the reports from Iraq continue to come in: '13 Bodies found dumped in a farm south of Tikrit', 'Iraqi journalist executed in Mosul', '39 citizens killed, injured in Kadhmiya suicide bombing', '17 Civilians killed by missile strikes in the north and east of Tikrit'. A journalist, an activist, a grandmother with her grandchildren, brothers, husbands and wives, police officers, the families of militia, farmers as they work, women as they shop. People like you. People like us. But whose blood is being spilt on someone else's battlefield, on someone else's path to empire.

Generation: war; Iraq 2017

'The battle of peace has to be fought on two fronts. The first is the security where victory spells freedom from fear. The second is the economic and social front where victory means freedom from want. Only victory on both fronts can assure the world of an enduring peace', said Edward Stettinius Jr, US Secretary of State in June 1945 (cited in UNDP, 1994, p 3). It was very much in the spirit of the UN, the spirit of cooperation to work towards peace and prosperity. It was only under those conditions, of peace and prosperity, that security was going to be achieved, in any country, in any community, in any area of human life. How was security in Iraq in 2017?

While the *invasion* of Iraq was 15 years before, the post-invasion *war* in Iraq continues to this day. Even the war's quietest months have been punctuated by moments of mass horror, and barely a day has passed without reports of civilians being shot or blown up. Despite any number of official declarations, there has been no 'turning point' towards peace, no 'mission accomplished' for 'Operation Iraqi Freedom'.

So it was that, 15 years after the invasion, with military battles having wrested Falluja and Mosul from ISIS's grip, and a democratically elected government in place, Iraqis still had good reason to be afraid. ISIS was not and is not the only threat to civilian lives in Iraq: were it to vanish entirely, violence against civilians would not vanish with it.

In 2017 there was an increase in kidnappings, along with all the family/community dread and anguish that each abduction involved. And even as longstanding perpetrators of lawless violence were fought off, new ones emerged. On 9 February 2018, Al-Baghdadiya reported:

> Human Rights Watch revealed on Friday new evidence that Kurdish Asayish forces carried out mass executions of detainees from a militant organization, calling it a war crime. 'There is new evidence that members of the al-Asayish branch in the west of the Tigris carried out mass executions against alleged al-Qa'ida militants in detention, which constitutes a war crime', the organization said in a report, seen by al-Baghdadiya. (Al-Baghdadiya, 2018)

The Peshmerga forces were holding the men, including Iraqis and foreigners, in a school in the village of Sahl al-Malahah, 70 kilometers north-west of Mosul, Neighboring Zammar, where they were executed. The evidence suggests that the Asayish forces collectively executed people suspected of belonging to Da'esh night after night for a week, meaning that they may have killed dozens or hundreds of male detainees (Middle East deputy director of Human Rights Watch, Lama Fakih, in Al-Baghdadiya, 2018).

Personal loss, the desire for retribution and numerous grievances ensured that multiple killings continued, unlawful killings as well as those sanctioned by the state. Deeply felt grievances related to ethnic and religious persecution and in them we saw the toxic residues of military occupation and foreign domination, economic disparity, political and judicial corruption. As state forces battled non-state forces, as insurgent groups battled each other and as militiaman coerced populations, civilians continued to be killed by all sides.

Just as freedom from fear remained perpetually over the horizon, so did freedom from want. Unsurprisingly, 2017 saw a rise in suicides in Iraq. The *Baghdad Post* noted on 4 March 2018: 'Not a day passes but new cases of suicide are recorded in various Iraqi provinces, in light of the difficult living conditions and high rates of poverty and unemployment, as a result of the failed government policies' (*Baghdad Post*, 2018).

An entire generation of Iraqi children has known little other than life in a country riven by violence, fear, hopelessness, internal displacement and poverty. All around them, the war's fearful legacy persists. The battle of Mosul may be over, but bodies are still being pulled from the rubble, the unavoidable and predictable outcome of the use of air- and ground-launched explosive weapons in populated areas. During the first seven months of 2017, until the Battle of Mosul ended, ISIS was contained and coalition airstrikes ceased, the monthly civilian death toll recorded by IBC averaged 1,580; in the seven months thereafter, it averaged 430. This lower monthly figure resembled those of the least-violent post-invasion period, 2009–2012. It was from this relative calm that ISIS burst bloodily onto the scene, and those monthly figures climbed to higher totals than seen even during the worst months of the occupation.

As the Iraqi media continued to report the violence daily, they became the only sources to provide any substantial amount of that consistent, incident-by-incident, person-by-person detail which humanizes and respects each victim in their individuality, and brings the circumstances of their death into focus. Western publics seem to be becoming ever more inured and desensitized to Iraqi suffering, in part thanks to the creeping 'normality' of the relentless daily death toll, as a generation in Iraq is growing up deprived of basic security or well-grounded hope, a generation of the orphaned and dispossessed.

At the 15-year mark of the invasion, as a generation of Iraqis born at the birth of the War on Terror was coming of age, the deaths of 193,000 civilians had been recorded. My own thoughts were with those whose deaths I had been documenting over the years, those men, women and children whose deaths may not have touched us here in the West, but whose lives had mattered as much as those of any other human being.

Each grave contains a death and bears witness to a life. The remains of the dead: their physical remains and what remains of their identity. Those who knew them will remember them and even those who did not know them will come to know something about who they were: their names, their affiliations, their faces. They are all elements of a person's identity, as each person is identified both as an individual and as a member of a group – familial, ethnic, religious, professional – through their name and title.

In the course of their lives, people may change their name to mark a change in identity or in line with local and traditional norms. A 'Miss' may become a 'Mrs', her husband's family name replacing her maiden name; a woman be named 'the wife of' the man she married, or she (and also he) become the 'the mother of' (or 'the father of') their eldest son; a fitting nickname may be gladly accepted for common and life-long use. Our names are at the core of who we are and of who we are perceived to be by others. When we die, we leave behind something of ourselves through our name, through the recollection of all that name meant. Nobody's name, identity, life, is of less value than another's. And nobody's loss is any easier to bear by those who knew and cared for them, those who will forever mourn their passing.

To remember and honour the dead is not only important for families; it is also important for nations. Nations have always commemorated their dead by making lists of those who gave their lives, or lost their lives, as members of that nation, and by building war memorials to honour them for their sacrifice. The British military has ensured those British soldiers who gave their lives in Iraq are not forgotten. A list of the 179 soldiers who died there can be found easily: Names, titles, the manner of their death, their images – some smiling, others serious, some holding a child that will have to grow up without the love of a parent.

Private Paul Lowe, just 19 years old, was killed on 4 November 2004 in Falluja, one of three soldiers killed in a suicide car-bomb attack. He was described as a keen footballer and keen volunteer who loved army life, but, just before his death, as 'just a boy who wanted to come home':

> days before he died, his family said, he told his mother, Helen, that he had had enough of Iraq and wanted to come home. He joined the regiment straight from Beath High School in Cowdenbeath, aged 16, to become a drummer

in the pipe band and play at the Edinburgh Military Tattoo.
(Kelbie, 2004)

Fusilier Kelan Turrington was even younger when he was killed in
action in Basra, on 6 April 2003. He was just 18 years old. Two days
after his death, the Ministry of Defence expressed the following:

> Our thoughts and prayers are with his family at this
> very difficult time. Fusilier Turrington was awarded a
> posthumous Mention in Despatches in the Operational
> Honours published on 31 October 2003 in recognition of
> the gallantry he displayed during the assault on an enemy
> trench that cost him his life. (Ministry of Defence, 2003)

Our victims of terrorism are also commemorated, those civilians
who tragically died as they went about their lives, those innocents
who met an untimely and violent end. Police named all 52 known
victims of the London bombers. Some families released statements,
paying tribute to loved ones lost in the attacks, as the site explains.
More names and photographs. More smiling faces. Some young and
bright-eyed.

Phil Beer, 22, from Borehamwood, Herts, was on the underground
with friend Patrick Barnes when the explosion struck between King's
Cross and Russell Square on 7 July 2005. His family said Mr Beer,
a hairdresser, was a 'fun-loving and colourful' character who had
red and black hair, a lip stud and a tattoo of a Celtic dragon on his
arm. Mr Beer's family requested that mourners wear bright colours
on the day of his funeral to reflect his personality. In a statement,
they said: 'His loss has left us feeling very empty and we miss his
infectious loud laugh' (BBC, 2005). A wonderful tribute to a son.
A loss indeed.

It is hard not to feel the pain of the loss of those lives. It is hard to
stay dry-eyed as you look at those names and those faces.

A memorial that fills one with both horror and a sense of loss is
the 9/11 Memorial in New York. The 2,983 names of the men,
women and children killed in the attacks of 11 September 2001, and
26 February 1993, are inscribed into bronze parapets surrounding the
twin memorial pools, located in the footprints of the Twin Towers.
Not a single name is missing.

The public recording of the deaths of civilians in Iraq has been
a different story, with only 1 in 12 of the deaths in the Iraq Body
Count database recorded with identifying details. The larger the

incident in which people are killed, the rarer it is for their names to be included, especially all their names. Rarest of all is that the loss of these Iraqi lives was illuminated by stories of their hopes and dreams, and who they were. Stories describing Iraqi victims in life, as well as the circumstances of their death, rarely appear in the Western and global media. The scale and the relentless nature of Iraq's violence have made it very difficult for journalists and others to report and record civilian deaths in appropriately humanizing detail. Every day more are added to this long list of violent deaths by guns, bombs and beheadings in a country that remains a battlefield. Most reports describe victims simply as 'policeman' or 'lorry driver'; of yet others – some two thirds of the victims in the IBC database – the public record contains nothing at all about the individual who lost their life, except that they were non-combatant, usually going about their ordinary daily business, and met a violent and premature death at the hands of others. Clearly their deaths must be counted, and matter, as much as the deaths of those who are better known. Their loss is largely represented in numbers.

Yet numbers alone cannot possibly represent human lives. Knowing how many have died cannot be enough without also knowing who has died, because figures cannot adequately communicate the loss of individuals. For many countries, public casualty reporting and recording often consists solely of statistics, of numbers. A poor representation of what is lost.

Whose children were they? Whose parents? How many miss them? What did they like to do? What kind of people were they? Did they have a talent?

Will we in the West directly and indirectly involved in the dissolution of the Iraqi state ever truly know what has been lost? Will we remember? Will the Iraqis know who all those people were whose blood was spilt in their streets? Will the identities of the thousands found as 'bodies in mass graves' be known?

The commemoration of a life lost must not have ethnicity, religion, colour, or monetary value. It cannot be reserved for the European, for the American, for the white, for the Christian, for the powerful, or for the well-to-do. It has to include the non-white, the poor, the Asian, the African, the illiterate, the beggar boy blown up, the elderly woman shot on her way to market and the Yazidi girl beheaded for not wearing her scarf. The commemoration of a life must know no boundaries or restrictions.

We all want to be remembered; we all want our death to be a loss to someone, just as much as we want our lives to have mattered.

Epilogue: Iraq and Its Casualties Today

> The original sin of the Iraq war was, perhaps, the neo-con belief that the invasion would be welcomed as liberation and a pro-US 'democracy' readily imposed.
>
> Hinnebusch, 2015, p 262

On 2 January 2020, a US airstrike killed a high-profile commander of Iran's secretive Quds Force, Qassim Suleimani, a commander of Iran's military forces in Iraq, Syria, Lebanon and elsewhere in the Middle East. Another man, Abu Mahdi al-Muhandis, deputy of the militias known as the Popular Mobilization Units and a close adviser to Suleimani, was also killed in the airstrike near Baghdad's airport. Al-Muhandis and Suleimani were killed when their vehicle was hit on the road to the airport. The Popular Mobilization had been fighting Islamic State forces alongside Iraqi government forces for years, and had increasingly come under attack themselves, with dozens of their fighters losing their lives in Iraq every year. Three days before the assassination of Al-Muhandis and Suleimani, 25 Popular Mobilization fighters had been killed by a US airstrike in Western Anbar. On 30 December 2019, Al-Baghdadiya reported the mass killing:

> The Popular Mobilization Directorate announced, on Monday, the outcome of the American bombing of the crowd camp, which rose to 25 dead and 51 wounded. 'The death toll from the martyrs and the wounded as a result of the American aggression that targeted the locations of the Popular Mobilization Forces in western Anbar is 25 dead and 51 wounded', Rabiawi said in a statement to the Popular Mobilization website. He added, 'The

number of martyrs can be increased due to the presence of wounded people in critical condition and severe injuries'. (Al-Baghdadiya, 2019)

Suleimani's Quds Force was a division of Iran's Revolutionary Guard, widely believed to support many Iran-backed terrorist groups, such as Hezbollah. This strike was aimed at deterring future Iranian attack plans, the Defence Department claimed. 'The United States will continue to take all necessary action to protect our people and our interests wherever they are around the world' (BBC, 2020).

This book has looked at what those interests are and what their protection has meant for the Iraqis. After nearly two decades of war, Iraq has experienced its least violent year: 17 years after the invasion, during 2019 2,392 civilian deaths were recorded by Iraq Body Count. In its worst year, 2006, Iraq had witnessed the violent deaths of more than 29,500 civilians. However, the monthly and yearly totals, assembled after the painstaking daily task of extracting the data from hundreds of reports, betray the true magnitude and impact of the war on Iraqi civilians.

The figures in Table 6.1 show that in 2019 the death toll was lower than any other year since the invasion. October witnessed the highest toll, with 361 killed; August the lowest, at 93. However, the killings were, yet again, almost daily, a fact that demonstrates the nature of the security situation in the country more than the actual figure – high or low. Of the 2,392 civilians killed during 2019, 92 were children. The previous year 110 Iraqi children had been killed.

Overall the violent deaths of 7,300 Iraqi children have been recorded by IBC. The number of women killed in Iraq since the invasion is a little higher, at around 9,000 identified as female in reports. The staggering figure of 190,000, however, represents the biggest victims of this war: Iraqi men.

The greatest perpetrators of violence in 2019 were government forces, which killed around 500 protesters during May, September, October and November. Another 25 protesters were massacred by a group of gunmen in Baghdad on 6 December. Airstrikes that killed civilians were few, with nine losing their lives in Turkish and US airstrikes:

25 January, four were killed by Turkish strikes in Dohuk;
24 March, one child was killed by US strikes in Oudan;
26 September, one was killed when Turkish planes struck in Dohuk;
4 November, three more civilians were killed in another Turkish airstrike in Sinjar.

Table 6.1: Civilian deaths by month 2003–2019

	Jan	Feb	Mar	Apr	May	Jun	Jul	Aug	Sep	Oct	Nov	Dec	
2003	3	2	3,977	3,438	545	597	646	833	566	515	487	524	12,133
2004	610	663	1,004	1,303	655	910	834	878	1,042	1,033	1,676	1,129	11,737
2005	1,222	1,297	905	1,145	1,396	1,347	1,536	2,352	1,444	1,311	1,487	1,141	16,583
2006	1,546	1,579	1,957	1,805	2,279	2,594	3,298	2,865	2,567	3,041	3,095	2,900	29,526
2007	3,035	2,680	2,728	2,573	2,854	2,219	2,702	2,483	1,391	1,326	1,124	997	26,112
2008	861	1,093	1,669	1,317	915	755	640	704	612	594	540	586	10,286
2009	372	409	438	590	428	564	431	653	352	441	226	478	5,382
2010	267	305	336	385	387	385	488	520	254	315	307	218	4,167
2011	389	254	311	289	381	386	308	401	397	366	288	392	4,162
2012	531	356	377	392	304	529	469	422	400	290	253	299	4,622
2013	357	360	403	545	888	659	1,145	1,013	1,306	1,180	870	1,126	9,852
2014	1,097	972	1,029	1,037	1,100	4,088	1,580	3,340	1,474	1,738	1,436	1,327	20,218
2015	1,490	1,625	1,105	2,013	1,295	1,355	1,845	1,991	1,445	1,297	1,021	1,096	17,578
2016	1,374	1,258	1,459	1,192	1,276	1,405	1,280	1,375	935	1,970	1,738	1,131	16,393
2017	1,119	982	1,918	1,816	1,871	1,858	1,498	597	490	397	346	291	13,183
2018	474	410	402	303	229	209	230	201	241	305	160	155	3,319
2019	323	271	123	140	166	130	145	93	151	361	274	215	2,392

The government of Iraq, a weak and vulnerable state, is still unable or unwilling to provide security and protection to its population from threats – internal and external.

The vast majority of deaths recorded were direct deaths from conflict violence, but many were also from violence and crimes resulting from the breakdown in security: robberies, kidnappings for extortion, executions. The perpetrators of those acts, increasingly Islamic State members, were committing criminal acts and associated violence in order to finance or otherwise support their conflict activities and objectives.

Anti-government protests have erupted on a regular basis in Iraq since 2015, but the protests of September–December 2019 are the largest and bloodiest since the overthrow of Saddam Hussein. For four months, protesters flooded the streets of Baghdad and towns and cities across the south of the country to demand jobs, basic services and an end to corruption. Hundreds of young people have been killed so far and thousands of others wounded in clashes with security forces. In a country rich in oil, Iraqis are without clean water and electricity, suffering in areas of both food and energy security. There is widespread poverty and high levels of unemployment. The young protesters, most of them 15–25 years old, demand the end of government corruption, lack of opportunity and deprivation, all of which leave them with dismal prospects. Regime security is at such low levels that many in Iraq are now longing for the days the dictator was controlling every aspect of life in Iraq. A 'Saddam nostalgia' is particularly noticeable among young people.

The protesters demand a country free of rule by small corrupt elites that maintain their power through patronage and sectarian identity; they demand an end to both US and Iranian interference in their country and control of the ruling elites; and they demand a new government that will provide security to the citizens and foster economic growth and opportunities. The demonstrations outside the American and Iranian embassies, during which thousands of people are prepared to lose their lives, show the determination of the protesters to have 'a true homeland' and to demand their right to 'a political process that is free from foreign malign influence and the corruption that both comes with it and fuels it' (Davison and Psaledakis, 2019).

The overwhelming motivations of the people who took to the streets in Iraq were the low standards of living, dismal economic and employment conditions, inefficient welfare state and food shortages, all of which can be seen in those 'Arab Spring' countries that witnessed serious protest movements from 2011: Tunisia, Egypt, Libya, Syria and others. During the previous couple of decades, these states in the Middle East and North Africa experienced economic transformation, imposed by the IMF and the World Bank, away from the state-command economy model of 'Arab Socialism' of the 1960s and 1970s, and towards market-dominated neoliberal capitalism in the 1980s and 1990s. Through the guidance and assistance of the IMF and the World Bank, the MENA region pursued neoliberal economic policies which led to great income inequalities and growing corruption.

The 2003 invasion of Iraq resulted in the breakdown of security, infrastructure and public health, as well as the deaths of hundreds of thousands of people, mostly civilians. The failure to make the security of Iraqis a priority; the imposition of puppet governments of mostly exiles; the mass unemployment; the flooding of the country with foreign mercenaries and contractors; the near-absence of post-war reconstruction; the brutal approach to counterinsurgency; the human rights abuses, indiscriminate use of force, food blockades, detention centres and humiliation; the widespread corruption and war profiteering not only convinced Iraqis that the 'liberators' were, in fact, occupiers, but also ensured that human security was neither a consideration nor an outcome.

The UN Development Programme's categories of human security (UNDP, 1994, pp 25–33) are economic security (an assured income), food security (access to food), health security (access to healthcare and protection against diseases), personal security (addressing threats from physical violence), community security (a sense of belonging and identity rooted in shared values) and political security (being governed in a way that protects basic human rights). As Iraq's power, wealth and collective purpose reached total collapse, security in all those areas was no longer possible. Moreover, the Sunni–Shia civil war spilled over to the wider region, resulting in the deconstruction of neighbouring states and the deaths of thousands more. Rather than empower Iraq, the War on Terror made Iraq weaker and more vulnerable. Iraq's vulnerability allowed first al-Qaeda and then ISIS to seize power and commit atrocities within its proclaimed 'caliphate', further violating the human rights of Iraqi civilians.

This book has narrated the witnessing of state collapse and its consequences by a casualty recorder. It has done so through discussions on the neoliberal system's effect on Iraq's security, on military interventions and the Western control paradigm, on individual and community trauma, on the value of Iraqi lives through compensation claims, on nation building and the human terrain project. It has asked questions around leadership and hegemony, the vulnerability of weak states, conceptions of 'winning' and 'losing', regime, energy, political and societal security, as well as the relationship between domestic, regional and international security. It has highlighted the tragic phenomenon of the 'cubs', the young children groomed for violence by the Islamic State. The weekly reports have told the daily story of Iraq: a story of tortures, of gruesome executions and mass graves, of airstrikes, raids and car bombs, of heroism and sacrifice, and of life carrying on regardless. It has stressed the legal and moral obligation of states to record the casualties of armed conflict.

The causes and weapons of the War on Terror, as they have been presented and debated since the 2001 terrorist attacks, provide us with different explanations of the 19-year-long violence in the region. Each colouring its narrative with shades and hues of ideology and culture, or of a clear morality and its imperatives, or of a cruel hegemon aggressively pursuing and protecting largely economic interests, or of a structural global power shift that inevitably led to a series of revolts against a weakening authority. It is in those ideological, political, moral and structural hues that we are invited to understand the deaths of hundreds of thousands of people, the starvation and flight of millions of others, the child soldiers, the blown-up street vendors, the killers and the victims. Does it matter if the deaths are attributed to a clash of civilizations? Does it matter if they are seen as 'death by capitalism'? Does it make a difference if we call them a consequence of morbid symptoms during an interregnum that led to global structural change? Finally, are they any less sad if we decide they were for a right moral cause?

This book covers a period of 15 years: 2003–2017. The 13,183 annual total of civilian casualties in 2017 was down to 3,319 in 2018 and 2019 witnessed 2,392 civilian deaths (Table 6.2).

Since it started its recording of civilian deaths in 2003, IBC has been used as a valuable source by the UK Home Office, the UNHCR, the Iraq War Enquiry, the BBC and many others, and has twice been nominated for the Nobel Peace Prize. The latest project was a report prepared for the European Asylum Support Office in 2019, with another one being on the way for 2020. There have been countless

Table 6.2: Civilian deaths by month 2018–2019

	Jan	Feb	Mar	Apr	May	Jun	Jul	Aug	Sep	Oct	Nov	Dec	Total
2018	474	410	402	303	229	209	230	201	241	305	160	155	**3,319**
2019	323	271	123	140	166	130	145	93	151	361	274	215	**2,392**

interviews and talks, during which I am sometimes asked: How do you know? What are your sources? Isn't the estimate much higher? The last question alludes to the controversy that started in 2004, in response to which Hamit Dardagan, John Sloboda and Joshua Dougherty released the following.

IBC Press Release: Reality checks: some responses to the latest *Lancet* estimates

A new study has been released by The Lancet *medical journal estimating over 650,000 excess deaths in Iraq. The Iraqi mortality estimates published in* The Lancet *in October 2006 imply, among other things, that:*

- *On average, a thousand Iraqis have been violently killed every single day in the first half of 2006, with less than a tenth of them being noticed by any public surveillance mechanisms;*
- *Some 800,000 or more Iraqis suffered blast wounds and other serious conflict-related injuries in the past two years, but less than a tenth of them received any kind of hospital treatment;*
- *Over 7% of the entire adult male population of Iraq has already been killed in violence, with no less than 10% in the worst affected areas covering most of central Iraq;*
- *Half a million death certificates were received by families which were never officially recorded as having been issued;*
- *The Coalition has killed far more Iraqis in the last year than in earlier years containing the initial massive 'Shock and Awe' invasion and the major assaults on Falluja.*

If these assertions are true, they further imply:

- *incompetence and/or fraud on a truly massive scale by Iraqi officials in hospitals and ministries, on a local, regional and national level, perfectly coordinated from the moment the occupation began;*
- *bizarre and self-destructive behaviour on the part of all but a small minority of 800,000 injured, mostly non-combatant, Iraqis;*
- *the utter failure of local or external agencies to notice and respond to a decimation of the adult male population in key urban areas;*
- *an abject failure of the media, Iraqi as well as international, to observe that Coalition-caused events of the scale they reported during the three-week invasion in 2003 have been occurring every month for over a year.*

In the light of such extreme and improbable implications, a rational alternative conclusion to be considered is that the authors have drawn conclusions from unrepresentative data. In addition, totals of the magnitude generated by this study are unnecessary to brand the invasion and occupation of Iraq a human and strategic tragedy.

187

There has been enormous interest and debate over the newly published Lancet *Iraqi mortality estimate of 655,000 excess deaths since the invasion, 601,000 of them from violence (and including combatants with civilians). Even the latter estimate is some 12 times larger than the IBC count of violent civilian deaths reported in the international news media, which stands at something under 50,000 for the same period (although the IBC figure for this period is likely to considerably increase with the addition of as yet unprocessed data). The new* Lancet *estimate is also almost the same degree higher than any official records from Iraq. This contrast has provoked numerous requests for comment, and these are our first observations.*

The researchers, and in particular their Iraqi colleagues who carried out the survey, should be commended for undertaking it under dangerous circumstances and with minimal resources. Efforts like theirs have consistently highlighted that much more could be done by official bodies, such as the US and UK governments, to assess the human suffering that has resulted from the invasion and occupation of Iraq. However, our view is that there is considerable cause for scepticism regarding the estimates in the latest study, not least because of a very different conclusion reached by another random household survey, the ILCS (the United Nations Development Programme Iraq Living Conditions Survey), using a comparable method but a considerably better-distributed and much larger sample. This latter study gave a much lower estimate for violent deaths up until April 2004, despite that period being associated with the smallest number of observed deaths in the latest Lancet *study. Additionally, claims that the two* Lancet *studies confirm each other's estimates are overstated. Both the violent and non-violent post-invasion death estimates are actually quite different in the two studies.*

What emerges most clearly from this study is that a multi-methodological approach and much better resourced work is required. Substantially more deaths have occurred than have been recorded so far, but their number still remains highly uncertain. We also take the view that far more recognition should be accorded the many other courageous people in Iraq, be they Iraqi or international journalists, hospital, morgue, and other officials, or relief workers, who are endeavouring to keep the world informed on the country's plight. Far too many have had to pay the highest possible price for their efforts. Ignorance of this catastrophic war would be far less endemic if their day-by-day contribution were consistently given the exposure it merits. The daily toll on civilian lives resulting from the Iraq war should be front-page news in the countries that instigated it, not inside-page news.

In October 2004, The Lancet *published a random cluster sample survey estimating that 98,000 Iraqis had died as a result of the invasion up to that point (an 18-month period), and that 57,600 of these deaths were from violence. The October 2006 study comes from the same research team and provides an estimate for the 40-month period from March 2003 to June 2006 of 655,000 excess deaths, 601,000 of them from violence. The data presented do not distinguish between civilian and combatant deaths.* The Lancet *researchers visited 47 neighbourhoods and conducted interviews in 40 adjoining households in each neighbourhood. About 1,800 households containing 12,000 Iraqis were surveyed. These households reported a total of 302 violent deaths, each of which has been multiplied by two thousand to provide an estimate of how many of Iraq's estimated 26,000,000 population would have died if this proportion of deaths were representative of the country as a whole. The study's central estimate of 601,000 violent deaths is exceptionally high. Even its lower bound 95% confidence interval of 426,000 violent deaths is shockingly large. If numbers of this magnitude are anywhere near the truth, then they reveal a disaster far greater than most could have conceived, and one which appears inconsistent with a considerable amount of other information that has emerged over the last three and a half years.* (Dardagan, Sloboda and Dougherty, 2006)

The Iraq Body Count data extracted from daily research suggests that smaller incidents are the ones that are most likely to be underreported. This means that the number of 'hidden' assaults implied by this study could be far greater. If, for example, the average number of people killed in each such assault were two, then the number of unreported deadly assaults would have to rise to 380 per day. Such a great number of small-scale unreported assaults could perhaps be explained by suggesting that many of them were secret killings resulting from abductions and executions. However, 42% of the 330,000 *Lancet*-estimated violent deaths in this final 13-month period were ascribed to 'explosives/ ordnance', car bombs, or airstrikes, all of which carry a fairly heavy and hardly 'secret' toll. As a daily recorder of violence, and having studied thousands of security reports over the years, I witnessed deaths ranging from 1 to 320, as a result of explosions and airstrikes. Very few of those explosions and airstrikes I documented only claimed one life; most single-victim incidents are, in fact, shootings.

The Lancet's 2005–2006 data generates an Iraqi average daily death toll of 350 from these explosions and air strikes, the IBC press release continues. Only a small fraction of these deaths are officially recorded or reported, *The Lancet* data claims.

More specifically, Lancet *data suggests large numbers of deadly car bombings occurring on a daily basis, of which only a small fraction are ever reported (and whose victims, including injured, fail to be recorded by hospitals).* Lancet *estimates 150 people to have died from car bombs alone, on average, every day during June 2005– June 2006. IBC's database of deadly car bomb incidents shows they kill 7–8 people on average.* Lancet's *estimate corresponds to about 20 car bombs per day, all but one or two of which fail to be reported by the media. Yet car bombs fall well within the earlier-mentioned category of incidents which average 6 unique reports on them. 'Baghdad-weighting' of media reports, even if applicable to car bombs, is unlikely to account for this level of under-reporting, as half of the car bombs IBC has recorded have been outside Baghdad. The Pentagon, which has every reason to highlight the lethality of car bombs to Iraqis, records, on average, two to three car-bombings per day throughout Iraq, including those hitting only its own forces or causing no casualties, for the period in question.* (Dardagan, Sloboda and Dougherty, 2006)

Is 207,645 (the current total documented) too low a number? Is the loss of so many innocent lives too small? Do millions need to have been killed for the world to be outraged by the catastrophic impact of the War on Terror on the Iraqis? The number of certain civilian deaths that has been documented to a basic standard of corroboration by 'passive surveillance methods' provides enough evidence to deem this invasion and occupation a complete security failure. On 11 September 2001, nearly 3,000 people were violently killed in attacks on the US. 9/11 was a terrorist attack that, for those of us who watched it live, will forever be etched in our minds, whatever our nationality. It was a crime against humanity that has been memorialized and is mourned still. In December 2005 President George Bush acknowledged 30,000 known Iraqi violent deaths in a country one tenth the size of the US, a death toll already 100 times greater in its impact on the Iraqi nation than 9/11 was on the US.

When I am asked the question 'Isn't the number much higher?' my response is usually: What do those that give the much higher number or estimate say about the violence last year? Last month? Last week? Have civilian deaths risen? What weapons are primarily used? Where is the conflict concentrated? Who are the victims? Who are most at risk and where? Who was killed yesterday? To these questions, they have no answers. In an *ongoing* war, casualty recording must be *ongoing* also. Iraq was not 'frozen' in 2007 and nor was the War on Terror. An alleged snapshot of Iraq of over 10 years ago can tell us nothing of Iraq or of the War on Terror now, or since. The methodology employed by IBC has meant that both short- and long-term effects of policies and interventions can be studied; that all relevant events can be broken down and assessed on their particular characteristics; that changes in pattern and frequency can be assessed over any given period of time; that any given period of time – a day, a week, a month or a year – can be compared and evaluated against any other, before or after an event, a policy, an intervention and so on.

An example of the usefulness of such ongoing research into civilian deaths is the collaborative work of IBC and *The New England Journal of Medicine*, which in April 2009 published the article 'The Weapons That Kill Civilians – Deaths of Children and Noncombatants in Iraq, 2003–2008'. 'Believing that a careful assessment of the effects of different kinds of weapons on civilians in Iraq was needed', the authors wrote, 'we used the database of the Iraq Body Count (IBC), a nongovernmental organization that documents civilian violent deaths in Iraq, to determine the nature and effects of various weapons on civilians in Iraq' (Hicks et al, 2009).

Casualty recording – body counting – has enabled us to see wars through the lens of civilian suffering and civilian loss. Despite criticisms, the usefulness and impact of the work of Iraq Body Count has changed the way we understand war. In 2017 an NGO called Save the Children asked me to provide some figures for Mosul in the January–April period: how many civilians have been killed and *how many of them were children* (and how they died). The latter is hard to ascertain, as reports tend to say 'among those killed were women and children', without giving figures for either. However, based on a very small number of reports that did mention the number of children killed, I came up with this list of 84:

- 12 starved to death;
- 38 were killed by coalition airstrikes;
- 4 were executed;
- 6 were shot dead;
- 11 killed by shelling and rockets;
- 2 killed in drone attacks;
- 10 by IEDs and car bombs;
- 1 by torture.

Why did these children die? Were their deaths a result of the struggle for hegemony and increased hegemonic penetration of the Middle East? Were they the outcome of clashing civilizations? Or of the ideology and actions of counter-hegemonic, anti-imperialist resistance movements? Or of the combination of discourse wars and hard wars? Perhaps, in a global context, their deaths were the consequence of a power vacuum and power shift during the crisis of a dying international order? Were they the sacrificial lambs in a battle between good powers and evil forces?

As I continue the body count in 2020, it is those innocents that have starved to death, that have been killed in airstrikes, blown up, shot and tortured that year, that month, that week or that day, I keep in my mind. As an academic, I often think of the world in terms of power, of states, of interests and of structures. As a casualty recorder, it is the 'boy in the orange shorts', whose three-year-old body was pulled from the rubble of his home, it is Ahmed Draiwel, who ran with the bomb in his arms, it is Shukran Ghanim Hussein, it is Nemat Rezaei, it is Fatima Talib Khazaal, it is those police officers, those teachers, farmers, children that drive me to search, to record, to document. It is ultimately to those Iraqis and to all Iraqis that this book is dedicated.

References

Advisory Service on International Humanitarian Law (2004) 'What is international humanitarian law?', [online] Available from: www.icrc.org/eng/assets/files/other/what_is_ihl.pdf

Airwars (2015) 'Coalition strikes and civilian casualty claims in Iraq and Syria, September 1st–30th, 2015', [online] Available from: https://airwars.org/report/coalition-strikes-and-civilian-casualty-claims-in-iraq-and-syria-september-1st-30th-2015/

Al-Baghdadiya (2018) 'Human Rights Watch reveals new evidence of mass executions by the Asayish forces in Nineveh', [online] 9 February, Available from: http://albaghdadiyagroup.com/news/akhbar-iraq/raets-ootsh-tkshf-2dlt-gdedt-ladamat-gmaaet-nfztha-qoat-al2saesh-fe-neno

Al-Baghdadiya (2019) 'The death toll from the American bombardment of Al-Hashd camp increased to 25 dead and 51 wounded', [online] 30 December, Available from: http://albaghdadiyagroup.com/news/akhbar-iraq/artfaa-hselt-alqsf-al2mreke-al-maskr-alhshd-l--qtela-o—msaba

American Anthropological Association (2008) *Final Report on the Army's Human Terrain System Proof of Concept Program*, Arlington, VA: American Anthropological Association.

Anderson, K. (2016) 'Cubs of the Caliphate: the systematic recruitment, training, and use of children in the Islamic State', Herzliya: International Institute for Counter-Terrorism.

Asharq Al-Awsat (2016) 'Mass suicide becomes only solution in Fallujah', [online] 29 March, Available from: https://eng-archive.aawsat.com/manaf-al-obeidi/news-middle-east/mass-suicide-becomes-only-solution-in-fallujah

Baghdad Post (2018) 'Suicide of a young man inside his home in central Basra', *Iraq News*, [online] 4 March, Available from: www.thebaghdadpost.com/ar/story/89507/احتراق-شاب-داخل-منزله-وسط-البصرة

BBC (2005) 'Obituary: Philip Beer', [online] 3 August, Available from http://news.bbc.co.uk/1/hi/england/london/4741127.stm

BBC (2020) 'Qasem Soleimani: "This will escalate an already volatile situation"', [online] 3 January, Available from: www.bbc.co.uk/news/av/world-middle-east-50980786/qasem-soleimani-this-will-escalate-an-already-volatile-situation

Benraad, M. (2011) 'Iraq's tribal "Sahwa": its rise and fall', *Middle East Policy Council*, 18 (1) [online] Available from: www.mepc.org/iraqs-tribal-sahwa-its-rise-and-fall

Berlin, I. (1958) *Two Concepts of Liberty*, Oxford: Oxford University Press.

Berti, B. and Osete, A. (2015) '"Generation war": Syria's children caught between internal conflict and the rise of the Islamic State', *Strategic Assessment*, 18 (3), [online] Available from: www.inss.org.il/wp-content/uploads/systemfiles/adkan18_3ENG%20(4)_Berti%20and%20Osete.pdf

Bin Laden, O. (2001) 'Text: Bin Laden's statement', *The Guardian*, [online] 7 October, Available from: www.theguardian.com/world/2001/oct/07/afghanistan.terrorism15

Bin Laden, O. (2002) 'Bin Laden's "letter to America"', *The Guardian*, [online] 24 November, Available from: www.theguardian.com/world/2002/nov/24/theobserver

Blair, T. (2014) 'Iraq, Syria and the Middle East', *Independent*, [online] 14 June, Available from: www.tonyblairoffice.org/news/entry/iraq-syria-and-the-middle-east-an-essay-by-tony-blair/

Breaking News (2006) 'Gates warns failure in Iraq would be a "calamity"', [online] 19 December, Available from: www.breakingnews.ie/world/gates-warns-failure-in-iraq-would-be-a-calamity-289915.html

Breau, S. and Joyce, R. (2011) 'The legal obligation to record civilian casualties of armed conflict', [online] June, Available from: www.everycasualty.org/downloads/ec/pdf/1st%20legal%20report%20formatted%20FINAL.pdf

Bull, H. and Holbraad, C. (eds) (1978) *Martin Wight Power Politics*, Leicester: Leicester University Press.

Bush, G.W. (2001a) 'Statement by the President in his Address to the Nation', The White House, [online] 11 September, Available from: https://georgewbush-whitehouse.archives.gov/news/releases/2001/09/20010911-16.html

Bush, G.W. (2001b) 'Bush addresses nation: full text', BBC News, [online] 12 September, Available from: http://news.bbc.co.uk/1/hi/world/americas/1539328.stm

Bush, G.W. (2001c) 'Transcript of President Bush's address', CNN, [online] 21 September, Available from: http://edition.cnn.com/2001/US/09/20/gen.bush.transcript/

Bush, G.W. (2001d) 'Text of George Bush's speech, State of the Union Address', *The Guardian*, [online] 21 September, Available from: www.theguardian.com/world/2001/sep/21/september11.usa13

Bush, G.W. (2001e) 'Bush gives update on war against terrorism', CNN, [online] 11 October, Available from: http://edition.cnn.com/2001/US/10/11/gen.bush.transcript/

Bush, G.W. (2001f), 'Proclamation 7513', [online] 9 December, Available from: https://en.wikisource.org/wiki/Proclamation_7513

Bush, G.W. (2003) 'President Bush announces "Volunteers for Prosperity"', White House, [online] 21 May, Available from: http://peacecorpsonline.org/messages/messages/2629/2013673.html

Bush, L. (2001) 'Laura Bush on Taliban oppression of women', *The Washington Post*, [online] 17 November, Available from: www.washingtonpost.com/wp-srv/nation/specials/attacked/transcripts/laurabushtext_111701.html??noredirect=on

Buzan, B. (1983) *People, States and Fear: The National Security Problem in International Relations*, Brighton: Wheatsheaf Books.

Chamayou, G. (2015) *Drone Theory*, London: Penguin.

Chomsky, N. and Achcar, G. (2007) *Perilous Power: The Middle East and US Foreign Policy*, London: Penguin.

Clark, R. (2005) *The Fire This Time: US War Crimes in the Gulf*, New York: International Action Center.

CNN (2007) 'Bush: "We need to change our strategy in Iraq"', [online] 11 January, Available from http://edition.cnn.com/2007/POLITICS/01/10/bush.transcript/

Cobban, H. (2006) 'Bush created a mess in Iraq. Here's how to clean it up', *The Christian Science Monitor*, 12 October.

Cockburn, P. (2014) *The Rise of Islamic State*, London: Verso.

Commission on Human Security (2003) 'Human security now', [online] Available from https://reliefweb.int/sites/reliefweb.int/files/resources/91BAEEDBA50C6907C1256D19006A9353-chs-security-may03.pdf

Connable, B. (2018) 'Human Terrain System is dead, long live … what? Building and sustaining military cultural competence in the aftermath of the Human Terrain System', *Military Review*, January–February, 25–33.

Cox, R.W. (1981) 'Social forces, states and world orders: beyond international relations theory', *Millennium: Journal of International Studies*, 10 (2): 126–155.

Dardagan, H., Sloboda, J. and Dougherty, J. (2006) 'Reality checks: some responses to the latest *Lancet* estimates', [online] Available from: www.iraqbodycount.org/analysis/beyond/reality-checks/

Davison, J. and Psaledakis, D. (2019) 'Washington blacklists Iran-backed Iraqi militia leaders over protests', Reuters, [online] 6 December, Available from: https://uk.reuters.com/article/uk-iran-usa-iraq-sanctions/washington-blacklists-iran-backed-iraqi-militia-leaders-over-protests-idUKKBN1YA209

Detter, I. (2000) *The Law of War*, Cambridge: Cambridge University Press.

Dobbs, M. and Goshko, J.M. (1996) 'Albright's personal odyssey shaped foreign policy beliefs', *Washington Post*, 6 December.

Dorrien, G. (2004) *Imperial Designs: Neoconservatism and the New Pax Americana*, New York: Routledge.

Doyle, M. (1986) *Empires*, Ithaca, NY: Cornell University Press.

EASO Country of Origin Information (2019), 'Iraq security situation (supplement) – Iraq Body Count – civilian deaths 2012, 2017–2018', European Asylum Support Office, [online] Available from: www.easo.europa.eu/sites/default/files/publications/EASO-COI-Iraq-security-situation-IBC-civilian-deaths.pdf

Economist (2003) 'Iraq's economic liberalisation: let's all go to the yard sale', [online] 25 September, Available from: www.economist.com/middle-east-and-africa/2003/09/25/lets-all-go-to-the-yard-sale

Edkins, J. (2003) *Trauma and the Memory of Politics*, Cambridge: Cambridge University Press.

Eide, E.B. (2013) 'Opening statement at Conference on Protection of Civilians under International Humanitarian Law', Ministry of Foreign Affairs, [online] Available from: www.regjeringen.no/en/historical-archive/Stoltenbergs-2nd Government/Ministry-of-Foreign-Affairs/taler-og artikler/2013/statement_conference/id727433/

Emberling, G. (2008) 'Archaeologists and the military in Iraq, 2003–2008: compromise or contribution?', *Archaeologies*, 4 (3): 445–459.

Every Casualty (2011a) 'Charter for the recognition of every casualty of armed violence', [online] Available from: www.everycasualty.org/campaign/charter

Every Casualty (2011b) 'Every Casualty campaign', [online] Available from: www.everycasualty.org/campaign

Fierke, K.M. (2007) *Critical Approaches to International Security*, Cambridge: Polity Press.

Financial Times (2013) 'Contractors reap $138bn from Iraq war', [online] Available from: www.ft.com/content/7f435f04-8c05-11e2-b001-00144feabdc0

Fine, M. (2018) 'Introduction', in M. Greene, *The Dialectic of Freedom*, New York: Teachers College Press, Columbia University.

Fouskas, V. and Gokay, B. (2005) *The New American Imperialism: Bush's War on Terror and Blood for Oil*, Westport, CT: Praeger Security International.

Fowler, M. (2014) 'The strategy of drone warfare', *Journal of Strategic Security*, 7 (4): 108–119.

Fukuyama, F. (1989) 'The end of history', *National Interest* 16: 3–18.

Fukuyama, F. (2006) 'After neoconservatism', *New York Times*, [online] 19 February, Available from: www.nytimes.com/2006/02/19/magazine/after-neoconservatism.html

Fukuyama, F. (2007) 'After neoconservatism', in D. Skidmore (ed), *Paradoxes of Power: US Foreign Policy in a Changing World*, New York: Routledge, pp 118–127.

Gabbatt, A. (2010) 'Last US combat troops leave Iraq', *The Guardian*, 19 August.

Gellman, B. (1991) 'US bombs missed 70% of the time', *Washington Post*, 16 March.

Geneva Convention relative to the Protection of Civilian Persons in Time of War (1949) Diplomatic Conference for the Establishment of International Conventions for the Protection of Victims of War, [online] Available from: www.refworld.org/docid/3ae6b36d2.html

Gerges, F.A. (2002) 'The "war" on terrorism: a cultural perspective', *Ethics and International Affairs*, 16 (1): 18–20, ABI/INFORM Global.

Gokay, B. and Hamourtziadou, L. (2015) 'Body counting and precision bombing in failed states', Open Democracy, [online] Available from: www.opendemocracy.net/en/body-counting-and-precision-bombing-in-failed-states/

Gourley, S., Johnson, N. and Spagat, M. (2006) 'Lancet Iraq Study flawed: death toll too high', [online] Available from: www.scoop.co.nz/stories/WO0610/S00436.htm

Green, C. (2015) 'Turnaround: the untold story of the Human Terrain System', *Joint Force Quarterly 78* (3): 61–69.

Grosscup, B. (2006) *Strategic Terror: The Politics and Ethics of Aerial Bombardment*, London: Zed Books.

The Independent (2003) 'Full text: Tony Blair's speech', Speech in House of Commons, [online] Available from: www.independent.co.uk/news/world/middle-east/tony-blair-iraq-essay-full-text-we-have-to-liberate-ourselves-from-the-notion-that-we-caused-this-9537514.html

Hacking, I. (1998) *Rewriting the Soul: Multiple Personality and the Sciences of Memory*, Princeton, NJ: Princeton University Press.

Hall, S. (2011) 'Race, culture and communications', in M.E. Green (ed), *Rethinking Gramsci*, London: Routledge, pp 12–18.

Hamourtziadou, L. (2006a) 'The price they pay for our humanity', [online] 8 October, Available from: www.iraqbodycount.org/analysis/beyond/week-in-iraq/10

Hamourtziadou, L. (2006b) 'Terrorists', [online] 26 November, Available from: www.iraqbodycount.org/analysis/beyond/week-in-iraq/17

Hamourtziadou, L. (2006c) 'Inside Pandora's box', [online] 17 December, Available from: www.iraqbodycount.org/analysis/beyond/week-in-iraq/20

Hamourtziadou, L. (2007a) 'The hero', [online] 18 March, Available from: www.iraqbodycount.org/analysis/beyond/week-in-iraq/36

Hamourtziadou, L. (2007b) 'Fighting terrorism in free Iraq', [online] 15 April, Available from: www.iraqbodycount.org/analysis/beyond/week-in-iraq/40

Hamourtziadou, L. (2007c) 'Tony Blair's legacy', [online] 13 May, Available from: www.iraqbodycount.org/analysis/beyond/week-in-iraq/44

Hamourtziadou, L. (2007d) 'The price of loss: how the West values civilian lives in Iraq', [online] 12 November, Available from: www.iraqbodycount.org/analysis/beyond/the-price-of-loss/

Hamourtziadou, L. (2008a) 'The vulnerable', [online] 3 February, Available from: www.iraqbodycount.org/analysis/beyond/week-in-iraq/48

Hamourtziadou, L. (2008b) 'The consequences of state collapse', [online] 24 February, Available from: www.iraqbodycount.org/analysis/beyond/week-in-iraq/51

Hamourtziadou, L. (2008c) 'The Charge of the Knights', [online] 30 March, Available from: www.iraqbodycount.org/analysis/beyond/week-in-iraq/56

Hamourtziadou, L. (2008d) 'For Ali, Sajad, Ayat and all the other children', [online] 4 May, Available from: www.iraqbodycount.org/analysis/beyond/week-in-iraq/61

Hamourtziadou, L. (2008e) 'Death of a child', [online] 2 November, Available from: www.iraqbodycount.org/analysis/beyond/week-in-iraq/73

Hamourtziadou, L. (2013a) 'The trenching of faults: Iraq 2013', [online] 1 January, Available from: www.iraqbodycount.org/analysis/beyond/2013/

Hamourtziadou, L. (2013b) 'Contains flashing images', [online] 19 March, Available from: www.iraqbodycount.org/analysis/beyond/flashing-images/

Hamourtziadou, L. (2017) 'Human security and the emergence of modern-day body counts: the law, the theory, and the practice of casualty recording', *Journal of Global Faultlines*, 4 (1): 57–70.

Herring, E. and Rangwala, G. (2006) *Iraq in Fragments: The Occupation and Its Legacy*, London: C. Hurst.

Hicks, M., Dardagan, M., Guerrero Serdán, G., Bagnall, P., Sloboda, J. and Spagat, M. (2009) 'The weapons that kill civilians – deaths of children and noncombatants in Iraq, 2003–2008', *New England Journal of Medicine,* [online] 16 April, Available from: www.nejm.org/doi/full/10.1056/NEJMp0807240

Hinnebusch, R. (2015) *The International Politics of the Middle East*, Manchester: Manchester University Press.

Hough, P. (2008) *Understanding Global Security*, New York: Routledge.

Hoare, Q. (ed) (2005) *Selections from the Prison Notebooks*, London: Lawrence and Wishart.

House of Commons (2014) 'Iraq: coalition against ISIL', Hansard Debates, [online] Available from: https://publications.parliament.uk/pa/cm201415/cmhansrd/cm140926/debtext/140926-0001.htm

House of Commons (2015) 'ISIL in Syria', Hansard Debates, [online] Available from: https://publications.parliament.uk/pa/cm201516/cmhansrd/cm151202/debtext/151202-0001.htm

Hoyos, C. and Morrison, K. (2003) 'Iraq returns to international oil market', *Financial Times*, 5 June.

Human Rights Watch (2003) 'Violent response: the US army in al-Falluja', [online] 16 June, Available from: www.hrw.org/report/2003/06/16/violent-response/us-army-al-falluja

Human Security Unit Office for the Coordination of Humanitarian Affairs United Nations (2003) 'Human security in theory and practice; application of the human security concept and the United Nations Trust Fund for Human Security', [online] Available from: www.unocha.org/sites/dms/HSU/Publications%20and%20Products/Human%20Security%20Tools/Human%20Security%20in%20Theory%20and%20Practice%20English.pdf

Huntington, S. (1993) 'The clash of civilizations?', *Foreign Affairs*, 72 (3): 22–49.

Ikenberry, G.J. and Kupchan, C.A. (1990) 'Socialization and hegemonic power', *International Organization*, 44 (3): 283–315.

Iraq Body Count (nd-a) 'About the Iraq Body Count Project', [online] Available from: www.iraqbodycount.org/about/

Iraq Body Count (nd-b) 'Data extraction', [online] Available from: www.iraqbodycount.org/about/methods/3

Iraq Body Count (2003) 'Over 1,500 deaths in occupied Baghdad', Press Release, [online] 23 September, Available from: www. iraqbodycount.org/analysis/numbers/occupied-baghdad/

Iraq Body Count (2005a) 'A dossier of civilian casualties 2003–2005', [online] 19 July, Available from: www.iraqbodycount.org/analysis/ reference/pdf/a_dossier_of_civilian_casualties_2003-2005.pdf

Iraq Body Count (2005b) 'A dossier of civilian casualties 2003–2005', Press Release, [online] 19 July, Available from: www.iraqbodycount. org/analysis/reference/press-releases/12/

IRIN News (2005) 'Death toll in Fallujah rising, doctors say', [online] 4 January, Available from: www.thenewhumanitarian.org/report/ 24527/iraq-death-toll-fallujah-rising-doctors-say

Jackson, R.H. (1998) 'Boundaries and International Society', in B.A. Roberson (ed), *International Society and the Development of International Relations Theory*, New York: Pinter, pp 156–172.

Jackson, R. (2013) 'Regime security', in A. Collins (ed), *Contemporary Security Studies*, Oxford: Oxford University Press, pp 200–214.

Jamail, D. (2006) 'Iraq: children pick their Christmas toys', IPS, [online] Available from: www.ipsnews.net/2006/12/ iraq-children-pick-their-christmas-toys/

Jamail, D. (2014) 'Iraqi government killing civilians in Fallujah', Truthout, [online] 3 March, Available from: www.truth-out.org/ news/item/22138-iraqi-government-killing-civilians-in-fallujah

Joseph, P. (2014) *'Soft' Counterinsurgency: Human Terrain Teams and U.S. Strategy in Iraq and Afghanistan*, New York: Palgrave Pivot.

Kagan, R. (2002a) 'Power and weakness', *Policy Review*, 113, June–July: 1–18.

Kagan, R. (2002b) 'The US–Europe divide', *Washington Post*, 26 May.

Kagan, R. (2003) *Of Paradise and Power: America and Europe in the New World Order*, New York: Alfred A. Knopf.

Kagan, R. and Kristol, W. (2001) 'Right war', *Weekly Standard*, 1 October, [online] Available from: https://carnegieendowment.org/ 2001/10/01/right-war-pub-791

Kaufman, S., Little, R. and Wohlforth, W.C. (2007) *The Balance of Power in World History*, New York: Palgrave Macmillan.

Kelbie, P. (2004) 'A boy who just wanted to come home', *The Independent*, [online] 6 November, Available from: www.independent. co.uk/news/uk/politics/a-boy-who-just-wanted-to-come-home-8002658.html

Kindleberger, C. (1981) 'Dominance and leadership in the international economy: exploitation, public goods, and free rides', *International Studies Quarterly*, 25 (2): 242–254.

Klein, N. (2003) 'Privatization in disguise', *The Nation*, 10 April.

Knights, M. (2009) 'The status and future of the Awakening Movements in Iraq', *Carnegie Endowment for International Peace*, [online] 2 June, Available from: https://carnegieendowment.org/sada/23190

Krauthammer, C. (1989) 'Universal dominion: toward a unipolar world', *National Interest*, 18: 46–49.

Krauthammer, C. (2001a) 'Voices of moral obtuseness', *Washington Post*, 21 September.

Krauthammer, C. (2001b) 'The war: a road map', *Washington Post*, [online] 28 September, Available from: www.washingtonpost. com/archive/opinions/2001/09/28/the-war-a-road-map/ 61cf9fa6-0f92-4949-b594-605bad624176/

Krauthammer, C. (2003) 'Coming ashore: the war is not just to disarm Saddam. It is to reform a whole part of the world', *Time*, 17 February.

Krieg, A. (2016) 'Externalising the burden of war: the Obama doctrine and US foreign policy in the Middle East', *International Affairs*, 92 (1): 97–113.

Kristol, W. and Kagan, R. (ed) (2000) *Present Dangers: Crisis and Opportunity in American Foreign and Defense Policy*, San Francisco, CA: Encounter Books.

Kumar, D. (2015) 'Imperialist feminism', *International Socialist Review*, 102, [online] Available from: https://isreview.org/issue/102/ imperialist-feminism

Lamb, C.J. (2013) *Human Terrain Teams: An Organizational Innovation for Sociocultural Knowledge in Irregular Warfare*, Washington, DC: Institute of World Politics Press.

Lebow, R.N. and Reich, S. (2014) *Good-bye Hegemony: Power and Influence in the Global System*, Princeton, NJ: Princeton University Press.

Mastanduno, M. (2005) 'Hegemonic order, September 11, and the consequences of the Bush revolution', *International Relations of the Asia Pacific*, 5: 177–196.

May, L. (2007) *War Crimes and Just War*, Cambridge: Cambridge University Press.

McClatchy (2007) 'Tens of thousands of Iraqis have disappeared without trace', 13 June, [online] Available from: www.mcclatchydc.com/ latest-news/article24462823.html

McClatchy (2008a) 'Suicide bomber attacks funeral in tiny Iraqi village, killing 60', 18 April, [online] Available from: www.mcclatchydc.com/ news/nation-world/world/article24481117.html

McClatchy (2008b) 'U.S. lists services it'll cut off if Iraq rejects pact on troops', 27 October, [online] Available from: www.mcclatchydc. com/article24507070.html

McFate, M. and Fondacaro, S. (2011) 'Reflections on the Human Terrain System during the first four years', *Prism*, NDU Press, 2 (4): 63–82.

McFate, M. and Jackson, A. (2005) 'An organizational solution for DODs cultural knowledge needs', *Military Review*, 85(4): 18–21.

McQuaig, L. (2004a) 'It's the crude, dude', *New Yorker*, 16–23 February.

McQuaig, L. (2004b) 'Crude dudes', *Toronto Star*, 20 September.

Ministry of Defence (2003) 'Operations in Iraq. Fusilier Kelan Turrington killed in Iraq', [online] 8 April, Available from: www. gov.uk/government/fatalities/fusilier-kelan-turrington

Montgomery, G.W. and McWilliams, T.S. (eds) (2009) *Al-Anbar Awakening Volume II Iraqi Perspectives: From Insurgency to Counterinsurgency in Iraq, 2004–2009*, Marine Corps University Press, United States Marine Corps, Quantico, Virginia, [online] Available from: www.hqmc.marines.mil/Portals/61/Docs/Al-AnbarAwakeningVolII%5B1%5D.pdf

Morse, L.E. (chair) and Myers Jaffe, A. (project director) (2001) 'Strategic energy policy: challenges for the twenty-first century', *Report of an Independent Task Force Cosponsored by the James A. Baker III Institute for Public Policy of Rice University and the Council on Foreign Relations*, [online] Available from: https://cfrd8-files.cfr.org/sites/default/files/pdf/2001/04/Energy%20TaskForce.pdf

New York Times (2006) 'Iraq was a "failure", Blix says', [online] 25 October, Available from: www.nytimes.com/2006/10/25/world/africa/25iht-invade.3285184.html?mtrref=www.google.com&gwh=C220280D0F81350AB16AA98EFDE2FDBE&gwt=pay&assetType=REGIWALL

Norrlof, C. (2010) *America's Global Advantage: US Hegemony and International Cooperation*, Cambridge: Cambridge University Press.

Nunez, C. (2019) 'Fossil fuels, explained', *National Geographic*, [online] 2 April, Available from: www.nationalgeographic.com/environment/energy/reference/fossil-fuels/

Obama, B. (2016) 'Executive Order – United States policy on pre- and post-strike measures to address civilian casualties in U.S. operations involving the use of force', The White House, Office of the Press Secretary, For Immediate Release, [online] 1 July, Available from: www.whitehouse.gov/the-press-office/2016/07/01/executive-order-united-states-policy-pre-and-post-strike-measures

Oklahoman (2008) 'Photographic icons of Iraq War', [online] 8 March, Available from: https://oklahoman.com/article/3213870/photographic-icons-of-iraq-war

Ortiz, X. (2006) 'Death in Iraq, with morning coffee', *The National Interest*, [online] 27 October, Available from: https://nationalinterest.org/commentary/death-in-iraq-with-morning-coffee-1245

Partlow, J., Scott Tyson, A. and Wright, R. (2007) 'Bomb kills a key Sunni ally of US', *The Washington Post*, 14 September.

Peters, R. (2007) 'Progress and peril: new counterinsurgency manual cheats on the history exam', *Armed Forces Journal*, [online] 1 February, Available from: http://armedforcesjournal.com/progress-and-peril/

Pitman, T. (2007) 'Sunni sheikhs join fight vs insurgency', *The Washington Post*, 25 March.

Podhoretz, N. (2004) 'World War IV: how it started, what it means, and why we have to win', *Commentary*, [online] September, Available from: www.commentarymagazine.com/articles/world-war-iv-how-it-started-what-it-means-and-why-we-have-to-win/

Poku, N.K. and Therkelsen, J. (2016) 'Globalisation, development and security', in A. Collins (ed), *Contemporary Security Studies*, Oxford: Oxford University Press, pp 262–276.

Radio Free Europe/Radio Liberty (2007) 'Iraq hails constructive conference', 10 March, [online] Available from: www.rferl.org/a/1075180.html

Rahim, A.H. (2011) 'Whither political Islam and the Arab Spring', *Hedgehog Review*, 13 (3): 8–22.

Raphael, S. and Stokes, D. (2016) 'Energy security', in A. Collins (ed) *Contemporary Security Studies*, Oxford: Oxford University Press, pp 343–355.

Relief Web (2006) 'Iraq: stress of violence leads to more suicides', [online] 27 December, Available from: https://reliefweb.int/report/iraq/iraq-stress-violence-leads-more-suicides

Report to Congress (2006) 'Measuring stability and security in Iraq', [online] Available from: https://archive.defense.gov/pubs/pdfs/9010Quarterly-Report-20061216.pdf

Reuters (2007) 'Iraqis vow to fight al Qaeda after sheikh death', [online] 14 September, Available from: www.reuters.com/article/us-iraq-anbar/iraqis-vow-to-fight-al-qaeda-after-sheikh-death-idUSL1477322720070914

Reuters (2008) 'Army issues new manual for nation-building', [online] 6 October Available from: www.reuters.com/article/us-usa-army-manual/army-issues-new-manual-for-nation-building-idUSTRE49570420081006?sp=true

Rich, F. (2007) 'The "good Germans" among us', *New York Times*, [online] 14 October, Available from: www.nytimes.com/2007/10/14/opinion/14rich2.html

Rubin, B. and Colp Rubin, J. (2002) *Anti-American Terrorism and the Middle East*, New York: Oxford University Press.

Rogers, P. (2019) 'The triple paradigm crisis: economy, environment and security', *Journal of Global Faultlines*, 6(2): 139–149.

Savell, S. (2019) 'This map shows where in the world the U.S. military is combatting terrorism', America at War, *Smithsonian*, [online] Available from: www.smithsonianmag.com/history/map-shows-places-world-where-us-military-operates-180970997/

Scott, P.D. (2007) *The Road to 9/11: Wealth, Empire and the Future of America*, Los Angeles: University of California Press.

Sims, C.J. (2015) *Human Terrain System: Operationally Relevant Social Science Research in Iraq and Afghanistan*, Carlisle, PA: Strategic Studies Institute and US Army War College Press.

Stewart, J. (2003) 'Towards a single definition of armed conflict in international humanitarian law: a critique of internationalized armed conflict', *International Review of the Red Cross*, 85 (850): 313–350.

Summerfield, D. (1998) 'The social experience of war and some issues for the humanitarian field', in P. Bracken and C. Petty (eds), *Rethinking the Trauma of War*, London: Free Association Books, pp 9–37.

Susman, T. and Ahmed, C. (2008) 'Sadr critical of draft plan on US troops', *Los Angeles Times*, [online] 23 August, Available from: www.latimes.com/archives/la-xpm-2008-aug-23-fg-iraq23-story.html

The Baltimore Sun (2003) 'Bush says U.S. must spread democracy', [online] 7 November, Available from: www.tribpub.com/gdpr/baltimoresun.com/

The Iraq Inquiry (2016) [online] Available from: https://webarchive.nationalarchives.gov.uk/20171123122743/http://www.iraqinquiry.org.uk/the-report/

The Iraq Study Group Report (2006) [online] Available from: www.iraqsolidaridad.org/2006/docs/gei-1.pdf

The White House (2006) 'President Bush meets with British Prime Minister Tony Blair', [online] 7 December, Available from: https://georgewbush-whitehouse.archives.gov/news/releases/2006/12/20061207-1.html

UNDP (1994) *Human Development Report*, New York: Oxford University Press.

UNHCR (2008) 'Iraq: latest return survey shows few intending to go home soon', [online] 29 April, Available from: www.unhcr.org/uk/news/briefing/2008/4/4816ef534/iraq-latest-return-survey-shows-few-intending-home-soon.html

Universal Declaration of Human Rights (1948) [online] Available from www.ohchr.org/EN/UDHR/Documents/UDHR_Translations/eng.pdf

US Department of Defense (2007) 'Concerned local citizens vastly improve security in Iraq's Diyala Province', [online] 12 October, Available from: https://web.archive.org/web/20090516190404/http://www.defenselink.mil/news/newsarticle.aspx?id=47783

Vale, G. (2018) 'Cubs in the lion's den: indoctrination and recruitment of children within Islamic State territory', [online] Available from: https://icsr.info/wp-content/uploads/2018/07/ICSR-Report-Cubs-in-the-Lions%E2%80%99-Den-Indoctrination-and-Recruitment-of-Children-Within-Islamic-State-Territory.pdf

Van der Pijl, K. (1984) *The Making of an Atlantic Ruling Class*, London: Verso.

Watani, H. (nd) 'The Sahwa / Awakening Councils / Sons of Iraq [SOI]', [online] Available from: www.globalsecurity.org/military/world/para/awakening.htm

Wolfowitz, P. (1996) 'Clinton's Bay of Pigs', *Wall Street Journal*, 27 September, [online] Available from: www.wsj.com/articles/SB843775850211826000

Index

CPSIA information can be obtained
at www.ICGtesting.com
Printed in the USA
BVHW041043080121
597355BV00010B/192